THE SOCIAL PRODUCTION OF SCIENTIFIC KNOWLEDGE

SOCIOLOGY OF THE SCIENCES

A YEARBOOK

VOLUME I – 1977

THE SOCIAL PRODUCTION
OF SCIENTIFIC KNOWLEDGE

Edited by

EVERETT MENDELSOHN, PETER WEINGART

and

RICHARD WHITLEY

D. REIDEL PUBLISHING COMPANY

DORDRECHT-HOLLAND / BOSTON-U.S.A.

Library of Congress Cataloging in Publication Data
Main entry under title:

The Social production of scientific knowledge.

(Sociology of sciences; v. 1, 1977)
Includes bibliographical references and index.
1. Science – Social aspects. I. Mendelsohn, Everett.
II. Weingart, Peter. III. Whitley, Richard. IV. Series.
Q175.5.S6   501   76–58390
ISBN 90–277–0775–8
ISBN 90–277–0776–6 pbk.

Published by D. Reidel Publishing Company,
P.O. Box 17, Dordrecht, Holland

Sold and distributed in the U.S.A., Canada, and Mexico
by D. Reidel Publishing Company, Inc.
Lincoln Building, 160 Old Derby Street, Hingham,
Mass. 02043, U.S.A.

TABLE OF CONTENTS

PART III:
Social Goals, Political Programmes and Scientific Norms

EDITORIAL STATEMENT

The Yearbook in the Sociology of the Sciences will publish collections of papers dealing with a particular topic each year. By publishing research from a number of perspectives and approaches on a specific topic, the Yearbook will provide an opportunity for the integration of different disciplinary strategies and their interrelated development. The term sociology in the title is thus meant broadly and includes historical and philosophical dimensions.

The basic standpoint of the Yearbook views the sciences as a plurality of socially constructed ways of comprehending natural and social phenomena. It therefore seeks to go beyond unitary and monolithic schematisations of scientific knowledge which reduce paths of development in all the sciences to a single process. It similarly considers the study of scientists inseparable from the study of developments in scientific knowledge and both as major parts of the general study of social change and development. Science is seen as a system of cognitive production which is related to other systems of production in determinate ways. Similarly, processes by which a particular system of cognitive production became institutionalised in particular periods as 'scientific' are regarded as important topics for investigation in an historical and comparative perspective. Relations between scientific knowledges and common sense beliefs and rationalities are relevant for the analysis of cognitive developments in the sciences and will be examined in the Yearbook.

Each volume of the Yearbook will be largely devoted to a single topic selected by the Editorial Board and edited by a group appointed by the Board. Additionally, general review articles of recent developments and papers which are considered particularly timely and appropriate will be published.

The Yearbook will be published in English but, in certain cases, translation of papers will be considered.

PART I

THE INSTITUTIONALISATION OF THE SCIENCES:
*Changing Concepts and Approaches in the History and
Sociology of Science*

THE SOCIAL CONSTRUCTION OF
SCIENTIFIC KNOWLEDGE

EVERETT MENDELSOHN

Harvard University

1. Introduction

In the closing pages of her remarkable study of Giordano Bruno, Frances
Yates set forth the critical problem of modern science:

The basic difference between the attitude of the magician to the world and the attitude
of the scientist to the world is that the former wants to draw the world into himself,
whilst the scientist does just the opposite, he externalizes and impersonalizes the world ...
Hence, may it not be supposed, when mechanics and mathematics took over from
animism and magic, it was this internalisation, this intimate connection of the *mens*
with the world, which had to be avoided at all costs. And, hence, it may be suggested,
through the necessity for this strong reaction, the mistake arose of allowing the problem
of mind to fall so completely out of step and so far behind the problem of matter in
the external world and how it works ... This bad start of the problem of knowledge has
never quite been made up (1).

The Scientific Revolution viewed from this perspective is fundamentally
flawed and its successive development bears the marks of this early 'mistake'.
The question we are immediately led to ask is, 'Why was the mistake made?'
And then, 'Who made it and in what circumstances?' We further confront the
basic question of the modern historiography of science: Shall we look wholly
within, to the intellect and its development as many generations of scholars
have urged? (2) Or, shall we venture without to examine the social and cultural context of knowledge itself?

2. Setting the Problem

My thesis is a simple one. Science is an activity of human beings acting and
interacting, thus a social activity. Its knowledge, its statements, its techniques
have been created by human beings and developed, nurtured and shared among

Mendelsohn/Weingart/Whitley (eds.), The Social Production of Scientific Knowledge.
Sociology of the Sciences, Volume I, 1977. 3–26. All Rights Reserved.
Copyright © 1977 by D. Reidel Publishing Company, Dordrecht-Holland.

groups of human beings. Scientific knowledge is therefore fundamentally social knowledge. As a social activity, science is clearly a product of a history and of processes which occurred in time and in place and involved human actors. These actors had lives not only in science, but in the wider societies of which they were members.

There is another dimension to the problem worth noting at once. The human approach to understanding, explaining and interacting with nature has certainly not been uniform through time, nor across cultures. It has not even been the same for all groups or classes within a single culture or society. Indeed, these very differences, appropriately studied, can provide the basis for a deeper understanding of the role(s) of science (or, more broadly, interpretation of nature) within a society or culture.

The techniques for the proper study of science as a human activity will thus encompass the historical and the sociological (and social-psychological) and be comparative in mode (3). The underlying assumption will link the cognitive and the social levels of science and the rigid bifurcation between mind and matter will be overcome. Of course, the study of science has not yet sufficiently broadened to reflect this multifaceted approach and, instead, science is still largely viewed as a very separate and almost holy activity (4). Indeed, the source of my interest in these problems comes from this continued failing in the historiography of science.

Historians of science (and most sociologists as well?) seem to have accepted the historiography and the mythology of science as devised by practising scientists themselves. Historians of science often have been self-congratulatory and righteous in their attitudes toward science, particularly in viewing science's confrontations with other forms of knowledge or other social institutions (5). The image that emerges from the historical studies is of unidirectional progress and a special quality of science as cumulative knowledge. This outlook is strengthened by the close focus of historians on the achievement of positive knowledge and the detailed study of its lineage. The historical community has generally expressed embarrassment at what lay at the fringes of established science — those activities that took place just beyond 'the edge of objectivity'. Only recently with the challenge raised from outside the fraternity of historians has any concerted attention been paid to the so-called 'pseudo-sciences' or the folk or popular sciences (6). Historians of science have tended to seek their own legitimation from within science itself, and have become in many instances the apologists for science rather than its analysts and critics. It comes as no surprise, then, that the approach taken to science has been to view the activity from the top down, and to follow the Newtonian vision of standing on the shoulders of giants and looking down the decades from one majestic achievement to another. By and large science has been represented by its luminaries with other practitioners often judged to be marginally necessary players of walk-on roles.

Lest it seem that the written history has been a total wasteland, it should be noted that some attempts have been made to establish a context for science notably involving the recognition of an intellectual context. Lynn Thorndike, for example, in his multi-volume study, noted the continuing interaction and demarcation between magic and science in the early modern period (7). More recently, others have joined in an exploration of this gray border area of science. Allen Debus has insisted upon the importance of alchemical and Paracelsian traditions, both as critics of older authority and as exponents of new methods (8). J. E. McGuire and P. M. Rattansi re-examined the work of Isaac Newton himself and found serious heterodox influences (9). The works of Frances Yates and Walter Pagel have justly received wide attention and a somewhat grudging and suspicious acclaim (10). What is striking to the reader of some of these unorthodox studies is the often embarrassed tone of the authors themselves.

In his exploration of Paracelsus, for example, Walter Pagel is well aware that in the works of this Renaissance physician the "mystical, magical and scientific elements are all blended together into a single doctrine" (11). Indeed, he demonstrates convincingly that Paracelsus can only be understood if all these elements are included and juxtaposed in Paracelsus's system of explanation in science and medicine. Nonetheless, Pagel warns his readers that "the theories, ideas and philosophies which will be discussed are difficult to digest and without obvious value today" (12). The historian's image of modern science accords with that of today's practitioners. Magic and miracle lend an air of quaintness to the period of transition from old to new. But even the context that Pagel *et al.* bring to early science are intellectual contexts and, to the extent that their role is examined and explained, the guides of intellectual history and the history of ideas are followed; ideas relate to, and interact with, other ideas. There is no exploration of the potentially different social role of the alchemist or the mystic, and the possibility of significant variance in social class origins of the orthodox and heterodox practitioners escapes real notice.

The very question of what lies behind the differentiation between the several traditions of the early scientific revolution remains untouched. Similarly, the institutional and social processes which established the boundaries of that which would ultimately be included within science remain unstudied. Yet it is just these boundaries, established in the course of history through a series of socially influenced processes, which give to science its distinctive case (so that it is today easily separable from magic and mysticism) and which in turn set the stage for many of the current 'crises' of science.

But how to grab hold of these issues? As I indicated above, science as a way of knowing and acting can best be understood as a socially constructed reality; the elements it includes are familiar — rationalism, empiricism and an underlying belief in a material reality. It had its origins in time, place, and circumstances. The framework capable of linking these parts, therefore, must be able to deal with ideas and concepts and modes of gaining knowledge, that is the cognitive structures and processes; but it must also include institutional forms and procedures; the social matrix, the structures and processes of the broader social order.

To date, the history of science has been most comfortable in focusing on interactions at the conceptual level, what has been called the 'historical filiation of ideas' or genetic history (13). Some historians, however, have joined the sociologists of science and worked on institutional developments (14). There have been several excellent histories of scientific and learned academies as well as some detailed studies of institutes, universities, and other sites of research and teaching (15). These works suffer, however, in that they offer almost no recognition that institutions, and the process of institutionalization itself, imply not only historical development but processes of control as well, social control (both positive and negative) of intellectual activity. Questions beg to be examined: what were the effects of the institutional forms on the cognitive processes harbored and regulated in these new institutions? (16) And, in turn, did institutional forms reflect cognitive activities and styles? Are there relationships between distinct national institutional structures and the often discerned national scientific-conceptual styles? The image of the institutional role of boundary definer and protector — separating the true from the pseudo-science — is suggestive of imagery projected by the anthropologist, Mary Douglas, who discusses the need to protect purity from contamination; pure science being guarded from both pseudo-science and such impurity as application (17).

There has, of course, been one serious effort, launched from within the history of science, to identify a social process of cognitive development in the sciences. Thomas Kuhn's seminal study, *The Structure of Scientific Revolution* (1962) gave dramatic focus to the role of various communities of scientists in creating both the consensuses of 'normal science' and the revolutionary thrusts of paradigm shifts or major conceptual changes. What is striking to the reader, however, is Kuhn's assumption of an almost total independence of the shape of the cognitive structures, or the content of the concepts, from either the institutional structures or the broader societal processes and structures. It is not that the question of links between the conceptual, institutional, and social levels were examined and nothing of note detected; rather, the question itself was never posed.

The other element, the role of social structures and processes in the matrix or framework of science, is certainly the most difficult to deal with and perhaps this provides partial explanation for the paucity of studies. Sociologists whose work encompassed the sociology of knowledge gave special place to science and left the decided impression that exact scientific knowledge had no sociology at all (18). There has been a small Marxist tradition which has sought social influences on scientific development, but much of it relies on social models much too simplified to provide understanding of the complex concepts alluded to. Boris Hessen's now classic seeking for the 'social and economic roots of Newton's 'Principia',' was a challenge to historians of the early 1930's but was too imprecise to have a lasting impact on any but committed Marxists (19). It is not enough to correlate a set of ideas with one social group or class and believe therefore that a social basis has been established. Historians have to delve more deeply and to recognize the historical processes which lay behind the explanations of the social group itself. They must examine the activities in which this group is engaged which in turn could make use of the ideas and techniques in question. Because social imperatives are not uniform for all times, places, and groups within a society, historians must attempt to identify specific activities and imperatives (20).

Two early and quite different attempts to provide historical examples, useful for our study, are worth identifying, albeit both were the products of historically oriented sociologists. Edgar Zilsel's sophisticated, Marxist studies of the social bases of the cognitive and epistemological styles of early modern science are only now being given the recognition they deserve (21). Seeking the social roots of the scientific methods of the High Renaissance and early modern epochs did not prove easy, but the lines of thought begun by Zilsel have proven to be more fruitful than his contemporaries acknowledged. A second important work of the 1930's, Robert K. Merton's *Science, Technology and Society in Seventeenth Century England*, left two trails one well traversed and the other largely ignored even in the later writings of Merton himself (22). The first path led through the now well known terrain of Puritanism and its role in the encouragement and shaping of the institutional structures of science; the second moved to explore 'extrinsic influences on scientific research' including social and economic influences and to provide some assessment of their role and strength (23). These two potential starting places, which were not obscure but which nonetheless were underdeveloped, raise an interesting problem for the sociology of knowledge: why were these trends, developed and fairly accessible in the 1930's, dropped or overlooked during the 1940's and 1950's and not 'rediscovered' until the more turbulent and questioning years of the later 1960's? (24)

Let me turn now to two examples where evidence can be developed which can help establish models useful for further studies of the sociology of knowledge in the sciences.

3. A Sociological Inquiry into Reductionism in Biology

In a recent study of the sources of physical reductionism in mid-nineteenth century biology, I attempted to examine the three interacting levels in the life of science (25). The period on which I focused was the 1840's in Berlin; the fields within science were physiology and medicine, and the conceptual structures involved a strong, new commitment to physical-mechanical reductionist explanations. The social and political context was the growing social instability and the emergence of reform and revolutionary movements (The milieu will be recognized as the same one that produced the young Karl Marx.) The *personae dramatis* were a group of young physicians and physiologists, prominent among them Rudolf Virchow, Hermann von Helmholtz, and Emil Du Bois-Reymond.

The question I asked was why during the few years around 1848 did such a strong commitment to physical reductionism emerge? **(26)** We are well aware, as historians, that mechanical reductionism was not an invention of Germany of the 1840's (albeit just this sort of claim was made by some at the time). Not only did reductionism become an issue among the physiologists, but they pursed it with great vigor. I would like to propose one social model/ explanation remembering, however, Horkheimer's injunction to be aware of the differing social imperatives of different times, groups and situations (meaning that the elements of one model may not be automatically transferred to all other situations). Rather than rehearse all the details (which are already in print), let me point to several critical factors.

First, when they took up the cause of reductionism *all* the proponents were young. They saw themselves engaged in the process of establishing a new method and new approach for the newly emerging disciplines of physiology and experimental medicine. They acted through public statements and lectures and often confided their hopes in private correspondence. Rebellion is what they were engaged in — rebellion against an older generation that they thought of as entrenched and moribund. I suspect that it was accident, but symbolically all the more meaningful, that at the height of the political rebellions of 1848, Johannes Müller, the acknowledged doyen of physiology (and the teacher of all the major young rebels), was the Rector of the much troubled Berlin University. A generational dispute, then, emerges as one factor, but it is not merely the young physiologists against the old. There was, in addition, a challenge to the internal institutional and intellectual controls. The extant institutional arrangements left little room for the advancement of the young and the construction of the discipline itself seemed too narrow and constricting. The old intellectual order in physiology seemed hopelessly idealistic and its ties to the Romantic philosophy through the strong commitment of many practitioners to *Naturphilosophie* (and attendant vitalism) as the core of scientific explanation seemed out of accord with the rising materialist explanations of the political radicals.

The step taken by the rebels was the construction of a conscious link between the reform of society and the reform of science and medicine. The same attempt to link intellectual and social reform sounds familiar to those of our own generation who have witnessed strenuous efforts to create 'radical' outlooks in fields ranging from English literature through anthropology and the natural sciences themselves (28). The young Karl Marx, whose radicalism had its roots in the same historical soil, was engaged in a similar project of philosophical revolution alongside the social revolution he heralded in his famous *Manifesto*.

Rudolf Virchow, the young physician-physiologist took direct aim, singling out for attack "... science for its own sake." His tone was radical and flushed with the enthusiasm which comes from 'movement' involvement: "It certainly does not detract from the dignity of science to come down off its pedestal and mingle with the people and from the people science will gain new strength." (29)

Like his confreres in the reductionist movement, Virchow came out of the *petite bourgeoisie* of Germany. We get the feeling that they saw themselves at the margin of wealth, power and authority, and in one way or another were involved in carving new space for themselves, especially intellectual space (30). (That in later life after achieving major positions in the educational establishment they became conservative politically as well as intellectually does not alter the significance of their early self-image and action.)

In the Germany of the 1840's, the marked political and social instablilities created, or at least coincided, with an alienated intellectual group. They were challenging authority in many ways and involved in attempting to replace the old order with a new ordering of their reality in the specific instances of how to explain and manipulate nature. The decline of social and intellectual authority which accompanied the societal instabilities permitted, encouraged, and perhaps even demanded, the creation of counter-concepts. Physical and mechanical reductionism was posited as a counter-concept by its proponents. Not only did this provide a significant change in explanatory mode in physiology and medicine, but it was claimed to be anti-autocratic (31).

Why should a crisis in society affect science? One way of answering is to suggest that the felt need to construct a new world view or social order affects not only philosophies regarding humans but of nature as well. This comes sharply into focus when we examine the activities and writings of Karl Marx and Friedrich Engels. The breakdown of older patterns of authority and traditionally held dogmas or consensus positions allows much broader boundaries for exploration and the staking out of positions previously proscribed (either tacitly or explicitly). But a crisis does something else as well: it amplifies and exaggerates; it brings conflicts to light and seems to demand choice. The young Virchow literally mounted the barricades of March, 1848, pistol in hand, and figuratively mounted the intellectual barricades with the sharpness of his new philosophic-scientific positions. Choice under this type of crisis condition is often more polarized and more radical. It appears that the individual is acting out internally and personally the tensions of the group and the society.

(I have wondered whether this is the same point that emerges from Paul Forman's very suggestive study of the emergence of quantum mechanics – a non-causal physics – during the years of social disintegration and instability of inter-war Germany? (32) I should add here that I am well aware that not all 'revolutionary' scientific innovations are the product of individuals who are themselves socially and politically radical or progressive. Nor do all socially unstable or revolutionary periods seem to create radical scientific change. Further, it seems almost obvious that not every field of science or intellectual endeavor is as deeply affected as are a few. But, then, the mix of social and intellectual imperatives and contradictions is never evenly dispersed.)

There is an additional point of historical importance worth noting, for it gives further emphasis to the interaction of cognitive and institutional forms and demonstrates the involvement of social and institutional elements in carving out new intellectual space. The 1840's reductionists not only constructed new conceptual and explanatory modes, but they were deeply involved in developing new institutional forms and loci for their activities. They were responsible for an important group of new journals (some with explicit political overtones), several new scientific societies which directly reflected their viewpoints, and new laboratories and institutes from which to influence subsequent generations (33).

But even as I bring this brief case examination to a close, there are several questions connected with it that are at present unanswered and, to me at least, as interesting and important as the ones already addressed. I pose just one. Why at almost the identical period in time and dealing with the same subject matter, physiology and experimental medicine, did there develop in France a strong and broadly influential organismic (or at least anti-reductionist) explanatory mode? The very existence of such a marked difference (national style?) almost demands a parallel investigation of the mix of cognitive, institutional and social factors west of the Rhine (34).

4. A Socially Constructed Epistemology

One of the important fallouts from Kuhn's *Structure of Scientific Revolutions* was recognition of the social nature of the procedures through which knowledge is achieved and explanations changed in science. Let me move now to stretch the boundaries of the social processes beyond the narrow confines of a community of scientists and indicate my own belief that the fundamental epistemology – way of knowing – of modern science has been socially formed and indeed is in continual interaction with the broader social order. To do this I will turn back in time to the period of the Scientific Revolution and the questions raised earlier in this paper about the setting of boundaries or limits as to what would be included and what excluded from the scientific way of knowing. Frances Yates set the problem well when she pointed to the exclusion of the problem of mind which might be extended to cover the subjective, the arational and the intuitive as alternate or supplementary ways of knowing.

Why did the problem of knowledge of nature develop the contours it did during the late 16th and early 17th centuries? One thing is certain – no simple answer will suffice, but it is helpful nonetheless to identify elements of an alternative perspective on this development. Historians have alluded to this period as a time of social, political, and intellectual instabilities; an era which witnessed a decline of the traditional sources of authority with both the church and the state caught in the chaos of schisms and civil wars; a period absorbed with the rise and the challenge of movements of reformation, rebellion, and restoration.

For those who were dealing with nature and explaining nature there was also turmoil and conflict; conflict between schools and traditions, between practitioners and professors. But several trends seem to me to be clearly discernible. Whether you were Paracelsus, Telesio, Ramus, or John Dee; whether you were Vesalius, Gilbert, Galileo, Descartes, or Francis Bacon, you joined in a rejection to one degree or another, of the formal training of the period. All were critical of the 'scholes' and the Schoolmen and all offered up 'new methods' to replace the old, albeit they differed one from another (35). Further they held in common a distrust of traditional learning and the seats of that tradition, the universities. Each set about enunciating a series of 'counter concepts' aimed at replacing those previously held to be authoritative. These challengers had very much the look of alienated intellectuals who found themselves at the margin or who consciously moved there. While there are certainly elements of a broad social-generational conflict visible, the shape of the new goals indicates something more specific at work as well. They were casting about for alternate ways of understanding, explaining and acting on nature. Almost all believed in one form or another that their new way of knowing and their newly gained knowlege would enhance the human ability to dominate and command nature. Francis Bacon and the hermetics, couching their arguments in different terms, both saw 'dominion over things' as possible and greatly to be desired (36). While it would be premature to attempt to identify a direct causal link between the seekers after new methods and command of nature on the one hand and the new commercial and technological practitioners on the other, the successes of the latter group certainly permeated their societies and the marked similarities in the structure of the thought and discourse of the two groups suggest the need for a much closer examination than we have as yet seen.

Among the challengers of the older ways of knowing, there was an almost universal call for some experiential or experimental basis for knowledge; albeit the range of experience might include magic and miracles as well as the more narrowly defined natural-experimental. But there is an additional dimension to the universal extolling of experience. It not only provides a link to the artisan and technologist, a point recognized quite clearly by Bacon and drawn in some detail by Zilsel, but at a more fundamental level it substitutes a new way of knowing which can be shared by any human being and gives those at the margin of traditional authority a new authority – experience – on which they can call (37). It had the marked effect of democratizing the process of gaining knowledge, opening wide the doors of the study of nature and breaking the control of an earlier hierarchy. Galileo's setting of his *Discorsi* in the Arsenal of Venice and writing it in the vernacular Italian take on an added significance when analyzed within this perspective (38). The move was not caprice on Galileo's part, but reflected a changed view of the locus of knowledge, the means of gaining it and the audience to be taken into account.

Another element held to be critically important by the challengers of authority was the goal of educational reform. The old institutions – the universities – were distrusted and indeed had often excluded the new seekers and certainly had not encouraged the new methods and practices. Therefore, plans were drawn in many quarters for new institutions. Francis Bacon's *New Atlantis* and its Solomon's House may be the most widely known alternate vision, but others, from different movements, also sought new homes for educational activity and for the conscious pursuit of new knowledge of nature (39). If truth by authority and revelation was to be replaced by truth gained experientially or through the combination of reason and experience, access to knowledge would have to be broached and institutions of markedly different social characteristics as well as intellectual substance would have to be designed and constructed. But even further, if a larger segment of the public was expecting to be able to 'know', there would be an added impetus toward literacy and, for the newly literate, toward new areas of knowledge and experience. Indeed, the figures show that the growth of literacy in northern Europe coincided with the rise of the new experiential interest in nature as it did with the increased activities of the new mercantilism and capitalism (40).

The social world in which the new approaches toward nature were being developed was a world of insecurity and anxiety. The idyllic image that some conjure of a pre-scientific age, of a pastoral and simple society embodying human harmony with nature is little more than a romantic myth. When the stabilities of an older order and its authority were gone, people felt themselves under constant threat and living at the mercy of natural hazards and catastrophies as well as human-made follies (41). War, famine, fire, weather as well as endemic and epidemic disease all added to the uncertainties of human life and death. Humans sought relief of their estate from numerous sources and encouraged many new forms as replacements for the old. They turned for assistance, for security and for an explanation of causes to such diverse systems as magic, alchemy, mysticism and other forms of religion; to medicine, science and technology; to metaphysics, occult philosophy and natural philosophy. Often of course, the demarcations between these activities, to which we have become accustomed, did not exist.

The 'first generation' of challengers to the old authoritative explanations of nature came from all of these sources. Their initial proposals for new cognitive orders and new institutional structures were cast in markedly diverse languages and concepts. The point I would make in adding to the reinterpretation of the Scientific Revolution is that we must be aware of at least two major stages. We must recognize that the nature of the period of breakdown that produced the early manifestations of revolution in human dealings with nature was quite different from the conditions and forces that accompanied the later consolidation, establisment and continuity achieved by the new system of explaining and manipulating nature. The restoration of civil order, the re-establishment of church authority, and the strengthening of the Counter-Reformation presented the 'second generation' revolutionaries with very different conditions from those of the earlier period.

The first generation of revolutionaries were creators of what might be thought of as the 'counter-cultures' of their day, often adherents to short-lived or transient movements or sects (42). They wore many intellectual garbs and had alliances, cognitive and political, with a wide order of other challengers of authority. Operating in periods of disintegrating order (actual civil war in England), they felt the freedom to adopt more radical and extraordinary positions. Allen Debus, in his very perceptive studies of several of these movements in England, pointed out that during the mid-years of the Civil War there was a significant increase in the number of philosophically revolutionary texts published. They were Hermetic, Paracelsian and Rosicrucian, and their authors felt greater ease at publication of works that they had previously withheld out of fear of suppression (43).

The second generation of the Scientific Revolution by contrast was made up of the establishers and institutionalizers of a newly ordered reality who adopted the task of setting limits and establishing controls. The limits and boundaries were by no means only of their own making, but reflected instead the constraints being asserted from the now more orthodox social order. This second generation inherited a mixed group of heretics, magicians and philosophers who had already challenged the traditional masters and authorities. This generation thus adopted the task of sorting; they restricted, they reordered and they created a new establishment of interpreters and manipulators of nature.

In the course of raising their challenge and developing alternate modes for explaining and acting on nature, the revolutionaries posed threats to the way of knowing of the established church (particularly true of Roman Catholicism) and often to established secular authority as well. These philosophical rebels were often enough marginal men drawn from the emerging bourgeoisies of England and the continent. By both birth and strategic alliance they were involved with the rising middle-classes and the closely related dissenting religionists. These were the same groups who were intimately involved in propounding a new image of social order and also deeply committed to making the commercial and, later, the industrial revolutions which swept England and the continent (44). That elements of this group should also be involved in constructing a new philosophy of nature should come as no surprise. Indeed, the vision they proposed of achieving human dominion over nature and mastery over things was an ideology in perfect harmony with the needs of the new capitalism and the nascent industrialism. No conspiracy theory of some special capitalist influence on the formation of the scientific way of knowing is necessary. The actors and their missions were drawn from the same segment of society and the same group conflicts and social forces for both the nascent scientist and the aspiring capitalist. The recent studies by Charles Webster and Christopher Hill provide added strength and supplemental dimensions to the earlier links drawn by students such as Weber, Tawney and Merton (45). The link with Puritanism as a marginal force striving toward the center has been well studied and the additional secular dimension of the religious urge makes a new sense of what earlier appeared to be a very special English phenomenon. But similar close scrutiny of the social class basis and the immediate social role of the others among the group of first generation revolutionaries seems all the more necessary now.

To point to one or another figure who seems anomalous because he is not immediately identified with marginality is to lose sight of specific position or role that an individual has fallen into or to miss what has often occurred in revolutionary situations – the actor who breaks class ranks and makes common cause with those whose interests initially seemed quite different. That someone is not by lineage a Puritan, for instance, but makes alliance with the religious movement may have more to do with the position in the immediate social conflict of Puritanism than with its specific belief structure at that moment.

But there is a problem, and it is indeed one of marginality. The revolutionaries trying to develop new modes for dealing with nature were at the same time trying to create social space for themselves, their concepts, and their activities. To the extent that secular and religious authority prevailed or regained strength, the revolutionaries existed very much at the sufferance of such authority. The Counter-Reformation on the continent made its position very clear in its condemnation of Galileo in 1633 (46). The example was not missed so that René Descartes suppressed his *Traité de Monde* and ultimately sought refuge out of range of the Church's authority.

In England, with the years of Cromwell, Civil War, and the Parliamentary control brought to an end, with the restoration of Charles II to the throne and the re-establishment of the Church of England, lines of authority became clearly marked once again. With Test Acts to bar dissenting religionists from the universities and other positions of preferment, elements of a new orthodoxy had to be considered. In response to those reassertions of position and power of both secular and religious nature, there emerged a series of withdrawals and compromises which directly affected the nature and dimensions of the new scientific way of knowing as it became established and institutionalized by the second generation of the Scientific Revolution. This has been referred to as the 'positivist compromise' (47).

It is clear that there were several sets of overlapping influences which helped draw the boundaries of what was to become the new science. Deep intellectual schisms existed among the first generation revolutionaries and some of the key figures were early proponents of a rationally based empiricism. Francis Bacon was a firm defender of the 'experimental philosophy and a very harsh critic of alternate mystical and magical traditions (48). He was anxious to demarcate the new phisolophy from other pursuits and, even as he was one of the major claimants for gaining human dominion over nature, he also expressed great concern about who, what sort of people, would exercise such domination (49). But it is equally true that in the year that Bacon died it would have been almost impossible accurately to discern the shape and borders of the new science. Would the image be that of Giordano Bruno and include miracles as part of the explanatory system? Would it be that of John Dee, the magus, and be deeply linked to Hermetic traditions, magic and conjuring? Or, would the new philosophy be more narrowly drawn along the empiricist lines of William Gilbert? Frances Yates posed the problem well in the paragraph quoted in opening, but the question now is, what tipped the balance? What drove Hermeticism, alchemy and magic from the system of knowing nature? It is not at all clear that intellectual strength by itself was creating the bifurcation.

My claim is that the consolidators among the second generation responded to the political realities of their day and consciously banished from consideration, in their new foundations, those areas which would transcend the authority of those whom they did not wish to offend.

The able Robert Hooke, in drafting a Plan for the nascent Royal Society of London, put the issue very bluntly:

This Society will not own any hypothesis, system, or doctrine ... (not meddling with Divinity, Metaphysics, Moralls, Politicks, Grammar, Rhetorick, or Logick) (50).

On the continent a similar note of caution was struck by the newly organized *Accademia del Cimento* and they closed the Preface to thier first volume of *Essayes of Natural Experiments* (1667) with the following 'Protestation':

That we never desire to entertain Controversie with any, or engage in any Nice Disputation, or heat of Contradiction; and if sometimes, as a Transition from one Experiment to another ... there shall be inserted any hints of Speculation, we Request they may be taken always for the thoughts, and particular sense of some one of the Members, but not imputed to the whole Academy, whose sole Design is to make Experiments, and Relate them (51).

Indeed, the very name of the Italian society gives indication of their narrow empiricist commitments (52). This is in marked contrast to their predecessor society (of which Galileo was a member) which bore the tantalizing title *Accademia del Lincei* (Academy of the Lynx) celebrating the animal that sees in the darkness (53). The ideology of the new science is given a detailed exposure in Thomas Sprat's early apologia, *The History of the Royal Society of London* (1667) (54). There the concern with the Baconian vision, the search for 'certain knowledge' is extolled and it is even suggested that an appropriate preface for the work would have been passages from Bacon's own works (55). The harking back to Bacon and his model of a 'New Atlantis' links the defense of the new science with a sharp delineation from suspect activities and sects.

The new science as it established an epistemology and institutionalized its activities foreswore interest in the normative, the subjective, the arational and, implicitly in many places and explicitly in Sprat's *History*, proclaimed a neutrality on the political and moral issues of the day. The outcome, of course, was to allow a pursuit of the power that Bacon and his contemporaries so correctly saw in the new science and also to encourage the seeking of dominion over things which gave a continual fascination to the pursuit of knowledge; all of this now devoid of responsibility and real accountability, with the moral, ethical and social dimension separated from what could seem like instrumental knowledge and technique.

The Academies and Societies which became the important institutional homes and supporters of science established the patterns of control and support and helped carve out the social space which allowed science to flourish. They were the focus for legitimation and also the more mundane, but absolutely critical, function of communication. They quite clearly chose the topics for discourse and publication.

The new societies and academies served as the gate-keepers for the new science and helped establish and regulate the routes of entry to the field as well as the audiences who would be addressed. From the earliest period there were battles about the boundaries which pitted the 'established' sciences against the fields at the margins – the 'pseudo-sciences'. The second generation of the Scientific Revolution was engaged in the task of consolidation and institution building. They made the best peace they could with secular and religious authority and they rigorously policed the boundaries. They sharpened their definitions of epistemology and method and self-consciously avoided the 'forbidden' territories until, finally, they were forgotten (56). Isaac Newton, certainly one of the towering figures of the consolidated science, explicitly studied and wrote on alchemical and theological subjects yet never published any of these works in his lifetime (57).

What I have tried to illustrate in this section is the manner in which forces active in the social order played a critical role (though not the only role) in the establishment of the scientific way of knowing – the epistemology of modern science. The sources of empiricism were clearly present at the cognitive level and perhaps, more importantly, at the practical level among the skilled craftsmen and the artist-engineers (identified by Zilsel) who bridged the chasm between scholarship and manual activity (58). But the very significant new role for experimentation seems to have been mediated by social forces, both positive advantages claimed by people like Bacon as well as constraints imposed by need for compromise with resurgent authority. The strong commitment to rationality certainly had roots in the growth of knowledge during the Renaissance, but the particular limits adapted to the fields considered suitable for rational enquiry and the specific disclaimer of interest in the arational and subjective reflect the very clear pressures of,

for example, the churches in the mode of counter-reformation and re-establish-
ed hegemony.

The search for new methods, new explanatory modes, new means of
gaining knowledge and a clear restatement of human domination of nature
coincide with the decline in social authority and the struggling to the top of
new social classes seeking means of achieving wealth and power. The social
instabilities definitely permitted, even encouraged, new social and cognitive
experimentation while the desire to consolidate gains and achieve social
space in the face of re-asserted authority necessitated the careful drawing
of boundaries and foregoing of many challenges. In short, the boundaries
chosen for the new knowledge and the social forms adopted for its practice
were boundaries socially imposed and self-consciously accepted.

Notes

1. Frances A. Yates, *Giordano Bruno and the Hermetic Tradition*, London, 1964 (Vintage Book edition, 1969, pp. 454–455).
2. This point of view was summed up recently by A. Rupert Hall, 'Merton Revisited, or, Science and Society in the Seventeenth Century', *History of Science* 2 1963, pp. 1–16. Hall cites with admiration historians who reject economic and social influences, and instead opts for 'The Ascendancy of the Intellect'. John U. Nef (pp. 9–10), Alexandre Koyré (p. 11), R. G. Collingwood (pp. 11–12) are all called to testify.
3. I have tried to identify some of the issues involved in comparative and cross-cultural studies in a recent paper, Everett Mendelsohn, 'Comparative Studies in Science and Medicine: Problems and Perspectives', in Arthur Kleinman *et al.* (eds.), *Medicine in Chinese Cultures: Comparative Studies of Health Care in Chinese and Other Societies*, Washington, D.C.: Dept. Health, Education and Welfare, 1975, pp. 659–667.
4. While many authors have argued this point, two collections of essays by Michael Polanyi especially stand out: *Science, Faith and Society*, Oxford, 1946 and *The Logic of Liberty, Reflections and Rejoinders*, Chicago, London, 1951.
5. This attitude becomes manifest most clearly in areas like the confrontation with the marginal or pseudo-sciences or in the supposed battles with religion. Since most historical activity has focused on the natural sciences, the historical treatment of the social sciences by the inner circles of historians of science has been most marked by neglect.
6. The challenge brought from the outside which was forcefully stated by Theodore Roszak, *The Making of a Counter Culture*, Reflections on the Technocratic Society and its Youthful Opposition, Garden City, N.Y., 1969 and *Where the Wasteland Ends*, Politics and Transcendence in Post-Industrial Society, Garden City, N.Y., 1972. Among the historians who have turned to serious examination of the nature and meaning of these marginal activities are Robert Darnton, *Mesmerism and the End of the Enlightenment in France*, Cambridge, Mass., 1968; Michael McVaugh and Seymour H. Mauskopf, 'J. B. Rhine's *Extra-Sensory Perception* and Its Background in Psychical Research', *Isis* 67, 1976, pp. 161–189, (this is part of a larger study to be published soon in book form); T. M. Parsinen, 'Popular Science and Society: The Phrenology Movement in Early Victorian Britain', *Journal of Social History* 8,

1974, pp. 1–20. One of the characteristics that has impressed me about these activities at the margin of orthodox and established science and medicine is the social movement nature of their organization and the intense commitment evidenced by both practitioners and lay participants. Political overtones are also often present. This emerges in Darton's study and also in Dora Weiner's work on F. V. Raspail, *Raspail, Scientist and Reformer*, New York, 1968.

7. Lynn Thorndike, *A History of Magic and Experimental Science*, New York, 1923–1958, 8 vols.
8. Allen G. Debus, *The English Paracelsians*, London, 1965. See also his review of alchemical studies in 'Alchemy and the Historian of Science', *History of Science* 6, 1967, pp. 128–138. In his Preface to a festschrift for Walter Pagel, Debus cites one of Pagel's defenses of his study of the heterodox:

> ... instead of selecting data that 'makes sense' to the acolyte of modern science, the historian should therefore try to make sense of the philosophical, mystical or religious 'side-steps' of otherwise 'sound' scientific workers of the past – 'side-steps' that are usually excused by the spirit or rather backwardness of the period. It is these that present a challenge to the historian: to uncover the internal reason and justification for their presence in the mind of the savant and their organic coherence with his scientific ideas.

See Allen G. Debus (ed.), *Science, Medicine and Society in the Renaissance*, New York, 1972, Vol. I, p. 7.
9. J. E. McGuire and P. M. Rattansi, 'Newton and the 'Pipes of Pan'', *Notes and Records of the Royal Society of London* 21, 1966, pp. 108–143.
10. The other volume by Frances A. Yates of most direct concern to the historian of science is *The Rosicrucian Enlightenment*, London, 1972. Walter Pagel's two major studies are *Paracelsus, An Introduction to Philosophical Medicine in the Era of the Renaissance*, Basel, 1958; and *William Harvey's Biological Ideas*, Basel, 1967.
11. Walter Pagel, *Paracelsus*, p. 4.
12. Walter Pagel, *Paracelsus*, p. iv. This modesty is all the more surprising in light of the view that Pagel enunciated (in note 8 above) in his later study of William Harvey (in note 10 above, p. 82).
13. I first became acquainted with the term 'historical filiation of ideas' in a paper by Robert K. Merton, 'Social Conflict Over Styles of Sociological Work', (1959) reprinted in Larry T. Reynolds and Janice M. Reynolds (eds.), *The Sociology of Sociology*, New York, 1970, p. 173.
14. The single best way to enter the now voluminous sociological/social historical literature is through the bibliographical study by Ina Spiegel-Rösing, *Wissenschaftentwicklung und Wissenschaftssteuerung*, Einführung und Material zur Wissenschaftsforschung, Frankfurt/M., 1973.
15. One of the earliest studies remains one of the best; see Martha Ornstein, *The Role of Scientific Societies in the Seventeenth Century*, Privately printed 1913. Chicago, 1928, 1938. Among recent detailed accounts are Maurice Crosland, *The Society of Arcueil*, A View of French Science at the Time of Napoleon I, London, Cambridge, Mass, 1967; Roger Hahn, *The Anatomy of a Scientific Institution*, The Paris Academy of Sciences, 1666–1803, Berkeley, Calif., 1971; Margery Purver, *The Royal Society: Concept and Creation*, London, Cambridge, Mass., 1967; Loren R. Graham, *The Soviet Academy of Sciences and the Communist Party, 1927–1932*, Princeton, 1967; Robert E. Schofield, *The Lunar Society of Birmingham*, A Social History of Provincial Science and Industry in Eighteenth-Century England, Oxford, 1963.

16. One very recent study makes a conscious effort to address the linkage between the institutional structures of science and the development of the concepts of life in seventeenth- and eighteenth-century France; see Claire Salomon-Bayet, *L'Institution de la Science et L'Experience du Vivant*, Méthode et Expérience à l'Academie Royale des Sciences, 1666–1793, Thèse pour le Doctorat d'Etat, Paris, 1976 (soon to be published). A brief example of this author's conscious approach to achieve a methodology for this form of study is 'L'Institution de la Science: Un Example au XVIIIe Siècle', *Annales*, No. 5, Sept.-Oct. 1975, pp. 1028–1044.

17. Mary Douglas, *Purity and Danger: An Analysis of Concepts of Pollution and Taboo*, London, 1966. The notion of 'pure' science itself has an interesting history. It is an invention of the nineteenth century and seems to reflect the necessity to separate science done within the context of and control by the scientific community itself. This was juxtaposed to science conducted in industry or 'applied' science. The imagery created by the terminology of 'pure' versus 'applied' seemed to carry the intended message. It was connected with the mid-century efforts to professionalize scientific activity and to gain a place for science within the university. The contemporary literature is filled with attempts to create a clear distinction between the pure and applied sciences and to claim for the former a special place. Lyon Playfair developed the theme in England: "... the progress of abstract laws, however apparently remote from practice, is the real benefactor to his kind: in reality far more so than he who applies them directly to industry". And Prince Albert reflecting in part the attitude developed toward science in Germany praised those scientists who adopted a "... self-conscious abnegation for the purpose of protecting the purity and simplicity of their sacred task". For a fuller discussion of this issue see Everett Mendelsohn, 'The Emergence of Science as a Profession in Nineteenth-Century Europe', in Karl Hill (ed.), *The Management of Scientists*, Boston, 1964, pp. 3–48.

18. See the essay by Karl Mannheim, 'The Sociology of Knowledge', in *Ideology and Utopia*, transl. Louis Wirth and Edward Shils, London, 1936. A recent attempt to confront this issue and provide an alternative perspective is made by Peter Weingart, *Wissenproduktion und soziale Struktur*, Frankfurt/M, 1976.

19. Hessens's paper appeared in collection of papers presented by the Soviet delegation to the International Congress of the History of Science, London, 1931, N. I. Bukharin *et al.*, *Science at the Cross Roads*, London, 1931. The setting of the presentation and the reactions of the participants is studied by P. G. Werskey in an Introduction prepared for a recent reprinting of the original volume, London (Cass) 1971. The British historian, G. N. Clark, took up Hessen's challenge (as did numerous others) and presented an alternate interpretation: *Science and Social Welfare in the Age of Newton*, Oxford, 1937, 2nd edition, 1949. The most sustained efforts at a Marxist interpretation of the development of science are those of the crystallographer, J. D. Bernal. The two most important works, one quite specifically focused and the other a wide canvas approach are: *Science and Industry in the Nineteenth Century*, London, 1953; and *Science in History*, London, 1954. While these works are enormously suggestive, they are flawed from the point of view of historical scholarship. A recent appraisal of Marxist scholarship in the field is to be found in Robert Young, 'The Historiographic and Ideological Contexts of the Nineteenth-Century Debate on Man's Place in Nature', in Miklas Teich and Robert Young (eds.) *Changing Perspectives in the History of Science*. Essays in Honour of Joseph Needham, London, 1973, pp. 344–438.

20. This point is elaborated in very useful fashion by Max Horkheimer, *Critical Theory*, Selected Essays, trans. M. J. O'Connell and others, New York, 1972. See especially, 'The Social Function of Philosophy', p. 263ff.

21. The critical papers by Edgar Zilsel are: 'The Origin of William Gilbert's Scientific

Method', *History of Ideas* 2 pp. 1–32, 1941; 'Problems of Empiricism', in G. De Santillana and Edgar Zilsel, *The Development of Rationalism and Empiricism*, *International Encyclopedia of Unified Science*, Otto Neurath (ed.), Vol 2, No. 8, 1941, pp. 53–94; 'The Sociological Roots of Science', *Amer. Journal Sociology* 47, pp. 245–279, 1942. A German translation of these and other papers has recently been published: Wolfgang Krohn (ed.), *Edgar Zilsel, Die sozialen Ursprünge der neuzeitlichen Wissenschaft*, Frankfurt/M., 1976. A collection of Zilsel's papers in English is being prepared by R. S. Cohen and E. Mendelsohn, to be published by Reidel in 1977.

22. Robert K. Merton, 'Science, Technology and Society in Seventeenth Century England', *Osiris* 4 pt. 2, 1938, pp. 360–632, reprinted Harper Torchbook, New York, 1970, with a new Preface by the author assessing the varied responses to the study through the three decades. See Merton's collected contributions to the field: *The Sociology of Science, Theoretical and Empirical Investigations*, edited by Norman Storer, Chicago, 1973.

23. Merton, 'Science, Technology and Society', especially chapters 7–11 and Appendix A for his treatment of 'extrinsic influences'.

24. Even when the movement for radical analysis of scholarship got underway in the 1960's, the critical approach in the natural sciences lagged significantly behind the activities developed in the languages, literature, history, and the social sciences.

25. Everett Mendelsohn, 'Revolution and Reduction: The Sociology of Methodological and Philosophical Concerns in Nineteenth Century Biology', in Y. Elkana (ed.), *The Interaction Between Science and Philosophy*, Atlantic Highlands, N.J., 1974, pp. 407–426.

26. The strength and clarity of the German reductionist claim is striking when compared to that of French contemporaries. See O. Temkin, 'Materialism in French and German Physiology of the Early Nineteenth Century', *Bulletin of the History of Medicine* 20, 1946, pp. 322–327.

27. Emile Du Bois-Reymond made just this claim in his lengthy obituary-biographical appreciation of Johannes Müller. He cited Theodor Schwann as the 'first of the physicalists'. See E. Du Bois-Reymond, 'Gedachtnissede auf Johannes Müller' (1858), *Reden*, Leipzig, 1887, Vol. 2, especially pp. 206–219.

28. See for example *Radical Science Journal* (London) 1974, Theodore Roszak (ed.), *The Dissenting Academy*, New York, 1968; Louis Kampf and Paul Lauder (eds.), *The Politics of Literature*, Dissenting Essays on the Teaching of English, New York, 1972; Bardon J. Bernstein (ed.), *Towards a New Past*, Dissenting Essays in American History, New York, 1968.

29. Rudolf Virchow, 'Über die Standpunkte in der Wissenschaftlichen Medizin', *Archiv pathologisches Anatomie* 1, 1847, translated in Leland J. Rather (ed.), *Disease, Life and Man: Selected Essays by Rudolf Virchow*, Stanford, 1958, p. 29.

30. A particularly interesting study of unrest and rebellion in the universities of Germany is, Konrad H. Jaransch, 'The Sources of German Student Unrest, 1815–1848', in Lawrence Stone (ed.), *The University in Society*, Princeton, 1974, Vol. 2, pp. 533–567.

31. See for example the claim made by Rudolf Virchow in one of his earliest lectures, 'Über das Bedürfnis und die Richtigkeit einer Medizin vom Mechanismen Standpunkte', *Archiv pathologisches Anatomie* 188, pp. 1–21, 1907. Although read in 1845, the paper was not published until 1907.

32. Paul Forman, 'Weimar Culture, Causality and Quantum Theory, 1918–1927: Adaptation by German Physicists and Mathematicians to a Hostile Intellectual Environment', *Historical Studies in the Physical Sciences* 3, pp. 1–114, 1971.

33. They were instrumental in founding the Berliner Physikalische Gesellschaft (1845),

Virchow himself was instrumental in establishing a new journal, the *Archiv für pathologische Anatomie und Physiologie* (1847), a medico-political weekly, *Die medizinische Reform* (1848) and the *Physikalische-medizinischen Gesellschaft* (Wurzburg, 1849).

34. One of the few studies to adopt a comparative approach to the institutional forms of European science is J. T. Merz, *A History of European Thought in the Nineteenth Century*, Edinburgh, London, 1897, Vol. 1.

35. This point is made by Allen G. Debus in several of his studies of alchemical learning and practice in the Renaissance. See particularly *The Chemical Dream of the Renaissance*, Cambridge: Churchill College Overseas Fellow Lecture, 1968, passim; the same point emerges in his introduction to *Science and Education in the Seventeenth Century* (see note 39 below). He cites one Paracelsian, R. Bostocke "... in the scholes nothing may be received nor allowed that savoureth not of Aristotle, Galen, Avicen, and other Ethikes, whereby the young beginners are either not acquainted with this doctrine, or else it is brought into hatred with them. And abroad likewise the Galenists be so armed and defended by the protection, priveledges and authorities of Princes, that nothing may be received that agreeth not with their pleasures and doctrine ..." (p. 16).

36. Frances Yates makes this point quite clearly in her explication of the role of the Hermetics. See 'The Hermetic Tradition in Renaissance Science', in Charles S. Singleton (ed.), *Art, Science and History in the Renaissance*, Baltimore, 1968, pp. 255–274.

37. See the papers by Edgar Zilsel (note 21, above) who traces the emergence of empiricism from being the daily tool of the technologist and artisan to its inclusion as part of the broader system of explanation and action in the sciences. Francis Bacon's plan for a 'History of the Trades' gives explicit recognition, to the methods of the artisan, in the scholarly and polite literature. See Paolo Rossi, *Francis Bacon, From Magic to Science*, (transl. Sacha Rabiovitch), London, 1968, especially chapter 1, 'The Mechanical Arts, Magic, and Science'.

38. Galileo Galilei, *Discorsi e Dimostrazioni Matematiche, Intorno à Due Nuoue Scienze ...*, Leiden, 1638. A recent English translation by Stillman Drake was published in 1974.

39. See the study by Nell Eurich, *Science in Utopia*, A Mighty Design, Cambridge, Mass., 1967, for a wideranging survey. In his introductory essay to the major tracts of the Webster-Ward debate, Allen G. Debus outlines the particular confrontation that was taking place between the orthodox and heterodox forces of the Scientific Revolution and the deep interest each had in education. He is particularly interested in the 'chemists' and attempts to correct earlier historical treatments which derided several of the educational reformers for their belief in magic and chemistry; *Science and Education in the Seventeenth Century, The Webster-Ward Debate*, London, New York, 1970.

40. See Carolo Cipolla, *Literacy and Development in the West*, London, 1969. See especially pp. 52–61.

41. In a review of a series of studies on magic, witchcraft and religion in the sixteenth and seventeenth centuries, Lawrence Stone examines these issues . See 'The Disenchantment of the World', *New York Review of Books*, December 2, 1971, pp. 17–25.

42. See Frances Yates' description of the Rosicrucians for an example: Yates, *Rosicrucian Enlightenment*.

43. Debus, *Chemical Dream*, p. 26 and *Science and Education in the Seventeenth Century*, p. 20.

44. See Christopher Hill, *Intellectual Origins of the English Revolution*, Oxford, 1965; Michael Walzer, *The Revolution of the Saints*, A Study in the Origins of Radical

Politics, Cambridge, Mass. 1965; Arthur Raistrick, *Quakers in Science and Industry*, London, 1950.

45. No discussion of the social and intellectual origins of the Scientific Revolution in England will be complete henceforth without consulting the brilliant new study by Charles Webster, *The Great Instauration*, Science, Medicine and Reform 1626–1660, London, 1975. A preliminary assessment of its importance is given by Quentin Skinner, 'Projectors and Practitioners', *Times Literary Supplement*, July 2, 1976, pp. 810–812.

46. See the account of Galileo's encounter with the church in Giorgio De Santillana, *The Crime of Galileo*, Chicago, 1955. Considering the interest that has been shown in the role of religion, especially Protestantism, in the development and reception of science, it is surprising that so little attention has been given to the Counter-Reformation and its interaction with the sciences in those countries of Europe where it became a source of authority. One of the few recent studies is Francois Russo, 'Catholicism, Protestantism, and the Development of Science in the Sixteenth Centuries', *Journal of World History* 3, 1956, reprinted in Guy S. Métraux and Francois Crouzet (eds.), *The Evolution of Science*, New York, 1963, pp. 291–320.

47. See the study by R. Lenoble, *Mersenne ou la Naissance du Mécanisme*, Paris, 1943.

48. Paolo Rossi stresses Bacon's role as a demarcator in a recent paper 'Hermeticism, Rationality and the Scientific Revolution', in M. L. Righini Bonelli and William R. Shea (eds.) *Reason, Experiment and Mysticism in the Scientific Revolution*, New York, 1975, pp. 247–273.

49. In the opening part of *De Angmentis Scientarum*, Bacon reviews contemporary attitudes to the men of learning and one comes away with the image of impracticality, contentiousness, obstinate and other less than praiseful assessments. On numerous other occasions he warns against the misuse of knowledge for private gain, pleasure of mind, contention etc. See e.g. *The Great Instauration*, 'Preface'.

50. See Robert Hooke, 'The Business and Design of the Royal Society', from Charles R. Weld, *A History of the Royal Society*, with Memoirs of the Presidents. Compiled from Authentic Documents, London, 1848, 2 vols.

51. Accademia del Cimento, *Essayes of Natural Experiments* (1667) transl. Richard Waller, London, 1684, 'Preface to the Reader'.

52. The Accademia del Cimento adopted a mode of working in which the group, numbering about nine, dealt with problems in concert and the volume they published gives no record of special authors for the different experimental reports. The attitude of uncompromising empiricism and their choice of their name deserve further scrutiny.

53. Ornstein, *Role of Scientific Societies*, p. 74.

54. Thomas Sprat, *History of the Royal Society*, London, 1667, reprinted and edited by Jackson I. Cope and Harold W. Jones, St. Louis, London, 1959.

55. *Ibid.*, p. 37.

56. The activities at the margins of science and medicine deserve serious attention beyond the little that has been given to date. Not only should there be study of the role played by the unorthodox fields in the shaping of early modern science, but also of the continuing interaction between the remnants of these beliefs and practices and science at more recent periods. That 'marginal', 'pseudo' and 'folk' beliefs have been harbored within the broader public is common knowledge, but we have yet to gain understanding of the implications of this dual system for the lay conception of science itself and the measure taken of its boundaries.

57. Interest in Isaac Newton's heterodox interests has grown in recent years as we have learned to be more tolerant of the non-positivist approaches to the formation of modern science. The most serious study to date is Betty Jo Teeter Dobbs,

The Foundations of Newton's Alchemy or 'The Hunting of the Greene Lyon', Cambridge, 1975. The historiography provided in the early pages of this work gives indication of the changing interpretations of Newton's activities. A recent brief assessment of Newton as alchemist by Richard Westfall is all the more interesting coming from a scholar whose earlier interest in Newton was uncompromisingly internalist; see 'The Role of Alchemy in Newton's Career', in Righini Bonelli and Shea, *Reason, Experiment and Mysticism*, pp. 189–232.

58. See the papers by Zilsel noted above (note 21).

THE SOCIAL CONSTRUCTION OF SCIENCE:
Institutionalisation and Definition of Positive Science in the Latter Half of the Seventeenth Century (1)

WOLFGANG VAN DEN DAELE

Max-Planck-Institut, Starnberg

1. Introduction

This essay is intended to contribute to the debate about the internal or external historiography of the rise of modern science. The internal-external distinction defines the contest between two explanatory programs. The one analyzes the scientific revolution of the seventeenth century as a cognitive transformation in the history of the endogenous development of intellectual structures, the other seeks the reasons for this transformation in the technical, economic and cultural conditions of the society (2). The point of contention between the two programs is that the internal program not only seeks to reconstruct the development of science logically but also to explain it historically. It assumes an independent history of intellectual structures; the development of the forms of knowledge is an independent variable of cultural evolution. The external program, on the other hand, views the social structures and the environment of science not simply as contingent boundary conditions or as a complementary dimension of the development of the logical structures of thought but regards them as constitutive of these.

In 1963 Rupert Hall published an article entitled 'Merton Revisited' in which he stated that the debate about the competing historiographic programs had come to an end. "Clearly, externalist interpretations of the history of science have lost their interest as well as their interpretative capacity", ... "the trend towards intellectual history is strong and universal" (1963, p. 13). This opinion, however, was refuted by later developments. Thomas Kuhn's 'Structure of Scientific Revolutions', which appeared in 1962, reopened the discussion within the philosophy of science (3).

Mendelsohn/Weingart/Whitley (eds.), The Social Production of Scientific Knowledge.
Sociology of the Sciences, Volume I, 1977. 27–54. All Rights Reserved.
Copyright © 1977 by D. Reidel Publishing Company, Dordrecht-Holland.

The works of Pagel, Rattansi, Yates, Debus, and others gave a new direction to the historiography of the rise of modern science in showing that the hermetic and magical traditions of the Renaissance were an essential component in the formation of rational science which then dissociated itself from everything magical and mystical as pseudo-scientific. According to Rattansi, "the resulting picture may be less 'rational' or secularized than the image of *New Science* which has been popular since the Enlightenment, but it does greater justice to its total character" (1968, p. 140) **(4).**

In a reconstruction of the emergence of modern science from the viewpoint of modern science itself it may be possible to separate the genuine scientists of the seventeenth century from the Mystics and from the Virtuosi, who were primarily concerned with technical problems and from the projectors of the social and political reforms who belonged to the scientific movement.

The logical reconstruction does not, however, do justice to the historical process. Historically, the forerunners of modern science were not only Galileo, Harvey, Descartes but also the Virtuosi and projectors of the scientific movement, and the chemical philosophers. The rise of science comprises not only the 'mechanization of the world picture' but it is also the definition and institutionalization of a social role which makes the technical and social elements of scientific behavior binding. Taking the example of the institutionalization of science in England I intend to show that within this process decisions were taken in respect of the program of the New Science and of elements of the concept of science. The normative (social, political, religious) neutralization of the knowledge of nature, which for us is an essential element of the 'positive', objective, and concrete character of scientific knowledge, was a condition for the institutionalization of science in the seventeenth century. The confrontation with alternative concepts and claims of natural knowledge was by-passed or ended by institutional decisions. If these decisions must be evaluated within the domain of intellectual history alone, they were not, however, taken within this domain alone.

2. '... not Meddling with Divinity, Metaphysics, Moralls, Politicks ...': Legitimation Through Demarcation

The thesis which will be developed here suggests that there is a connection between the rise of science as a cognitive program and the rise of science as a social structure.

A decisive step in the social history of science toward the institutionalization of science was the foundation of the Royal Society in London in 1662 and of the Académie des Sciences in Paris in 1666 (5). The particular element of these foundations was the *political incorporation* of science by royal edict. The Charter of 1662 ensured the Royal Society the Royal favour and patronage and accorded it a number of privileges, in particular "the full power and authority ... to print such things, matters and businesses, concerning the said Society ... to anatomize dead bodies of Persons executed, to all intents and purposes and in as ample a manner and form as the Colledge of Physicians, and Company of Chirurgions of London ...", and finally "to hold Correspondence and Intelligence with any Strangers, whether private Persons, or Collegiate Societies or Corporations, without any Interruption or Molestation whatsoever'. (Sprat, 1667, p. 142) (6).

For the internal organization of scientific conduct, the incorporation of the Royal Society and of the Académie des Sciences gave birth to institutions which defined scientific standards and began to exercise social control over the observance of such standards. Science was metropolized and hierarchized. The Académie and the Royal Society became 'centres of excellence', gathering outstanding scientists. They functioned as arbiters of the work of other scientists, repeated their experiments and evaluated their writings. With the 'Philosophical Transactions' the Royal Society was in control of the most important publication of the period. Laboratories and observatories were set up. Regular meetings fostered co-operation and communication among the members. The activity of the Secretaries and the periodic scientific journals stabilized the flow of information to other scientists and to the public at large (7). Consequently for the first time there developed an infrastructure ensuring the relative continuity of scientific work.

Externally the incorporation of the new science into the political structure of absolutist society guaranteed social visibility and prestige and political protection vis-à-vis institutions with rival claims. The social functions of science, however, were marginal and, by the same token, the degree of institutionalization was low. Science remained isolated from the traditional educational system (the schools and universities); the great promises of technological advances which had been an essential element in the campaign for the institutionalization of science were not realised except perhaps for technical expertise with respect to patents for 'new and useful devices' (8). Institutionalization did not transform science into a regular occupation not to speak of a professionalization comparable to the classical professions (such as medicine or jurisprudence). In the Royal Society only Hooke as its Curator received a salary, while in the Académie some twenty of the 'Pensionaires' enjoyed this privilege. In general, however, experimental philosophy was not an occupation or a career. The normal scientist of the seventeenth century was an amateur.

According to Ben-David (1971) the institutionalization of the experimental philosophy in the seventeenth century is constituted by the ermergence of the scientific role. To be sure, this role does not yet comprise all the technical aspects which characterize science from, say, the end of the eighteenth century onward. Its essential technical element is the method of experience, i.e., experiment and measurement (9). Given this reservation, the definition of the institutionalization of 'experimental philosophy' as the emergence of the scientific role has the advantage of indicating that the social acceptance of science was not confined to concrete institutions (Royal Society or Académie des Sciences) but refers to a type of social action.

'Institutionalization of science' in the present analysis is the social organization of the technical activities of expert scientists: the definition of norms, the establishment of social control, provisions made to ensure the continuity of scientific acitivity. A different point of reference is chosen by Ben-David. According to him institutionalization will only be achieved when the cultural patterns of the society become transformed in line with the values and norms of the scientific movement (10). But this can only hold true given a complete cultural homogeneity of the society. Yet as a rule societies are segmented sufficiently to allow for the social reproduction of culturally marginal or deviant activities (cf. Eisenstadt, 1965). Certainly this applied to France in the era of Absolutism and to Restoration England. The rise of modern science did not result in the adaptation of the cultural value-system to scientific values and orientations either in France or in England. The stability of institutionalized science rested on its capability to mobilize political power without itself being anchored in the cultural system (11). Science did not achieve cultural legitimacy by exporting its values to the whole of society, but by guaranteeing non-intervention in the prevailing institutions and ideologies of political and cultural legitimation.

Most of the projects for the institutionalization of science set out clear demarcation lines from religion, politics, morality, and education. Hooke's draft Statutes of the Royal Society (1663) stated: "The Business and Design of the Royal Society is: To improve the knowledge of natural things, and all useful Arts, Manufactures, Mechanics, Practices, Engynes and Inventions by Experiments (not meddling with Divinity, Metaphysics, Moralls, Politicks, Grammar, Rhetoric, or Logick)" (Ornstein, 1938, p. 108). The Charter of the Society itself makes evident that observing these limits is the condition for the privileges the Society and its Fellows enjoyed. These are granted: "... Provided that this Undulgence or Grant be extended to no further use than the particular Benefit and Interest of the Society in Matters Philosophical, Mathematical and Mechanical." (Sprat, 1667, p. 142). In the opinion of the English natural philosophers this limitation to 'harmless" matters offered advantages to the 'Philosophical Transactions' as compared to the French 'Journal des Savants'. In a letter to Huygens Moray points out that the 'Philosophical Transactions' "will be much more philosophical" ... "and will not interfere with legal or theological matters" (1665, cited by Brown, 1934, p. 201) (12).

The only cognitive sphere from which institutionalized science did not dissociate itself were the 'useful arts'. The development of experimental philosophy and the development of technology were not yet programmatically separated. And this fact could be exploited by those planning to institutionalize science since it appealed to the utilitarian concerns of the Absolutist rulers. By contrast, the propagandists of the new science in the 1660's had very good reasons for dissociating their science from politics, from religion, from social and educational reform. In the scientific movement of the seventeenth century no clear-cut division had been made between these spheres and what was later to become positive science. Under conditions of political restoration science could only hope for official acceptance if it was ready to draw its distance from the culturally revolutionary aspects of the New Learning.

3. The Scientific Movement

From the stance of modern science it seems easy to identify cognitive factors

through which positive science prevailed against other alternatives: the limitation of the inquiry to Nature as its object, the methodical character of the
investigations (experiment, induction, hypothesis), the separation of secular
from religious knowledge, the renouncement of explanations based upon
'first principles', the predominance of mechanical philosophy over Christian
and magical natural philosophies. From this viewpoint a reconstruction of the
rise of positive science will try to trace the effects of these principles back
to their precursors and only those who advocated these principles will be
accepted as forerunners of science.

The historical process, however, is more complex. In the movement that
preceded institutionalized science, the separation of science from politics,
morality, education, and religion, which became constitutive for positive
science, had not yet taken place. For Puritan England of the pre-Restoration
period (the 1640's and 1650's) Baconianism was not only a strategy of
empirical science in the modern sense but a method and a program of social
and political reform as well. The 'Advancement of Learning' (Bacon, 1605)
was associated with the idea of an 'Allgemeine und General-Reformation der
ganzen weiten Welt' (13), and with the search for a unity of Christian truth.
The reformist philosophy of the Commonwealth as it was formulated by
Hartlib, Dury, and Comenius, and the so-called 'chemical philosophy', provide examples of this relationship.

In what follows we are not concerned with the various projects of the
Puritan era in the domains of law, education, and health, but rather with the
ideological relationship between the reform movement and the New Learning.
We are interested in the vision of science that underlies the Baconian
movement, in the concepts of the social functions and of the legitimacy of
science it implied. The distinctive features of the reform movement were anti-
authoritarianism, progressiveness, anti-elitism, pedagogic idealism, and humani-
tarian spirit. All of these features can be related to the structures of the New
Learning.

3a. *Anti-Authoritarianism*

The battle against the philosophical authority of the ancients (Aristotle,
Ptolemy, Galen) was the precondition for the revival of learning. It was the
battle of Paracelsian physicians, of alchemists, of mystical-hermetic thinkers

and of mechanical philosophers as well. All these were unified by their common reference to personal experience as the instance of cognition. Acceptance of this had become possible since experimental observation had supplied a method by which experience could be made reproducible and thus universal. A deeper foundation lay in the modified evaluation of subjectivity, articulated paradigmatically both in the Protestant Reformation and in the Cartesian rationalistic philosophy. The new self-confidence of the individual was the basis of intellectual resistance to antiquity.

The battle for the emancipation of learning was not confined to the rejection of philosophical systems. It implied contest with the classic ideals of scholarship and education and of classical style with its emphasis on eloquence and logic. Above all, it implied opposition to the laws, statutes and privileges by which the schools and universities and the monopolies of knowledge exercised by the corporate professions (medicine in particular) were shielded from the freedom of philosophical thinking. In addition, the newly-won subjective self-confidence and the resulting anti-authoritarian mood were a fertile soil for political claims to emancipation. R. Jones cites a certain Agricola Carpenter (1652) "I am a Free-born subject; and the Law of Nature which is indispensible knows no slaverie" ... "I could never resolve my Reason into the Opinion of Antiquity, or surrender my Experience upon a different determination ...". (1961, p. 127)

3b. *Progressiveness*

The scientific movement was supported by the awareness that progress is necessary and possible. The geographic discoveries of the fifteenth and sixteenth century had literally refuted the 'ne plus ultra' which is said to have been inscribed in the Pillars of Hercules, and which was symbolic for the conviction that all essential knowledge was contained in the tradition from the ancients. Progress, however, does not only mean novelty, but also accumulation and perfection. The 'advancement of learning' was conceived as an approximation to the true philosophy and methodical investigation and cooperation of researchers were the means of this progress.

The consciousness of progress clashed with the static mind of the conservative culture. The latter saw the development of Nature and of the World as in general representing a history of decay in which everything becomes the more corrupt the farther it proceeds from its source (14). The return to the perfect state of the beginning is a subliminal theme of many reform schemes of the time, as e.g. in Bacon's characterizing the renewal of science as *Instauratio Magna* (cf. Rossi, 1968, p. 127ff.). Yet, the dominant dynamic elements of the reform movement are the idea of an open future, the critical scrutiny of the old and the accumulation of the new. And the New Learning supplied the paradigm for such progress.

3c. *Anti-Elitism*

The Baconian advancement of learning has many features which accord with the democratic, participatory impulse of the Puritan era. It places perception of the senses and real things above rhetoric brilliance and speculative wit. It makes the phenomena of every day life and the products and procedures of craftmanship the objects of scientific investigation. It emphasizes the role of work as the source of cognition and insists on a clear and plain style and intelligible language in the communication of scientific findings.

There thus comes into being a vision of science which is not the monopoly of an esoteric elite of the learned. Speaking of his method, Bacon says: "... the course I propose for the discovery of sciences is such as leaves but little to the acuteness and strength of wits, but places all wits and understandings nearly on a level." And "For my way of discovering sciences goes far to level men's wits, and leaves but little to individual excellence; because it performs everything by surest rules and demonstrations." Even for Bacon this holds true only for the beginning of any science and no longer for the step of induction by which one ascends from the facts to true philosophy of nature. Presumably, the new learning had egalitarian traits only in regard to the appropriation and the reproduction of its findings (15).

Nonetheless, the turn against the elite of the learned men and a revaluation of the respective importance of intellectual and manual labor were undeniable. It was precisely the combination of natural philosophy with manual work in measurement and experiment that provoked derision from reactionary scholars. In a polemic against the 'chemical physicians' Alexander Read, a Fellow of the College of Royal Physicians and an exponent of Galenical medicine, said that "they are meerly factive, commonly called mechanicall, and so unworthy of a Philosopher" (16).

3d. *Educational Reform*

For the proponents of the new experimental philosophy it was self-evident that the 'advancement of learning' implied a critique and a reconstruction of the established scholastic educational institutions. The philosophy of real, concrete things, the emphasis on experience of the senses, and the valuation of manual labour underlying the New Learning demanded radical alternatives to the traditional schools and universities. The reform projects which were most developed came from the Hartlib Circle (cf. Webster, 1970, pp. 55–60). Educational reform for this group was not only an inevitable consequence of the New Learning but also the means towards a profound intellectual regeneration of society. They sympathized with Comenian 'pansophia', aiming at the unity of all knowledge flowing from the sources of experience, of reason, and of revelation. Didactic reform, universal language and universal knowledge were the means of social renewal. For the Hartlib circle, Bacon's proposal of a "College dedicated to free and universal studies of the Arts and Sciences" was the model and the institutional basis of reform (Webster, 1970, p. 23). The Society was to be more than an academy of experimental philosophers, it was to be a 'spiritual brotherhood', aiming both at the advancement of learning and of piety, at the reform of schools and of churchs. The 'learning' which the Baconians of the 1640's and 1650's intended to promote embraced all "knowledge of divine and humane things which by humane industrie in a rational way is attainable". It excluded – in accordance with Puritan principles – the immediate knowledge of divine things, which is "different from natural, moral and civil perfections". The divine knowledge is taught by God himself and must not be mediated by human learning. The perfection of natural, moral and civil knowledge, in contrast, is part of the educational program of the scientific movement **(17)**.

The reformation of natural knowledge through the experimental method is symbolic for a purification of all knowledge from prejudice and corruption. The investigation of nature was taken as the model of how the application of method might lead to truth and unity also in religious and political matters **(18)**.

An important effect of the new natural philosophy on education was the emergence of a social orientation: replacing the ornaments of scholastic learning by ideals of public service (cf. Webster, 1970, p. 11). The bridge thereto was the intrinsic relation assumed by the Baconian Movement between empirical knowledge of nature and the promotion of the public good, in particular the improvement of the lot of the poor.

3e. *Humanitarian Orientation*

Apparently the New Learning was related to the public good by the technical potential of experimental inquiry. The experiment is the pathway both to the discovery of the secrets of nature and to the multiplication of useful inventions. This coincidence is a main theme of the Baconian writings. The Puritan Baconians made the utilitarian perspective a norm of the New Learning. The aim of knowledge was the 'relief of mankind from outward miseries' (John Dury, 1649, cited by Jones, 1961, p. 92). 'Not useful' becomes equated with 'false' and 'vain' — features attributed to the peripatetic philosophy **(19)**. The New Learning was related to the public good, but in the Puritan era 'public good' had redistributive implications. The predominant theme was the improvement of the condition of the poor: questions of nutrition, of work opportunities in the towns, of health care. The significance of the New Learning was not confined to its potential for technical progress. Within the context of the Puritan reform movement experimental science was embedded in a normative structure which stipulated the universal dissemination and free disposability of knowledge. The universality of the New Learning was explicated in the postulate of universal enlightenment in the educational reform schemes, it was also developed into the demand for public and universally useful knowledge in the social-political reform projects of the Baconians, in particular those relating to health care. These demands presupposed free, non-monopolized application of knowledge. Therefore, the monopolistic practices of the Galenist physicians associated in the College of Royal Physicians become a main target of the Puritan reform movement (cf. Webster, 1967, pp. 16–41). The College's Fellows were the physicians of the rich and for as long as they controlled who was admitted to medical practice the countryside and the lower classes were practically deprived of medical care. The experimental chemical medicine was, under these conditions, for the Baconians not only a scientific, but also a social alternative to traditional medicine. It was held to promise chemical medication (a possibility largely overestimated at the time), that could be produced cheaply and would be easy to apply. Medical knowledge was to be made available to the public, and (at least in the more radical projects) treatment was to be free. Robert Boyle wrote in 1649 'An Invitation to Communicativeness', "inviting all true Lovers of Vertue and Mankind to a free and generous Communication of their Secrets and Receits in Physick". The campaign for free medicine postulates christian charity as an element of the usefulness of the New Learning (**20**).

3f. *The Unity of Theological and Philosophical Truth*

Although in principle they dissociated religious insight from scientific explanation, the Puritan Baconians always spoke of the 'advancement of piety and learning' in one breath. For them, the progress of science coincided with the truth of the Christian faith and without this was neither true, nor legitimate, nor useful. Robert Boyle is aware of the objection that the new science may lead to atheism "by making it possible for men to give themselves such an account of all wonders of nature, by the single knowledge of second causes, as may bring them to disbelieve the necessity of a first". And he replies: "... if this apprehension were well grounded, I should think the threatened evil so considerable, that instead of inviting you to the study of natural philosophy, I should very earnestly labour to dissuade you from it. For I, that had much rather have men not philosophers than not Christians, should be better content to see you ignore the mysteries of nature, than deny the author of it." (**21**)

The conviction that the truth of revelation and the truth of natural philosophy must not fall asunder, and that philosophy too could achieve absolute truth and certainty was shared by all the proponents of the new science (**22**). But hermetic natural philosophy did not only postulate the congruity of religious and scientific knowledge and the equivalence of their truth claims. It also constructed, on the one hand the experimental method as the means to arrive at knowledge of spiritual matters and, on the other, considered mystic and religious illumination to be the ultimate ground for true natural knowledge. In his answer to attacks by Marin Mersenne against mystical chemistry Robert Fludd insisted that true chemistry seeks explanations of man and of the universe and that, in this sense, its objects of inquiry were the same as those of theology. In this view there was a close link between the natural and the supernatural and chemistry was the key to both (cf. Debus, 1975, pp. 31–32). Correspondingly, for Hermetic chemistry, experience and experiment comprise not only the practical manipulation of objects but they presuppose the intervention of divine illumination without which the secrets of nature cannot be uncovered (23).

To sum up: in the scientific movement of Puritan England, we find the idea of experimental natural knowledge embedded in schemes whose claims and norms range far beyond what, to our mind, the concept of positive natural science delimits. Chemical philosophy developed the vision of a mystical and religious knowledge of nature as a Christian alternative to the idle speculation of scholastic philosophy. The Baconian reform movement linked and identified the New Learning with moral, educational, and social aspects. In all the social utopias of the period the learned societies of the new philosophy, Bacon's 'fraternity in learning and illumination' (Advancement of Learning, 1605, cf. Yates, 1972, p. 118), are regarded as the basis for a reconstruction of social life. The advancement of science achieved through the co-operation of the philosophers is the means of universal progress, the scientific method is the paradigm of unity through truth. The legitimacy of the New Learning remained bound to the orientation to Christian piety and social progress. Reflection upon the effects of science is part of, or condition for, science itself.

We might nowadays tend to dismiss the magic-religious overtones of the chemical philosophy as unscientific and to regard the social and cultural claims of the Baconian reformers as alien to the concept of science. This kind of criticism had already been made by contemporaries, by J. Kepler, by the mechanical philosophers (e.g. M. Mersenne), and by the Oxford Club for experimental philosophy which had come into being sometime around 1648, and which Sprat considered a direct precursor of the Royal Society (24). They advocated a reductionist concept of experimental science with no social cultural or educational implications. But in the judgment of the period this was not the only justifiable concept of science. The period was undecided. "There was still room in the third quarter of the seventeenth century for serious disagreement over the choice of the new science which nearly all agreed must supersede the Peripatetic philosophy of the past." (Debus, 1970, p. 62).

The iatrochemists were an active part of the scientific movement and in the middle decades of the seventeenth century chemical philosophy appeared as a scheme of the new natural philosophy equivalent to that of mechanical philosophy (25). Similarly, the Baconians of the Puritan Reform Movement cannot be said to have been outside the real scientific activities. Admittedly, none of the Projectors (Hartlib, Dury, Comenius) was a productive scientist, but until the end of the Commonwealth Hartlib and his circle were in close contact with the various experimental circles in England. In the 1640's Hartlib's house was the meeting place of the chemical physicians and the Virtuosi (26). Theodore Haak who established a club of experimenters in London in 1645 (which was later joined by the F. R. S. Wilkins, Ent, Goddard, Glisson, Wallis and which according to John Wallis was the group to which the immediate rise of the Royal Society is to be traced), was Hartlib's friend and ally (27). Both Robert Boyle and Sir William Petty, the one the dominant figure of the natural philosophy side of the scientific movement, the other the most dynamic of the practically oriented Virtuosi, remained Hartlib's close friends until the Restoration.

The diverse schemes of the scientific movement for defining the philosophical, normative and social connections of experimental study of nature are variants of a new science. They shared forms of thought and consciousness which distinguished them from all traditional forms of learning. Some fundamental elements of this new cognitive and cultural paradigm are: experimental method, the assumption of laws of experience, self-confidence of the subject, constructive model thinking, consciousness of progress and universalistic evaluation of assertions.

The historical choice between the variants of the new science cannot adequately be described as a process of cognitively controlled selection. Prior to 1660 there was no discernible tradition belonging to the positive experimental philosophy within which its superiority over other concepts of the new science could have been demonstrated. Nor was there, prior to the founding of the Royal Society, any institutional forum in which evaluations of the particular sciences could have visibly taken place. Moreover, the criteria according to which the primacy of positive science was established were only made cognitively binding through the institutionalization of this science. Controversies regarding the various concepts of science were often a mixture of, in the modern sense, 'scientific' and political-religious arguments. The political assessment of the scientific programs, fear of magic and heresy, and the risk of witch hunts were factors in these controversies (28).

To assume that the choice in the seventeenth century between the different programmes of the New Learning was made according to twentieth century criteria is a reconstructive circle. Historically it was the *institutionalization of science* which put an end to the cognitive contest between the various programs.

4. The Conformity of Institutionalized Science

The end of the Puritan Revolution with the Restoration in 1660 also marked the end of the association between science and social, political or educational reform, and of the call for an integration of scientific with religious knowledge. Charles II rescinded the laws of the Interregnum, revoked Cromwell's legal reforms, revised the social policy, abolished the national Puritan Church, purged the Universities of the adherents of experimental natural philosophy (cf. Trevor-Roper, 1967, p. 291). The political and social setting of the new science was fundamentally changed (29).

Above all, if there was to be a chance of royal protection and support for the experimental philosophy its educational dimension had to be abandoned. Education had become one of the chief targets of the conservative reaction. The scientists adjusted themselves "... they were willing to relinquish that element in the scientific movement which had most outraged conservative thought" (Jones, 1961, pp. 270–271).

Already in the Puritan era prominent exponents of the new philosophy had rejected the call for a radical reorganization of the universities, in particular those established in Oxford and Cambridge who felt their own position threatened by the attacks on Aristotelianism (30). After the Restoration all scientists agreed that the reformation of the schools and the universities was not their business. Literature and moral philosophy came to dominate the scene of public education (cf. Rattansi, 1972, pp. 28/29). Thomas Sprat, it is true, still made cautious allusions to the educational value of 'teaching by practice and experiments' (1667, p. 329) but the Royal Society avoided advocacy of any educational scheme that would bring it into opposition to the established institutions (31).

For the Baconian philosophers of the Puritan era the new science had been both a means to revive true religious knowledge and to keep out of the controversies between the Puritan sects (cf. Shapiro, 1968, p. 28). In the program of the Royal Society only the emphasis on the neutrality of the new science is left, no scope is offered for the revival of religiosity. Experimental philosophy is a field of inquiry freely admitting men of different faiths (Sprat, 1667, p. 63) (32). To be sure, at a time when the official culture and the learned professions were under the orthodoxy of the Church of England it was indubitably an achievement to maintain a sphere of learning that was culturally neutral due to the universalistic character of experimental knowledge (33). The price institutionalized science had to pay was the renunciation of all those 'subversive' educational, cultural and social claims and goals, which, in the past had been associated with the New Learning. Science continued to be a system which deviated from the dominant culture. It held fast to the rejection of traditional authority, to esteeming manual labour and experience of the senses rather than scholastic erudition, to the demand that its discussions and findings be made public, to universalistic evaluation and to the freedom of communication and exchange. However, the normative implications of science were more or less reduced to the functional conditions of experimental research. The clash with the conservative culture was limited to natural philosophy itself. The demands of the Baconians of the Puritan scientific movement had been "release from the restrictions of the ancien régime, liberty of religious association, liberty of the press, free trade, reform of monopolistic professional practices, leading to free and socially reoriented medicine, education and law" (Webster, 1970, p. 41). The virtuosi of the Royal Society for their part were seeking a niche within society, not the reform of that society.

No wonder they cancelled their relations with Samuel Hartlib. In 1660 Hartlib had in vain appealed to Charles II to renew his state pension. In his petition he cited among other things his merits for "erecting a little academy for the education of the Gentrie of this Nation to advance Pietie, Learning, Moralitie and other Exercises of Industrie not usual then in Common Schools" (cf. Webster, 1970, pp. 5/6). But these were precisely the activities the Crown was no longer willing to tolerate in connection with the new natural philosophy and which the Virtuosi were eager to dissemble. Hartlib had no part in the plans for the founding of the Royal Society, he was not proposed as one of its Fellows, nor does his name appear in the official 'records' nor in the 'History' of the Society. His death in 1662 went largely unnoticed (cf. Webster, 1970, pp. 63f, 69).

In 1667 Thomas Sprat still eulogized "... the Universal Light, which seems to overspread this Age ..." but this light is different from that which illuminated the 1640's and the 1650's and its universality had less meaning. One third of Sprat's 'History' is devoted to proving that there is no reason "to suspect the change, which can be made by this Institution; or the new things it is likely to produce" (1667, p. 321). Institutionalized science "will be so far from hurting, that it will be many waies advantageous, above other studies, to the wonted Courses of *Education*; to the Principles and instruction of the minds of Men in general; to the *Christian Religion*; to the Church of England; to all Manual Trades; to *Physics*; to the *Nobility* and *Gentry*; and the Universal Interest of the whole *Kingdom*." (1667, pp. 322/323).

The cultural and political conformity of institutionalized science was brought about in the seventeenth century by the very same structural properties which, with time, were to become a predominant trait of science: the reduction of explanatory claims and the identification of the emancipatory effect of knowledge with knowledge as such.

Contrary to the radical proposals made by R. Hooke who initially intended to eliminate all discussion of hypotheses from the program of the Royal Society, the real aim of institutionalized science was the establishment of the 'true natural philosophy', Additionally, the problem was posed whether the philosophical conception of the cosmos was in accordance with the ontology of the Christian world picture and what its practical consequences for religion would be. Yet in the theory which by the end of the seventeenth century had become the model for natural philosophy, i.e. in Newtonian mathematical mechanics, the claim to ontological explanations had already been forsaken.

In deriving his fundamental terms (space, time, motion, mass) Newton had translated the ancient philosophical distinction between 'true" (verum) and 'appearing to be' (apparens) into the distinction between the mathematical and the vulgar view of phenomena. For him the true phenomena are those that are determined relative to absolute space and absolute time (i.e. determined mathematically). Newton, it is true, still required that in the true natural philosophy his merely mathematical *Principia* be supplemented by physical principles which would explain the cause of gravitation. But the need for such a causal explanation had been 'forgotten' already by the following generation and d'Alembert eventually dispensed with the question of forces as a metaphysical one, and defined the mathematical description of phenomena as the proper task of physics.

As a result the retreat from ontological knowledge into the mathematical means 'to save the phenomena', by which A. Osiander, the publisher of Copernicus' 'De revolutionibus ...' hoped to shield his author against the verdict of the Church, became virtually *the* method of science. To be sure, in the seventeenth century the renunciation of ontological claims was largely a matter of tactics for the scientists.

Descartes, for instance, emphasized that his mechanical principles were only the construction of a *possible* world although he was convinced that he had discovered the true laws of nature. From Galileo to Newton scientists did not view their hypotheses merely as fictions, appropriate at the most for the calculation or production of phenomena. Nonetheless, already Newton had laid a foundation from which science ultimately came to understand the truth of hypotheses functionally and to identify it with the capacity to calculate and produce phenomena. The 'undercommitment' in the conception of scientific truth developed which later came to a head in modern positivism and in conventionalism (cf. de Santillana, 1968, pp. 179f, 187) (34).

In the seventeenth century compatibility with the practical requirements of Christian piety and morality was a *conditio sine qua non* for any science. The normative sting of this condition, however, was removed by supposing that Christian humility and devotion would be an inexorable consequence of the new natural knowledge. Robert Boyle emphasized that he had "much rather have men not philosophers than not Christians ...", but in fact he pretended that a break between knowledge of nature and religious duty was impossible. In view of the then current debates about the admissibility of vivisection and of medical experiments (blood transfusions) with human beings (cf. Ornstein, 1938, p. 118) such certainty may already be seen as ideological. It indicates that religious reservations were no longer accepted as the boundaries of the legitimacy of scientific inquiry.

This process by which an external condition for the legitimacy of the experimental search for truth becomes identified with the concept of positive knowledge itself, applies also to the relation between the new science and human needs. The normative reference of true natural knowledge to human needs remains a topic of the seventeenth century view of science. But for institutionalized science it is evident that social progress does not set any limits to scientific inquiry, but on the contrary, is *a priori* associated with it. Science rids itself of the normative goals which the scientific movement associated with the concept of true natural knowledge by identifying the social, political and educational value of knowledge with the objectivity of knowledge itself. The association with human progress is held to be ensured by the technical potential of knowledge, by which we can make ourselves "masters and possessors of nature" (Descartes). But with that it is not usefulness but only functionality of positive knowledge that is laid down. There are no methodical or social mechanisms in science to secure a link of this functionality with human progress. Knowledge and emancipation in fact fall asunder. When this can no longer be denied, the blame is put upon the applications of science, not upon science itself.

5. The Separation of the Scientists from the Philosophers

The demands for political-social and moral regeneration which the scientific movement had associated with the New Learning and which were not institutionalized in the official science organizations survived in the diffuse institutions of the literary public in bourgeois society. Partly they were driven into illegality, as was the case with the movement for experimental education in England and for rational religion in France (35).

The Enlightenment of the eighteenth century revived many of the impulses immanent to the scientific movement of the Puritan epoch prior to 1660. 'Scientia' is again propagated as a means of moral and political reconstruction of the society, scientific spirit and method is expected to uproot ignorance and prejudice, the progress of knowledge is to transform man's capabilities to use and control technology and universal education is seen as the path leading to virtue and happiness. (cf. Dieckmann, 1969, pp. 87ff.; Hahn, 1971, 36ff.)

But the addressees of these expectations were not the experimental philosophers, the mathematicians, the astronomers all by then institutionally established in the Royal Society or in the Académie des Sciences. The torchbearers of freedom and reason were the intellectuals, the 'philosophes', and the 'Société des Gens de Lettres' formed by them. The 'philosophes' were not identical with the natural scientists, nor did their community coincide with the then emerging network of cooperation and communication among the latter. The basis for the Enlightenment in England was a combination of moral philosophy and literature (**36**). In France the spirit and method of science, Newton's philosophy in particular, represented the paradigm of free and autonomous thought. But the moral and political impetus which impelled this thinking (with the Encyclopédistes, for instance such as Diderot and d'Alembert) could have no normative effect on the social and the methodical construction of the institutionalized natural sciences. The social role and conception of positive science drew an irreversible demarcation between the experimental philosopher and the movement for cultural and social emancipation. What was left was a biographical combination of the diverse intellectual dimensions in particular individuals (as for instance Newton, Leibniz, d'Alembert) (**37**). But expert science and emancipatory science, the scientific community and the scientific movement had fallen apart (**38**).

6. Consequences

It remains for me to discuss the systematic significance of the historical arguments. Let me first sum up the historical analysis. Historically the principles underlying the 'new science' (the assumption of laws of experience, consciousness of progress, thinking in terms of constructive models) did not unequivocally determine the modern form of natural knowledge. The scientific movements which had preceded the institutionalization of science by the Academies and Societies of the seventeenth century developed several variants of the new science on the basis of the above principles, embracing mechanical philosophy and empiricist 'experimental philosophy', as well as programmatic currents which associated the 'New Learning' with educational, social, and political goals. In the course of institutionalization science was differentiated from politics, morality, social reform and religion. The separation of natural knowledge from normative reflection became methodically binding and was institutionally established in the social role of the scientists. This separation, which in logical reconstructions of the development of science is described as an internal achievement, is a historical compromise that follows not only from scientific purposes but also from the exploitation of opportunities for institutionalization offered within the context of Absolutism. The confrontation with alternative conceptions and claims of natural knowledge was suspended by institutional decision. If one accepts this

historical interpretation, the immediate consequence is that the conceptual
scheme of internal and external explanation cannot be applied in the usual
manner to the rise of positive science. An internal historiography, which is
not simply a rational reconstruction of cognitive transformations in which the
real history stays in the footnotes (Lakatos), presupposes the real (social)
existence of a 'context of justification': a context which not only operates
as a logical principle of evaluation but is a real context of argumentation and
communication among researchers in which the applicability of concepts, the
claims to validity of statements of fact and of theories are decided by means
of discourse. For the transition from the diffuse programs of the scientific
movement to positive science there existed no such 'context of justification'.
Only the institutionalization of positive science created the social structures
on the basis of which it then developed. The rise of the modern structures
of science is not an event of the internal history of science but rather is the
step with which the internal history of science originates.

I shall not go into the question of the systematic consequences of this
historical analysis for the assessment of positive science as a cognitive program.
Here two contrasting positions are possible. The first asserts that, on the
grounds of the cognitive principles of the modern era, positive science was the
only possible, because the only true, form of natural knowledge, and that
historical analysis can only throw light upon the contingent circumstances
of its emergence. The second position views the institutionalization of
positive science as a decisive judgement on the cognitive and social structure
of science which determined its further development; the selection of one
variant of modern natural knowledge at the expense of others and the limiting
of the development of possible alternatives. The burden of proof between
these two positions is distributed very unevenly in favour of the internalist
argument and we seem to lack the methodological means for a decision
between them. The internalist position as a rule refers to the successes of
positive science and is supported by the prevailing view of the world which
is itself, in part, the consequence of science. The separation of practical from
theoretical discourse, the separation of claim to the validity of norms of
human action from claims to the validity of assertions about the objectivity
of nature, is a constituent element of our world view. For us there exists a
categorical distinction between knowledge of nature and social enlightenment.
Therefore, if the seventeenth century in fact elaborated an alternative

cognitive program of modern knowledge of nature, we ourselves, if for no other reason than because this program was not historically realized, have a strong likelihood of either not discovering it, or of not understanding it.

What the scientific movement of the seventeenth century did imply was the idea of an alternative social structure of science; a structure wherein scientific work would at least institutionally and normatively be associated with the requirements of human progress, enlightenment and emancipation; a structure in which reflection upon the social potential and consequences of science is part of the social role of science. Medicine offers the paradigm for such a role. In medical research, interests in knowledge are governed by normative purposes. Through the institutionalization of positive science a different social structure was realized. Scientific work became incorporated into the tradition of specialized scholarship and organized in institutions whose dynamic favours self-centered interests of scientific inquiry and results in its reproduction as 'pure' science. The ethos of institutionalized science is specialist, differentiated and (tends to be) professional. It legitimizes maximum exploitation of the advantages the separation of science from the normative spheres of culture affords, the maximization of knowledge irrespective of its social meaning. The definition of the social context of scientific work establishes — and it is this which justifies speaking of the 'social construction' of science — that the reflexive horizon of science is the growth of knowledge and not its social meaning. Obviously, science does have a social meaning. This, however, remains external to science itself — as the effect or application of knowledge (39).

The political and moral valuation of the normative neutralization of science has been ambivalent throughout history. Even the medical and technical advances of natural science since the nineteenth century have not been able to dissipate the fears that the development of science may diverge from the needs of man. In 1668 Comenius warned the virtuosi of the Royal Society that their work, should it not pursue aims transcending the mere knowledge of nature, might well turn out to be a "Babylon turned upside down, building not toward heaven, but towards earth" (cited by Yates, 1972, p. 191).

The feeling that the tower of science might be built into the earth has recently been revived. The shock of atomic weapons, the threats to the ecological balance through scientifically produced technology, the role of scientists in the Vietnam war, the visions of genetic manipulation have all given rise to severe criticism of the existing form of science. The demand for an analogue of the Hippocratic Oath for natural scientists, such movements as 'science for the people', the demand for 'free clinics' which appeared in the United States of America at the beginning of the seventies, the programs of the Chinese cultural revolution for 'de-academizing' science, and the attempts to make scientific research socially relevant by means of science policy, are all different expressions of the demands for an alternative social role of science. None of these demands abandons the foundation of the cognitive principles of modern scientific thought. What they do, however, is to revive within the horizon of these principles the postulate of a link between natural knowledge and human emancipation and the satisfaction of human needs. Whether this can produce a cognitive alternative to positive science is uncertain and perhaps improbable (40). Presumably the alternative to the established science is positive science within a modified social context. The call for such a change may in our society be as illusory for political reasons as were the demands of the scientific movement of the seventeenth century to associate objective natural knowledge with the strategies of cultural, political and social emancipation. But the limits for a social reconstruction of science lie first in the society and not in science.

Notes

1. I am indebted to Everett Mendelsohn for the idea of investigating the 'social construction' of science. He outlined the theme in a lecture at the Max-Planck-Institut in Starnberg in December 1974. The manuscript was finished at the end of 1975. Therefore I could not take into account Webster's (1976) which is probably the most comprehensive analysis of Puritan Science. Cf. also Hoppen 1976.
2. A characteristic example of the internal program is the approach of E. Dijksterhuis (1955) who reconstructs the rise of modern science as the 'mechanization of the world picture'. For the external program one may refer to R. Merton (1970) who attributed the rise of scientific thought in the seventeenth century to the emergence of the Protestant ethic and to the technological and economic needs of the society. E. Zilsel provides another variant of the external explanation. According to him the roots of modern science have to be seen in a social de-differentiation of the Renaissance society by which the competences of various strata of intellectuals (the free artisans and engineers, the humanists, and the traditional scholars) became amalgamated (1942) (cf. Krohn 1976).
3. Cf. I. Lakatos and A. Musgrave (1970), S. Toulmin (1972), Stegmüller (1973). See also G. Böhme, W. van den Daele, and W. Krohn (1972).
4. See also the debate in *Changing Perspectives in the History of Science – Essays in*

Honour of Joseph Needham, M. Teich and R. Young (eds.) (1973), and M. Righini Bonelli and W. Shea (1975).

5. None of the early academies and learned societies prior to 1660 achieved a stability and paradigmatic character comparable to the Royal Society or the Académie des Sciences. In England and in France 'experimental philosophy' evolved in the diffuse and private form of associations characteristic of the emerging bourgeois society – in the clubs, salons, the 'Invisible College'. In the rigid feudal society of France scientific societies were more politically dependent on a strictly private character than in puritan England before 1660 (cf. Brown, 1934, pp. 12, 20, 30). In Italy the Counter-Reformation suppressed all attempts at institutionalization. The Florentine Academia del Cimento (1657–67) which was certainly the most important foundation prior to 1660, lacked a basis in a more general scientific movement and in a milieu that was hostile to the new science depended on the Grand Duke's patronage and interests. Its influence was confined largely to the court of Tuscany.

6. The relations between the Académie des Sciences and the French Crown were closer. The meetings were to be held in the King's Library, at least until proper laboratory facilities had been completed. Its members were appointed by the State and received their 'pensions' from the Treasury (Hahn, 1971, pp. 4, 14, 16).

7. The rising social prestige of the Académie and the fact that it could choose its members from any part of France enabled, at least in the case of the Académie des Sciences, a purposeful recruitment of members. In the Académie a number of 'students' each attached to a pensioned academician, were allowed to attend meetings, as passive members (Hahn, 1971, p. 16).

8. As early as 1662 the King declared that no patents should be granted for any philosophical, mechanical invention, until examined by the Royal Society (Ornstein, 1938, p. 21). But nothing seems to have come of this. In 1664 the Society requested the King to issue an edict according to which all mechanical inventions would be presented to it for testing, to see "whether they were new, true and useful" (cf. Clark, 1948, pp. 14f.). By contrast the Académie des Sciences did act as a kind of patent office for the French Crown (Hahn, 1971, p. 22).

9. The objection that Thomas Kuhn (1972, p. 174) raises to Ben-David's thesis is "that the scientific role came into unequivocal existence not earlier than the end of the eighteenth century when (primarily in French science) the tools of the more mathematical scientific tradition were applied to the product of a matured empirical movement of which the primary home had been, and for a time remained, Britain". (cf. also Ben-David, 1975).

10. "Neither scientistic movement nor institutionalization of science refers to expert scientific activity, but to the behavior of people in general in relation to science. The scientistic movement consists of a group of people who believe in science (even though they may not understand it) as a valid way to truth and to effective mastery over nature as well as to the solution of the problems to the individual and his society. Empirical and mathematical science, in this view, is a model for the solution of problems in general and a symbol of the infinite perfectability of the world. The word 'movement' implies that the group strives to spread its views and to make them acceptable to society as a whole. Institutionalization follows when the movement achieves its aim and has its values actually adopted by society". (Ben-David, 1971).

11. Cf. Downey, 1967. The assumption that normative integration with the society is the condition for the institutionalization of science is influenced by Merton's (1957) attempt to establish that liberal democracy is a functional precondition for science.

12. French scientists, in their plans to secure the King's patronage and support, were also ready to assure him of their abstention from political and cultural activities. The project for a Compagnie des Sciences et des Arts (1663 or 1664) contains a clause: "In the meetings there will never be a discussion of the mysteries or religion or of the affairs of state; and if there is at time talk of metaphysics, morals, history, or grammar, it will only be in passing and in relation to physics or to exchanges among men" (Hahn, 1971, p. 12).

13. From the title of the first manifesto of the so called 'Rosi-crucians' (1614), see F. Yates, 1972, p. 236. For the scientific movement in England see H. Trevor-Roper, 1967; R. Jones, 1961, pp. 87–180; M. Purver, 1967; C. Webster, 1970, pp. 1–72; P. Rattansi, 1968; C. Hill, 1968; M. Boas and R, Hall, 1968; for the chemical philosophy see especially the works of A. Debus, 1968, 1975; C. Webster, 1967; P. Rattansi, 1963, 1964.

14. The theory of the decay of nature and the controversy with the Baconian movement are dealt with in R. Jones, 1961, pp. 22f.

15. The repetition of experiments that had been invented by others was a popular occupation of the virtuosi in the Baconian movement. The egalitarian presupposition that everybody was capable of understanding the New Learning is implied in Descartes' assumption in the beginning of the *Discours de la méthode* (1637) that reason is universal and nothing in the world is more evenly distributed than common sense.

16. R. Jones, 1961, p. 80; for other examples of this attitude see *ibid*. 43, 76.

17. See John Dury's 'Some Proposals Towards the Advancement of Learning' (1653), reprinted in C. Webster, 1970, pp. 165f.

18. The certainty of experimental natural research is a paradigm for the certainty of religious knowledge. John Everard (1653) criticizes the scholasticism of Christian dogmatists and praises the experience of those who "know Jesus Christ and the scriptures *experimentally* rather than grammatically, literally or academically" (see C. Webster, 1967, p. 27).

19. The feeling of illegitimacy vis-à-vis knowledge for the sake of knowledge, as can for instance be found in astronomy, is expressed by Robert Boyle in a famous letter to S. Hartlib: "... if there be no such use at all of the motions of these bodies, as that which I may call physical, viz. for predicting, ... it would very much lessen and depreciate with me that toil, cost, pains, watchings, and continual exercises and endeavors, that have been used for the gaining of exact observations in astronomy. Seeing, when we have done all, ... we can propound no end, benefit, use or advantage, ... and if so, we know them only to know them." (R. Boyle, *Works* V, pp. 638f.) The utilitarian evaluation of natural knowledge holds true also for the 'invisible college' of experimenting virtuosi in London, to which R. Boyle refers in a letter from 1646: "The other humane studies I apply myself to, are natural philosophy, the mechanics and husbandry, according to the principles of our new philosophical college, that values no knowledge but as it has a tendency to use". (R. Boyle, *Works* I, p. 20.)

20. See C. Webster, 1967, p. 32. In contrast to Boyle and the other Baconians of the Hartlib circle the majority of the chemical doctors refused to communicate their prescriptions for commercial reasons and because of their relation with the esoteric hermetic tradition. Nonetheless Hartlib's house was a centre of the movement of the chemical doctors. A practical example of a social medicine is offered by the 'Conférences du Bureau d'Adresse' which the French chemical doctor Théophraste Renaudot held in Paris from 1631 on (see H. Brown, 1934, pp. 18ff.). The conferences had the function (among other things) of a 'free clinic' for the poor. Renaudot gave public and free consultation and distributed medicines gratis.

21. 'The Excellency of Theology' (written 1665), see M. Boas Hall, 1965, p. 142.
22. B. Nelson (1968) points out that fictionalism (the construction of 'saving the phenomena') was not accepted by Copernicus, Galilei, Descartes. For Bacon see *Works*, Vol. 5, p. 511: "... it is not merely calculations or predictions that I aim at, but philosophy: such a philosophy I mean as may inform the human understanding, not only of the motion of the heavenly bodies and the period of that motion, but likewise of their substance, various qualities, powers, and influences, according to natural and certain reasons, free from superstition and frivolity of traditions; and again such as may discover and explain in the motion itself, not what is accordant with the phenomena, but what is found in nature herself, and is actually and really true". In the 'Fama Fraternitatis' of J. Andreae, which is written in the hermetic-mystical tradition, the call for unity of scientific and religious truth is expressed in the following way: "... seeing the truth is peaceable, brief, and always like herself in all things, and especially accorded by with Jesus in omni parte and all members. And as he is the true Image of the Father, so is she his Image. It shall not be said, this is true according to Philosophy, but false in Theology. ... All that same concurreth together, and makes a sphere or Globe, whose total parts are equidistant from the Centre." (Reprinted in F. Yates 1972, p. 250).
23. See C. Webster, 1967, pp. 27f., and M. Purver, 1967, pp. 207f. for Comenius' concept of knowledge.
24. See A. Debus, 1975, pp. 26, 31; M. Purver, 1961, pp. 106ff.
25. In the middle of the seventeenth century Paracelsian and Helmontian chemistry had an increasing part in the plans for a New Learning. In the sixteen fifties more Paracelsian and mystical chemical texts were translated than in the century before 1650. See A. Debus, 1970, p. 33, and, 1975, pp. 35ff.
26. R. Wilkinson, 1968, pp. 54ff. in addition to Boyle and Petty includes the Fellows of the Royal Society Henshaw, Digby, Whintrop in the Hartlib circle.
27. The significance of the London association of virtuosi for the development of institutionalized science is controversial, see M. Purver, 1967, pp. 161ff.; Hill, 1968, pp. 144ff. G. Frank indicates that the work of the virtuosi in Oxford was hardly less practically oriented than the work of those in London (1973, pp. 193ff.).
28. In the Novum Organum Bacon had refuted the attempts of the hermetic tradition to connect religious and natural knowledge, for "from this unwholesome mixture of things human and divine arises not only a fantastic philosophy but also a heretic religion" (cited by P. Rattansi, 1972, p. 13). Similarly Marin Mersenne in 1625 had warned Robert Fludd that the religious theological and philosophical speculations had to be dropped from alchemy if this science was to be accepted by the catholic church (see A. Debus, 1975, p. 31). See Also F. Yates (1972, p. 113).
29. See also R. Jones, 1961, pp. 270ff.; C. Webster, 1970, pp. 63-72; F. Yates, 1972, pp. 188ff.
30. This applies in particular for such proposals of the Hartlib circle that aimed at a de-institutionalization and a de-professionalization of secular and religious education (see C. Webster, 1970, p. 56). In the debate with the chemical philosopher John Webster the two professors of astronomy John Wilkins and Seth Ward (both members of the Oxford Philosophical Society) opposed the magical-christian elements of Webster's proposals for a reformed curriculum and denied the necessity to reform the universities altogether. They conclude their defence of the university with the opportunistic warning: "Which of the Nobility or Gentry, desire when they send their Sonnes hither, that they should be set to Chymistry, or Agriculture, or Mechanicks? ... the desire of their friends, is not, that they be engaged in those experimentall things, but that their reason, and fancy, and carriage, be improved by lighter Institutions and Exercises, that they may become Rationall and Gracefull

speakers, and be of an acceptable behaviour in their Countries". (Vindiciae Academiarum, 1664, p. 50; reprinted in A. Debus, 1970). The reason for this 'defence' was the fear that the reform of the universities would less serve the promotion of experimental philosophy but rather the strengthening of the influence of the Puritan sectarians. (See B. Shapiro, 1968, pp. 23, 27).

31. In 1661 the poet Abraham Cowles put forward a plan for erecting a 'philosophical college', which according to Sprat very much furthered the foundation of the Royal Society (1667, p. 59). In this plan the education of the youth in the spirit of the New Learning was to be an essential element of the institutionalization of science. The virtuosi of London cancelled the educational scheme.

32. In this respect, the difference from the pre-restoration period must not be exaggerated. The institutional combination of development of religion with the new science was ruled out, but the significance of scientific attitudes for the development of a rational, natural religion was not denied. Many members of the Royal Society continued to advocate 'latitudinarian' religious policies (tolerance in theological and liturgical subtleties). (See M. Purver, 1967, pp. 143ff.; B. Shapiro, 1968; J. Jacob, 1975).

33. "For they openly profess, not to lay the foundation of an English, Scottish, Irish, Popish or Protestant philosophy, but a philosophy of mankind".

34. In R. Boyle's chemistry, too, the possible shift from substantial to functional reasoning is indicated. Instead of explaining the phenomena from their true, first causes and principles, science can explain them from secondary causes, that contain the conditions under which they can be produced with certainty. It is true that explanation from first principles is the proper aim of science, but for the use and the domination of nature an explanation of the second kind is sufficient. See 'Certain Physiological Essays', written 1657, Works, Vol. I, p. 310.

35. Included in the jurisdiction of institutionalized science are, however, such 'arts' as alchemy and astrology, they are discarded as non-science.

36. This applies, for instance, to John Locke, one of the fathers of the English enlightenment. For him in 1690 natural philosophy does not yet deserve the qualification 'scientific' whereas he regards "morality the proper science and business of mankind in general" (1690, p. 327) (cited by P. Rattansi, 1972, p. 29).

37. Newton never tried to integrate his theological activities with his membership in the Royal Society. The statutes of the reorganized Academy of Friedrich II in Berlin (1746) did provide a common organization for a class of theoretical and practical philosophy together with classes for experimental philosophy, mathematical philosophy and fine arts which was unique in Europe. However, the mathematical and physical classes never had common meetings with the philosophical one. See A. v. Harnack, 1901, Vol. I, pp. 2, 300ff.

38. J. Ben-David, 1971, p. 85f. remarks that in several European countries the institutionalization of science was organized 'from above' without any basis in an emancipatory scientific movement.

39. Efficiency and growth have, in a similar way, come to be the constitutive rationale of the system of scientific production as the accumulation of capital has come to be the rationale of the economic system.

40. A revision of the concept of objective, neutral natural knowledge might possibly be necessary in the domain of (psychosomatic) medicine.

References

Bacon, F., Works, ed. by J. Spedding, R. Ellis, and D. D. Heath, Boston: Brown & Taggard, 1860/64.

Ben-David, J., *The Scientist's Role In Society: A Comparative Study*, Englewood Cliffs, N. J.: Prentice Hall, 1971.

Ben-David, J., 'Probleme einer soziologischen Theorie der Wissenschaft', in P. Weingart (ed.), *Wissenschaftsforschung*, Frankfurt, N.Y.: Campus, 1975, 133–161.

Böhme, Gernot, van den Daele, W., and Krohn, W., 'Alternativen in der Wissenschaft', *Zeitschrift für Soziologie* 1, 1972, 302–316.

Bonelli, Rhigini, M. and Shea, W. (eds.), *Reason, Experiment and Mysticism*, New York: Science History Publications, 1975.

Brown, H., *Scientific Organisations in Seventeenth Century France*, Baltimore: The Williams and Wilkins Company, 1934.

Boyle, R., *Works* (1744), (ed. by Thomas Birch), Neudruck: Hildesheim: Olms, 1965.

Clark, G., *Science and Social Welfare in the Age of Newton* (1970), Second Edition, 1949, Reprinted, 1970. Oxford: Oxford University Press.

Debus, A., 'Palissy, Plat, and English Agricultural Chemistry in the 16th and 17th Centuries', *Archives Internationales d'Histoire des Sciences* 21, 1968, 67–88.

Debus, A., *Science and Education in the Seventeenth Century: The Webster-Ward Debate*, London and New York: MacDonald & American Elsevier, 1970.

Debus, A., The Chemical Debates of the Seventeenth Century: the Reaction to Robert Fludd and Jean Baptiste van Helmont', in M. Righini Bonelli, W. Smea (eds.) *Reason, Experiment and Mysticism in the Scientific Revolution*, New York: Science History Publications, 1975, 19–47.

Dieckmann, H., 'The Concept of Knowledge in the Encyclopedie', Dieckmann, Herbert *et al.*, *Essays in Comparative Literature*, St. Louis, Missouri: Washington University Studies, 1961, 73–107.

Dijksterhuis, E., *Die Mechanisierung des Weltbildes*, Berlin, Göttingen, Heidelberg: Springer, 1956.

Downey, K., 'Sociology and the Modern Scientific Revolution', *The Sociological Quarterly* 8, 1967, 239–254.

Eisenstadt, S., 'Transformation of Social, Political, and Cultural Orders in Modernization', *American Sociological Review* 30 1965, 659–673.

Frank, R., 'John Aubrey, John Lydall, and Science of Commonwealth Oxford', *Notes and Records of the Royal Society* 27, 1973, 193–217.

Hahn, R., *The Anatomy of a Scientific Institution, The Paris Academy of Science, 1666–1803*, Berkeley, London: University of California Press, 1971.

Hall, M. B., *Robert Boyle on Natural Philosophy: An Essay with Selections from his Writings*, Bloomington: Indiana University Press, 1965.

Hall, R., 'Merton Revisited or Science and Society in the Seventeenth Century', *History of Science* 2, 1963, 1–16.

Harnack, A. v., *Geschichte der Preussischen Akademie der Wissenschaften*, 3 vols., Berlin: Akademie der Wissenschaften, 1900.

Hill, Ch., 'The Intellectual Origin of the Royal Society, London or Oxford?' *Notes and Records of the Royal Society* 23, 1968, 144–156.

Hoppen, Th., 'The Nature of the Early Royal Society', Part I, II, *British Journal for the History of Science* 9, 1976, 1–24, 243–273.

Jacob, J. 'Restoration, Reformation and the Origins of the Royal Society', *History of Science* 13, 1975, 155–176.

Krohn, Wolfgang, 'Die sozialen Ursprünge der neuzeitlichen Wissenschaft', foreword to Wolfgang Krohn (ed.), *Edgar Zilsel, Die sozialen Ursprünge der neuzeitlichen Wissenschaft*, Frankfurt: Suhrkamp, 1976.

Jones, R., *A Study of the Rise of the Scientific Movement in Seventeenth-Century England*, St. Louis: Washington University Studies, 1961.

Kuhn, T., *The Structure of Scientific Revolutions*, Chicago: University of Chicago Press, 1962.
Kuhn, T., 'Scientific Growth: Reflections on Ben-David's 'Scientific Role',' *Minerva* 10, 1972, 173–4.
Lakatos, I. and Musgrave, A. (eds.), *Criticism and the Growth of Knowledge*, New York: Cambridge University Press, 1970.
Merton, R., *Science, Technology and Society in Seventeenth-Century England*, New York: Fertig, 1970.
Nelson, B., 'The Early Modern Revolution in Science and Philosophy: Fictionalism, Probabilism, Fidelism, and Catholic 'Prophetism',' in R. S. Cohen and M. Wartofsky (eds.), *Boston Studies in the Philosophy of Science*, Vol. III, Dordrecht: Reidel, 1968, 1–40.
Ornstein, M., *The Role of Scientific Societies in the Seventeenth Century*, reprint of the third edition of 1938. London: Archon Books, 1963.
Rattansi, P., 'Paracelsus and the Puritan Revolution', *Ambix* 11, 1963, 24–32.
Rattansi, P., 'The Helmontian-Galenist Controversy in Restoration England', *Ambix* 12, 1964, 1–23.
Rattansi, P., 'The Intellectual Origins of the Royal Society', *Notes and Records of the Royal Society of London* 23, 1968, 129–143.
Rattansi, P., 'The Social Interpretation of Science in the Seventeenth Century', in P. Mathias (ed.), *Science and Society 1600–1900*, Cambridge: Cambridge University Press, 1972, 1–32.
Rossi, P., *Francis Bacon. From Magic to Science*, London: Routledge & Kegan Paul, 1968.
Santilliana, G. de, *Reflections on Men and Ideas*, Cambridge, Mass: The M.I.T. Press, 1968.
Shapiro, B., 'Latitudinarianism and Science in the Seventeenth Century England', *Past and Present* 40, 1968, 16–41.
Sprat, T., *History of the Royal Society* (1667), (ed. with critical apparatus by Jackson Cope and Harold W. Jones), St. Louis, Missouri: Washington University Studies, 1958.
Stegmüller, W., *Theorie und Erfahrung (Probleme und Resultate der Wissenschaftstheorie und analytischen Philosophie Bd. II)*, 2. Halbband, Theorienstrukturen und Theoriendynamik. Berlin, Heidelberg, New-York: Springer, 1973.
Teich, M. and Young, R. (eds.), *Changing Perspectives in the History of Science. Essays in Honour of Joseph Needham*, London: Heinemann, 1973.
Toulmin, St., *Human Understanding*, Vol. I. Oxford: Clarendon Press, 1972.
Trevor-Roper, H., *Religion, the Reformation and Social Change*, London: Macmillan, 1967.
Webster, C., 'English Medical Reformers of the Puritan Revolution: A Background to the 'Society of Chymical Physitians',' *Ambix* 14, 1967, 16–41.
Webster, C. (ed.), *Samuel Hartlib and the Advancement of Learning*, London: Cambridge University Press, 1970.
Webster, C., *The Great Instauration. Science, Medicine and Reform 1626–1660*, New York: Holmes & Meier, 1976.
Wilkinson, R., 'The Hartlib Papers and Seventeenth Century Chemistry', *Ambix* 15, 1968, 54–69.
Yates, F., *The Rosicrucian Enlightenment*, London: Routledge & Kegan Paul, 1972.
Zilsel, E., 'The Sociological Roots of Science', *American Journal of Sociology* XLVII, 1942, 245–279.

PROBLEMS OF A HISTORICAL STUDY OF SCIENCE

WOLF LEPENIES

Free University of Berlin

1. Introduction

Within a relatively short period of time the study of science (Wissenschaftsforschung) has become a unified discipline. The philosophy of science, the
history of science (1) and the sociology of science no longer dismiss one
another as auxiliary disciplines but exchange essential elements of their
conceptual apparatus. As examples one might take Weizsäcker's conception
of the history of science as being a philosophy of science, or Thomas Kuhn's
attempt to establish a scientific-historical theory on the basis of a sociological
category ('scientific community'). In this respect the study of science
furnishes, from its own development, proof of the thesis that changes in the
system of science are characterised less and less by the emergence of completely new disciplines or interdisciplinary programmes but rather by exchanges of parts of disciplines within established subjects and by an amal-
gamation of disciplines.

Both in its subject-matter and in its methods the study of science is able
to shift concerns. These can be of a scientific-theoretical, sociological or historical nature. Moreover, thematic and methodological emphasis can be
combined. A sociological problem, for example, can be dealt with historically
or, on the other hand, theoretical conclusions can be drawn from historical
research. In this way combinations of approaches in the broad field of the
study of science could be outlined.

Here, however, I merely want to draw attention to the fact that in
principle these combinations are possible and that their legitimacy can no
longer be disputed. In the following, I confine myself to the problem of *one*
of these possible combinations and discuss some points concerning the key
problems of a historical study of science.

Mendelsohn/Weingart/Whitley (eds.), The Social Production of Scientific Knowledge.
Sociology of the Sciences, Volume I, 1977. 55–67. All Rights Reserved.
Copyright © 1977 by D. Reidel Publishing Company, Dordrecht-Holland.

2. History of Science and the Historical Study of Science

An open relation between sociology and history has largely contributed to
the increasing importance of the historical study of science. After all, the
humanities and the social sciences can to-day, more than ever before, be
identified by a specific set of cross-references. While historical studies on the
one hand are being understood more and more as a social science, the
tendencies to a historical approach in sociology on the other hand can no longer
be disregarded. Some authors, in describing this state of affairs, have gone so
far as to talk about a reversal of methodology. This suggests that a nomoth-
etic history would be contrasted with idiographic sociology. Although this
characterisation surely goes too far, it indicates an alteration in the relations
between history and sociology, a change from which the historical study of
science has undoubtedly benefited.

At this point a terminological remark, though of far-reaching consequence,
seems to be appropriate. Why talk of the historical study of science and not
simply of the history of science? The answer depends on one's assessment of
the extent to which history lends itself to a theoretical approach (Theorie-
fähigkeit). Jürgen Habermas has suggested that we should distinguish between
theoretical research in history (Geschichts*forschung*) and historical writing
(Geschichts*schreibung*). For the time being, I would like to use this distinction, although I do not accept all the conclusions Habermas draws from it.
Habermas sees the main characteristic of historical writing in its narrative
form. This dependence on form restricts its ability to lend itself to a theoretical approach insofar as narratives do not predict anything, and forecasts
cannot be narratives. Compared with this, theoretical research in history
plays a more instrumental part. It "acts as a useful corrective against the
provincialism of time, region and matter of present social research" (2). In
the end, however, the theoretical value of research in history is not greater
than historical writing. It has the mere advantage of being able to offer its
assistance to more theory-oriented disciplines.

Habermas thinks he is able to show that sociology can demonstrate its
theoretical capacity, both towards historical writing and theoretical research
in history, only if it concentrates on the construction of a theory of social
evolution. Such a theory of social evolution is no part of 'history' as a discipline although its task, like that of universal history, can be described with the

catchword 'reconstruction'. But while universal history describes *previous events*, a theory of social evolution necessarily reconstructs *previous stages of development*. Habermas thinks that, with the assistance of this differentiation, he can show that a theory of social evolution, as distinguished from universal history, can in principle make a forecast. The evidence does not seem to me to be conclusive on this point. Furthermore, I do not think that theoretical research in history, as Habermas puts it, really has to be content with the role of Cinderella as a universal subsidiary discipline. Yet the differentiation between historical writing and theoretical research in history is useful because, by using it, history of science and historical study of science can be also distinguished.

3. Reconstruction

With Imre Lakatos' research, the term 'reconstruction' has become a central conception in the study of science. By contrast, the history of science — also in terms of its self-understanding — is to a large extent confined to a narrative function. In this context one should not forget that Comte, who was in vain to ask Guizot to establish a professorship for the history of science, sometime ago drew a distinction between the history of science and the historical study of science. I believe, at any rate, that the following quotation from his letter to Valat from September 8th, 1824 can be interpreted in this way (3). "Rappelle-toi qu'en physique on ne remonte jamais au-delà de Galilée, en chimie au-delà de Black et de Lavoisier, etc., et tu verras que, non pour l'histoire d'une science, mais pour sa culture, ce qui est fort différent, l'usage de regarder comme nuls et non avenus tous les travaux qui ont précédé l'époque où la science est devenue positive, est très-raisonnable; le reste ne ferait qu'entraver le savant, et ne doit etre pris en considération que par l'historien de la science".

Here the history of science is restricted to antiquarianism which makes the historian eagerly eat even the "dust of bibliographical trifles", to quote Nietzsche's malicious terms in *Vom Nutzen und Nachteil der Historie für das Leben*. On the other hand there is the culture of science, as Comte calls it, in which a discipline's actual stock of knowledge is represented. The aim of the historical study of science is to trace the genesis of this stock of knowledge and the obstacles to its process of maturation. In this respect, the conceptual apparatus of the historical study of science is not new. It was formulated at exactly the same time as the first attempt was made to institutionalise the history of science as an academic discipline.

Compared with the traditional history of science, which was oriented more towards a single scientific discipline — and thus pursued the development of this one discipline over a longer period — the historical study of science is oriented towards several disciplines. It reconstructs the development of complexes of disciplines in shorter, more coherent periods. The awareness that continuity of a discipline's name does not lead to any clear conclusions on cognitive or institutional identities was crucial for this change in the angle of approach.

So it was less unpretentiousness or concentration on a clearly limited question which caused François Jacob not to write a history of biology but rather a logic of the living with the sub-title 'A History of Heredity', but more the understanding that problem-fields show more stability than disciplines (4). This obviously does not mean that problem-fields do not change — this would make an analysis which uses historical comparison meaningless. It does mean, however, that certain basic problems remain comparable even over longer periods of time, whereas it is not very sensible to compare, for example, the 'Biology' of Buffon with that of Darwin, not to mention molecular genetics.

All this does not mean, however, that a history of problems can simply replace a history of disciplines. It is rather the appreciation that different disciplines in an observable period can have more similarities that the different stages of a single discipline over a longer period which is decisive. Michel Foucault, for example, wanted to show that linguistics, biology and economics at the end of the 18th Century had more in common than the 'Biology' of Buffon and Darwin or Ricardo's economics and Marx's political economy. Without accepting all of Foucault's premises and conclusions, I think that his approach is of special importance for a historical study of science. If the historical study of science is going to pursue the reconstruction of previous historical stages of development, it cannot confine itself to a single discipline or simply connect reconstructions of several disciplines. If it wants to be more than a mere recapitulation, the historical study of science must rather prove the necessity of the discipline's development. This can probably be

done in different ways but at least it becomes plausible if steps in the development of different disciplines can be pointed out; steps which are analogous
and perhaps complementary, but in any case connectable with one another
in a systematic way.

4. Disciplinary Relations

Thus it would be important for a historical study of science to construct a
theory of relations between scientific disciplines. It is not possible to write
a history of a discipline without taking into account developments in neigh-
bouring disciplines, whether they have been models or rivals for it. In this,
neither the social philosophy of the 17th Century, nor the social science of
the 19th Century can be written without looking at mechanics and biology
respectively as their model disciplines. And in any case, historiography in its
different forms must be taken into consideration, having constantly been a
rival discipline for sociology. In this respect the isolated history of a single
discipline is completely repudiated by the historical study of science. It rather
is always the history of complexes of disciplines whereby the emphasis can of
course change according to the specific demands one makes on such a history.
Georges Canguilhem convincingly demonstrated how different disciplines – in
this instance physiology and sociology – can benefit from such a history of
complexes of disciplines (5).
  He has proved that at the beginning of the 19th Century medicine and
physiology were characterised by the idea of only a gradual difference
between health and illness, normality and abnormality. He shows that these
so called 'quantitative' conceptions of normality were in the first instance,
adopted by positivist sociology, then were transformed and, in an altered
form, brought back into physiology. There the idea of a fundamental and
not only gradual difference between normality and abnormality, using the
'qualitative' conception of normality, again comes to the fore towards the
end of the 19th Century. Neither a traditional history of medicine nor a
history of sociology records such a transformational process. But still, this is
the only possible way to explain why basic conceptions of physiology changed
relatively quickly and why sociology in this period both influenced, and was
influenced by, physiology.

5. Thematic Categories

Therefore, a theory of relations between disciplines must search for common thematic categories (6); that is, for categories which structure problem-fields, in the same way as the history of complexes of disciplines does. 'Normality' is one of these thematic categories. It can be traced back through all the different fields of the humanities and the social sciences, physiology and medicine in the 19th Century and later. Only with the help of these thematic categories can histories of complexes of disciplines really be written. Thematic categories can, but do not necessarily need to, have a metaphorical character. Neither must every metaphor, which is important in a scientific-historical way, fulfil the function of a thematic category. In any case the historical study of science needs semantic analyses, but these must be different from those used in the traditional history of science which has relied on historio-semantic analyses. These analyses traditionally use the principle of continuity; that is, they record the origin, the development, the alterations and finally the decay of a concept. The semantic surveys which the historical study of science relies on, however, imply discontinuity from the very beginning. Their aim is to find semantic 'breaks' and revolutions which can be taken as evidence for a change of theoretical and conceptual basic assumptions without presupposing a fundamental correspondence between them.

Thus another, and perhaps the most important, difference between the historical study of science and the history of science is identified. The history of science relies on continuity and can be characterised by its narrative form; the historical study of science, however, reconstructs discontinuities as do, for instance Piaget in his cognitive psychology of development or Darwin in his theory of evolution.

The traditional history of science's illusion of continuity has been deprived of its foundations at least since the writings of Kuhn. Meanwhile it has been forgotten that thinking in terms of discontinuities ('scientific revolutions') can be found in the history of science at least since Condorcet. It has also been forgotten that in French epistemology, represented mainly in Gaston Bachelard's writings, a theory of discontinuous development of science has been in existence for more that 30 years.

In his attempt to write a psycho-analysis of objective cognition (as the subtitle of 'Formation de l'esprit scientifique' says) Bachelard outlined this theory as well as explaining it in many other works. Among others Georges Canguilhem and Michel Foucault also follow this tradition. Although I cannot deal with this in more detail here, I should like at least to give a terminological clue. In France the history of science is usually translated as 'histoire des sciences'. Without over-emphasising the difference between linguistic usages in France on the one hand, in England and Germany on the other, the French term seems closer to the history of complexes of disciplines with which a historical study of science is identified. It is one of the peculiarities of the study of science that this branch of a discontinuously oriented history of science has been largely ignored to the present day.

In his 'Formation' which has already been mentioned, Bachelard identified, as he thought, a crucial threshold of an era: that transition to the modern era which took place at the beginning of the 19th Century and which separated the natural science finally from their links with the living world. From now on science became the 'science ennuyeuse' of Coulomb. Common sense cannot in principle understand it any longer. Bachelard does not cease to stress the epochal importance of this transition towards the modern era. The tone at least in which he talks of the pre-history of natural-scientific disciplines and the extent to which he deals with this 'useless' prelude of modern scientific thinking makes one wonder where his sympathies really are. Be that as it may, Bachelard at least emphasised the topic of the connection between scientific development and common sense rationality which is important for a historical study of science.

6. Historical Anthropology

A historical study of science should benefit from this, but differently from Bachelard's suggestion. According to Bachelard the connection of common-sense rationality with the development of science ceased at the end of the 18th Century. To deal with it is, for him, only possible from an antiquarian interest in the pre-history of science. I think, however, that the vitally important close interconnections of scientific processes and common sense orientations should be a topic for the historical study of science (7). For this purpose the historical study of science could refer to historical anthropology, a discipline with which it has in common at least one methodological basic assumption: the idea of discontinuous processes of development.

In talking of historical anthropology, I mean neither a new discipline nor a combination of disciplines but rather a method of describing and defining historical periods. In doing this I follow a suggestion of Reinhart Koselleck (8). It seems to me to be promising to look at changes of anthropological structures as an indicator for the transition of historical periods. Thus 'historical anthropology' must be understood as some kind of collective term which should include historical research on the family as well as historical demography.

Historical anthropology at present aims for something like a theory of the middle range, to use Robert Merton's expresssion. It tries to historicise facts close to biology, that is, facts which are on the one hand rooted 'deep' enough to suggest a kind of biological substratum and, which, on the other hand, require a comprehensive cultural shaping for their full development, and that means an evolution or historical unravelling.

In this way, historical anthropology studies the variability of patterns of behaviour which seem at first glance to be 'constant'. If alterations of behaviour can be found in great number, it takes them as evidence of a change of an historical era. This evidence must be related to elementary patterns of behaviour if a connection with anthropology is to be sustained. It must be determinable for an observable period if historiography is to be able to find criteria for the determination of the periodicity of historical processes. Historical anthropology thus makes it its business to describe, and if possible to explain, the alteration of elementary patterns of behaviour in an observable period (9).

The closeness of historical anthropology and a historical study of science is clearly to be seen. In addition, one can find at least some hints about the relation of historical anthropology and historical study of science in one of the earliest and, to the present day, most convincing works in historical anthropology, namely Norbert Elias' 'Über den Prozess der Zivilisation' (On the Process of Civilisation). These hints have been made explicit by the author in the second edition (10). Here Norbert Elias has drawn attention to connections between the development of a scientific way of acquiring knowledge on the one hand, and the development of new attitudes of men towards themselves, of new personality-structures, but mainly of the progression towards more control of emotion and self-detachment on the other hand. Elias stresses, for example, the fact that great control of emotion was necessary to allow the transition of the geocentric into the heliocentric view of life. I think this approach is still too restrictive, however, because basically it simply takes alterations in the range of behaviour as an allusion to structural changes in views of life. This assumption can be demonstrated even more precisely. When Elias in fact regards the 'damping down' of spontaneous outbursts of feeling, the restraint of emotion and the range of thought beyond the immediate moment to the sequences of past causes and future consequences, as the crucial pre-condition for the development of civilisation, then he simultaneously depicts the basic perceptual and intellectual pre-conditions of the typical modern, experimental attitude towards scientific work.

In the 17th Century, John Wilkins and Seth Ward set the universities the task of educating the students to have 'acceptable behaviour' and to become 'rational and graceful speakers'. This corresponds exactly to the type of behaviour which Elias has characterised as typical for the process of civilisation in Western Europe. The victory of a 'detached' over a so-called 'enthusiastic' attitude is reflected in the overall advance of an internalised control of emotion. Here we find another explanation for the fact that science in its 'modern', experimental form was only developed in Western Europe. On the other hand, historical study of science which is connected to the historical anthropology as shown above obviously needs to incorporate the comparative analysis of cultures. Its fruitfulness has been shown long ago, not least in answering the question of the specific character of scientific development in Western Europe (11). The possibility of a socio- and ethnocentrism in semantic surveys must in the same way be corrected and put right by comparative studies.

A historical anthropology that wants to contribute to the identification of thresholds of historical epochs can support a historical study of science which more and more focusses on discontinuity. That is, it mainly analyses stages of the development of science and no longer shows this development as a continuous history of progress. Two examples will make this clear. Since the development of modern science, a period that can be dated as from 1775 to 1825, a historical approach has become generally accepted in many scientific disciplines (12). Within linguistics the transition from the tradition of common general grammar to historical philology occurred at about 1800. In economics categories like labour and production gain importance and it must be added that working time as a common source of value is of special importance. In Marx's terms all economy will dissolve in the economy of time. 1775 is seen as the date of birth of the so-called 'dynamic psychiatry' (13). Anticipated by the relativisation and thereby the historisation of the conception of beauty (in the 'Querelle des anciens et des modernes'), the temporalisation of the history of art can be dated back to Winckelmann's 'Geschichte der Kunst des Altertums' (History of the Arts in Ancient Times) (1764).

In the history of music the late 18th Century can be characterised by the final formulation of the temporally structured tonality in major and minor modes and the irreversible arrangement of works (11). Even Utopia gains a temporal structure and becomes 'Unchronie'. In 'L'An deux mille quatre cent quarante', published in 1770/71 Mercier projects Utopia into time for the first time. Several aspects of this 'temporalisation', which characterises the development of science at the beginning of the modern era are remarkable. For example, the universality of this developmental stage taking place in nearly every discipline, and the chronological precision of the transition towards the historical way of thinking of which the 'Sattelzeit', as Reinhart Koselleck calls the period between 1775 and 1825, is typical.

This change in basic scientific assumptions, the importance of which can only be compared with the scientific revolution of the 17th Century, cannot be explained here. The transition to a historical way of thinking in the sciences at the end of the 18th Century is remarkable for yet another reason. The 'temporalisation' which characterises the scientific development at this epoch corresponds with a new relation to time which apparently determined the everyday actions of people living at the end of the 18th and the beginning of the 19th Century. In everyday life a stronger sense of time was developed; one example is the introducing of fixed visiting hours.

Children are now more and more carefully planned and on the basis of such a 'calculation' the family becomes mapped out and the child's future anticipated. Processes of infantile growth become the focus of the human sciences. The first life insurances were established, the introduction of which demanded an elaborate probability-calculation as well as a conception of life and its processes of developement, a conception which only now is gradually being achieved. Both these references and the following example I borrow from the works of Philippe Ariès (14).

There appears to be a connection, which seems to be closer than hitherto supposed, between basic scientific assumptions and historically dominant mentalities. Although scientific processes doubtlessly influence psychical and social structures, certain states of conciousness and feeling on the other hand form limits beyond which even scientific explorations cannot be effective. Thus the popularity of old age – especially of the 'vieillard' in France – at the end of the 18th Century precedes the medical progress which brought about a longer life expectancy, it is more its pre-condition than its result. The late application of certain techniques of diagnosis is probably due to the lack of a certain way of thinking which could have enabled their application. So Leopold Auenbrugger (1722–1809) had already employed the percussion of the thorax-surface, but not before 1808 did percussion become a widely accepted diagnostic aid through Corvisart, Napoleon's personal physician. Soon afterwards, Laënnec's introduction of auscultation and the use of the stethoscope followed.

Another example, again used by Philippe Ariès, has to do with the so-called 'dangers des sépultures' (the title of a book of Vicq-d'Azyr, published in 1778). In the second half of the 18th Century, people suddenly became aware of the "threat of infections transmitted by corpses as well as poisonous gases that are formed in graves ... as a source of danger". It could be assumed that progress in medical and hygienic findings made the continuation of such phenomena, to which they had reconciled themselves for centuries, unbearable for men. In fact it is rather the opposite, changed attitudes towards death and burial directed attention to phenomena hitherto overlooked, phenomena which only now could become objects of research for medicine.

The resort to a historical anthropology may facilitate the necessary connection between internalist and externalist explanations of processes of scientific development. First of all it would be necessary, within a history of complexes of disciplines, which to a large extent still proceed in an internally reconstructive manner to ascertain thematic categories which define the development of various disciplines over longer periods of time. These thematic categories would have to be attributed to thresholds of historical epochs to be revealed by historical anthropology according to significant changes of behaviour. Only then could one try to consider external factors, such as economic ones, as further explanations. In the earlier mentioned example of

the success of historical thinking in science at the turn of the 18th/19th
Centuries, the following would have to be done:

Firstly, altered temporal structures in the range of objects (Gegenstands-
bereich), in theory structures and scientific organisations, at this time would
have to be described and possibly brought into relationship with one another
(internalist reconstruction).

Secondly, parallel development as alterations of temporal structures in the
everyday world of the same era would have to be described (determination
of epochal thresholds by historical anthropology).

Thirdly, attempts would have to be made to connect the altered temporal
structures of the everyday world with external factors such as changed
conditions of production and employment relationships, and, accordingly,
an altered understanding of time.

Thus, the internalist reconstruction of developments in a discipline and
external factors of scientific processes could be connected within the historical
study of science. If the historical study of science is understood in this way it
can, at present, benefit less from traditional history of science than from the
more recent theoretical developments within historiography, such as a theory
of historical times. As for the rest, the historical study of science must urge
a revision of the history of the sociology of science. Even though Robert
Merton was right in some aspects of his critique of the sociology of knowledge and therefore hardly wanted to establish the sociology of science as a
successor to the sociology of knowledge – within the historical study of
science the sociology of knowledge will doubtlessly experience a renaissance.

Acknowledgement

This paper has been translated by Ludwig Orians.

Notes

1. In the German version of this paper, I talk of 'Wissenschaftsgeschichte', a term
   which is broader than the English 'history of science' and includes the social sciences and the humanities as well as the natural sciences.
2. J. Habermas, *Zur Rekonstruktion des historischen Materialismus*, Frankfurt a.M.:
   Suhrkamp, 1976, p. 202.
3. A. Comte, *Correspondance générale et confessions. Tome I: 1814–1840*, Paris/La
   Haye: Mouton, 1973, p. 130.
4. F. Jacob, *La logique du vivant. Une histoire de l'hérédité*, Paris: Gallimard, 1970.

5. G. Canguilhem, *Le normal et le pathologique*, Paris: Presses Universitaires de France, 2nd ed., 1972.
6. In the German original, I use the term 'durchlaufende Kategorien', which goes back to the philosophy of Nicolai Hartmann and was further developed by Arnold Gehlen in his anthropology. By 'durchlaufende Kategorien' Gehlen meant categories 'which cut right across the human constitution' and by which it is possible to describe almost every form of behaviour; the 'element of language' being one of those categories. Cf. A. Gehlen, 'An Anthropological Model', *The Human Context* 1, 1968, pp. 11–20.
7. I have tried to describe some of these interconnections in my book *Das Ende der Naturgeschichte. Wandel kultureller Selbstverständlichkeiten in den Wissenschaften des 18. und 19. Jahrhunderts*, München: Hanser, 1976.
8. R. Koselleck, 'Wozu noch Historie?', *Historische Zeitschrift* 212, 1971, pp. 1–18.
9. W. Lepenies, 'History and Anthropology: a historical appraisal of the current contact between the disciplines', *Social Science Information* 15, 1976, pp. 287–306.
10. N. Elias, *Uber den Prozess der Zivilisation. Soziogenetische und psychogenetische Untersuchungen*, Bern/München, 2nd. ed. 1969.
11. I refer only to B. Nelson, 'Sciences and Civilizations, 'East' and 'West': Joseph Needham and Max Weber', in R. S. Cohen and M. W. Wartofsky (eds.), *Boston Studies in the Philosophy of Science* XI, 1974, pp. 445–493.
12. Cf. Note 7.
13. H. F. Ellenberger, *The Discovery of the Unconscious. The History and Evolution of Dynamic Psychiatry*, New York: Basic Books, 1970.
14. Ph. Ariès, *L'Enfant et la vie familiale sous l'ancien regime*, Paris: Plon, 1960.
Ph. Ariès, *Essais sur l'histoire de la mort en Occident du moyen âge à nos jours*, Paris: Editions du Seuil, 1975.

SCIENTIFIC IDEOLOGY AND SCIENTIFIC PROCESS:
The Natural History of a Conceptual Shift

ROGER G. KROHN

McGill University

1. Introduction

This paper attempts to outline the process and significance of a shift from a
positivist to a social and historical understanding of science. From the viewpoint of an adherent to the new perspective, the positivist model appears as
an external, philosophers' image of what is natural science, one which takes
at face value what its spokesmen, and to a lesser degree what its practitioners
say it is. To identify this line of externally addressed philosophy of science
and internalist intellectual history, I would mention Bacon, Sarton, Cohen,
Popper and the logical positivists generally. Even recent and formidable
sociologists of science (Merton, Ben-David) share key elements of the positivist
assumption, that positivism is an accurate reflection of scientific practice and
that science is intellectually and internally self-determined (autonomous).

A newer social history and sociology of science has been developing in
recent years which links intellectual development within science to those
outside, and finds science to be a vital social process, not only within science,
but also as part of the larger society. To identify this newer perspective I
would mention Kuhn, Mendelsohn, the Roses, Blume, Sklair, Mulkay, Whitley.
The theme here is that we are moving rapidly through a three stage process in
the conceptual development of a reseach specialty. We are proceeding from
(a) a general ideological debate, in dialectical form, on the nature of science,
through to (b) a stage of the criticism of the existing vocabulary of the
specific terms of everyday *talk* about the scientific process and to the invention of a new and more precise vocabulary, one more suitable to the third
phase of the dialectical argument that is emerging. (c) Finally, we are, less
clearly, beginning to see the development of a new set of problems and

*Mendelsohn/Weingart/Whitley (eds.), The Social Production of Scientific Knowledge.
Sociology of the Sciences, Volume I, 1977. 69–99. All Rights Reserved.
Copyright © 1977 by D. Reidel Publishing Company, Dordrecht-Holland.*

research programs, the generation of new data, and the re-interpretation of
old data in the new terms. Practically, the paper attempts to expedite the
movement securely beyond stage one and into stages two and three.

I think we can see at least six major issues that have been debated, serially
and concurrently, in the philosophy of science; three concern the internal
nature of science and three the relation of science and society. The three
issues in the nature of science concern the relation of data and theory, the
objective or subjective origin of innovative ideas, and the norms and counter-
norms of the scientific community.

2. On the Relation of Data and Theory

From very early days the new natural philosophers believed that they, as opposed to traditional philosophers and theologicans, were reading nature
instead of books, making observations, and making straight deductions from
observations to theoretical conclusions. The Renaissance artist-students of
nature "held that man was the eye for which reality had been made visual —
the ideal eye, the eye of the viewpoint of Renaissance perspective" (1). Later
the empirical philosophy and then the positive philosophy assumed an open
but one way relation of observations to theory in which the immediate
theoretical implications were recognized by all competent people who made
the observations. This is true from Bacon to Popper, and in its contemporary
version it is true of Merton and Ben-David. Ben-David has written expressly
to refute the possibility of social forms or carriers of knowledge entering into
the specific formulation of ideas, giving a firm 'no' to his own question, "Is
a Sociology of Knowledge Possible?". Again in 1971 he argued for the strict
limitation of what is explainable in natural science theory in terms of the
social occasion of its formulation (2).

We can see a counter-conceptual movement to positivism in structuralism.
Structuralist writers do not see science as proceeding only from a series of
observable items, or from isolated bits of experience, to a specific series of
concepts and hypotheses, but in perspective giving wholes, sets of beliefs,
'Gestalten', or paradigms, or even world views.

Michael Polanyi believes that intellectual life is based on a number of
'fiduciary programs', which need not be true, but in any case must underly
any theoretical interpretation, "... some such set of beliefs is clearly indis-

pensible" (3). Further, Polanyi believes that no structure of knowledge can be made wholly explicit both because the meaning of language in use lies in a tacit component, and because "to use language involves actions of our body of which we have only a subsidiary awareness." The aspect of experience 'A' about which we can be most explicit is that about which we are 'focally aware', but we are at the same time subsidiarily aware of 'B', or several B's, less identifiable but which give the meaning and relevance of the object of attention. This gives rise to a 'structure of tacit knowing'. "Hence, tacit knowing is more fundamental than explicit knowing: we can know more than we can tell and we can tell nothing without relying on our awareness of things we may not be able to tell." (4)

This is clearly a basic revision of the traditional empiricist philosophy of science. Polanyi sees knowledge as not only structured, but as ultimately biologically located and emotionally relevant, and in its most important dimensions never entirely articulated. Kuhn follows Polanyi's program, adding (a) an historical or processual perspective by which one operative paradigm and accompanying research program (Polanyi's 'fiduciary program') is carried on by a communicating group of scientific workers, and (b) that periodic change from one paradigm and research program to another is punctuated by internal confusion about just how data is to be interpreted, by conflict and debate, and concluded by a minor political revolution within science.

This debate between the atomistic and structuralist philosophies of science shows signs of being dialectically — and empirically — resolved with the concept of 'branching'. Mulkay and associated workers have observed that more often than internal 'revolution' and paradigm replacement occurring within specialties, science actually develops by new problem and topical areas being uncovered by scientists at work in one or several existing research specialties (Hagstrom's 'dispersion and isolation', Mullins' 'networks') (5). These new problem areas are first explored by scattered people from several fields who 'migrate' to the new topic and gradually build a new social network of communication as they discover their common interests, problems, and contributions. More effective communication launches a more effective scientific discussion and debate, resolving on certain key issues, concepts, definitions, and useful techniques, which begin to look like an effective scientific consensus and a working research program.

3. On the Origins of Innovative Ideas ('Truth')

From the empiricist philosophy to the positivist, creativity in science creates
a special problem. The (subject) scientist has only to accurately perceive the
object and to make adequate inductive generalizations to discover the Truth.
If the object determines the subject, the subject is passive, as in the 'tabula
rasa' metaphor. The subject is not culture bearing, but rather shares a common human nature which is the ground of common experience and common
knowledge. Thus, throughout the history of the naturalist philosphy the
question of the origins of innovative ideas has been begged with concepts
for abstract ability on the one hand — 'genius' or 'talent' or 'intelligence'
— and an 'objective' stance on the other; the social and psychological sources
of the 'hunch', the 'hypothesis', or the 'insight' have been unexplored.

The traditional sociology of knowledge reverses empiricism; the subject
determines the object, but only in an expanded sense of the sources of error.
Individual and/or institutional interests are conceived and articulated in
'ideologies', that is, they are appeals for public support and legitimacy. The
subject here is active, and projects his views upon the object. The subject is
not only culture bearing, but confined, as in 'relativism', in 'incommensurable paradigms', and in 'perspectivism', and sees only through the distor-
ting lens of a partisan or local culture. Of course, the problem is always left,
why should a class, even though exploited, or an intellectual stratum even
though socially 'free floating', or scientists, even though deliberately objective, be able to see and to say more than people in other social locations?

To resolve this dilemma I believe we have to see the scientific (intellectual)
process as having four aspects, not two. These are traditional concepts, but
not traditionally invoked to understand science. Besides the 'observation',
'data', 'experience', of traditional attention in the philosophy of science, and
the 'interest', 'class', 'institution', or 'social organization' attended to by the
critics of social thought, it is equally important to pay close attention the the
purpose, worry or problem behind a specific example of social thought. That
is, we need to see that there is an emotional source of intellectual effort as
there is of all human effort. It is increasingly common in the literature to pay
attention to the emotional source of scientific work, as when we speak of
'sense of direction' or 'sense of problem' when it has reached only partly
intellectualized form. Most recently, and most strongly, Mitroff has sought

to add 'bias' and 'commitment' as positive sources of scientific work, especially in the elaboration and criticism (but still not the origin) of theories (6). Kuhn has also spoken of commitment to paradigms and to worldviews. Mendelsohn and Buck have gone the key step further and traced scientific innovation to revolutionary initiative, and Feuer has traced 'iso-emotional lines' between socio-political and scientific problems and theories (7).

The last determinant in the scientific process to be introduced is intellectual. Whether one speaks of 'paradigms', 'intellectual traditions', 'structures', or 'perspectives', two key assumptions are made. One is that concepts are not isolated and endlessly re-arrangeable in the mind but rather cohere in patterns which place limits on intellectual change until the whole pattern is abandoned or re-arranged in some determinant way. In the areas of myth analysis (Levi-Strauss), language (Chomsky), and dreams or other psychological process (Lacan) the formulation of the rules of 'transformation' or of 'transition' between such structures has been attempted.

These terms of analysis, emerging in studies of science, are versions of four elements or aspects of social process which have been perennially referred to in one way or another. I believe these concepts can be stated more systematically to bring out their bearing on problems in the sociology of science and to by-pass certain traditional but no longer productive problems in the sociology of knowledge generally.

(a) The bio-emotional process is the social elaboration of human physiology, and bio-emotional structures are the results of past experience carried forward to the future.

(b) Social organization is the set of patterns of reciprocity and loyalty among the participants in a social process, and among these units of process (or organization) as in 'institutions', 'movements', or 'groups'.

(c) Culture is the learned skills, concepts, etc. used in social life; it is the social elaboration of perceptual and motor abilities.

(d) Environment is the material basis of social life, the aspects of geography, climate, plant, animal, human life, etc., that have been socially perceived, elicited and used.

The point of this exercise is to avoid the traditional dichotomies of individual/group, man/nature, subject/object, and rational/irrational that have given rise to and been carriers of perennial debates. They suggest unresolveable problems, arising from the question of which side is the more basic, with the others to be reduced or explained away. Each side in each debate has had hold of part of the truth, and at the same time afforded its opponent ample material for refutation or convincing counter-argument. In short, neither in social life generally, nor in science specifically can we decide on such permanent directions of determinism, or even of 'influence'. There has been a powerful impetus toward such 'false generalization', based on a too quick, too complete, or too 'interested' a resolution of the social-political problems behind the invention and use of the dichotomies. In science, as in all intellectual life, the question of a predominant influence of one aspect of scientific or macro-social process is an empirical question to be determined in a case by case analysis.

For example, there are historical periods, classes, institutions, individuals, who are more alert to and perceptive of their environment, and who rapidly respond and adjust to changes in it and to changes in their perception and knowledge of it. And other periods, classes, institutions, individuals who are culturally determined, who see and interpret events in the same way, regardless of changes, and who learn little additional about it. But to try to say that periods, classes, or institutions determine interpretations generally is a false effort, opening one to refutation by a counter school, and intellectual life to a perennial and fruitless dialectic. Nor is our task to try to sketch an example of these complex, multi-directional processes. We will only try to show that historically our attention has been partial, to some aspects of social and scientific processes and not to others, and our theories have been one-sided, missing the backflow of consequences in any postulated determinism or direction of influence.

4. On the Place of Scientific Norms and the Ethics of the Communication of Original Work

We will use here Merton's much cited four norms as a discussion point. Mitroff adds two further norms but they apply primarily to the investigation phase, which I want to treat separately (8). The institutional or manifest norms of science concern:

1. Universality: the nature of knowledge, its truth status.
2. Communism: individual and collective rights in knowledge.

3. Disinterestedness: the legitimate individual motives in scientific work.
4. Organized skepticism: the acceptance of innovation vs. established theory.

4.1. *Universalism: The Nature of Knowledge*

"Universalism (is) the canon that truth claims ... are to be subjected to pre-established impersonal criteria, consonant with observation and previously confirmed knowledge" (9). Claims for the universality and permanence of knowledge have a complex history; it is sufficient here to say that European theology and science have both claimed to identify a universal and eternal truth. This is contrasted by Needham with the Chinese concepts of Yin and Yang, the female and the male principles, which postulate a relation as well as a tension ('the Yang harbours a colony of the Yin within itself') between principles, not a sharp contradiction, and complementary as well as contrasting forces, not only antagonism (10). In the West we have elaborated 'the Persian dualism' (Light/Dark; Heaven/Earth; Good/Evil), abstracting True and False Gods in the logic of $A/-A$ and in the epistemology of True/False.

In recent times this has been challenged persuasively politically, notably under the concept of 'ideology', by Marx and Engels in the 1840's. This political critique was expanded upon and phrased in more general sociological terms by Mannheim's 'perspectivism' in the 1920's, at least implied or approached in anthropology, e.g. by R. Benedict's 'cultural relativity' (a relativity of tribe or ethnic group) in the 1930's, and finally brought home to science itself by Kuhn's use of 'paradigm' to replace 'theory' in 1962.

I won't detail the way the point was phrased in each case — they are all well known — but only say that each located and attempted to explain the precise formulations of mental-intellectual process in a specific social context. This, of course, opposed to the older, total claim to permanent truth the assertion that only partial, contextually specific and temporary claims to knowledge can *ever* be phrased.

That leads to the conundrum of 'relativism'. How do we have any more confidence in the critic's statements than in the statements he criticizes? Because many have been unwilling to yield the felt superiority of European science to other knowledge systems, and yet are, or will be, unable to maintain scientific knowledge as a category of exception to increasingly sociological explanations of human conceptual processes, a third position is being sought.

The dilemma is resolved if we conceive science as an open-ended search for an assumed *eventual* coherence of the various scientific specialties. This is one sense of Kuhn's characterization of science as "a process of evolution from (our) primitive beginnings ... a process (of) ... an increasingly detailed and refined understanding of nature, (but not) a process of evolution *toward* (italics in original) anything" (11).

Here science has had a creative utopianism. Because its program stated that it was progressing *toward* truth, this removed the requirement of logical coherence — and the consequent intellectual closure. Scientists could continue to explore ever-opening branches of learning, and delay until another day, and even remove to another role, the task of making all this new knowledge selfconsistent, i.e. "consonant with ... previously confirmed knowledge."

I would like to underline the view here that science is complex rather than coherent in both its overall conceptual and social structure, in contrast both to the positivist and to the counter positivist assumptions of the radical and structuralist views being outlined here. Pointing to this as yet little described complexity, and to the task of discovering unities within it, is one theme of this essay.

4.2. *Communism: the Relation of Individual and Collective Rights in Knowledge*

"Communism (is) the ... common ownership of goods, (the belief that the) substantive findings of a science are a product of social collaboration and are to be assigned to the community (as) a common heritage" (12). I would like to note two things here. The first is the ambiguity between the scientific (the "... findings of science are a product of social collaboration") and the general community ("... and are assigned to the community [as] a common heritage"). Although the scientific community states its rights in knowledge it does not state any general community rights, nor oblige itself to translate esoteric knowledge into publically useable form. This omission would seem more characteristic of the later (academic) than the earlier (amateur, or pre-academic) versions of the ethic (13). Second, just as the quest for truth is utopian, the communal ownership of knowledge is romantic — the price of communal control has to be the popular appropriation of knowledge which is incompatible both with rapid scientific advance and the elitist structures assumed by Merton himself. European science rapidly evolved during the academization of science, first in Germany in the mid 19th century, to make 'communism', the common ownership of intellectual property, even within the scientific community, impossible.

Merton himself entered the first qualification on the community's rights to all discovered knowledge, noting the individual's 'credit' for discovery upon publication. 'Property rights in science are whittled down to a bare minimum ... of recognition and esteem ... commensurate with the significance of the increments ...'' (14). Additionally, Mitroff has called attention to secrecy as a counter-norm in science. His informants told him (in the Apollo research on the geology of the moon) of the widespread practice of protective secrecy in science. It is implicit, but worth noting, that such rights to privacy of intellectual property pertain before publication, until the researcher is ready to announce his 'results' and to claim his 'credit' (15).

This is a step toward resolving the contradiction; the norms are not exactly counter-norms but rather pertain to different phases of the scientific process — privacy and self-control (and intellectual freedom) before and credit (and responsibility) for the contribution after publication. To take a further step, we could see science as involving at least three major phases — investigation, publication and evaluation-criticism — the latter directed to a hoped for and eventual consensus on the most promising lines of investigation and the most credible interpretation of any given range of phenomena or events.

Common to all three phases is a 'gift ethic', that is, science is a system of exchange by 'prestations' as defined by Mauss (16). In science there is also the obligation to give — to make a contribution, to receive — to be current with all relevant contributions to the literature, and to return a gift — to acknowledge all important and non-obvious contributing pieces of information and ideas to one's own work.

This formulation will allow us to see privacy, secrecy, contribution, property rights and credit, as non-contradictory elements in the sequential ethics of scientific communication, with varying rights and responsibilities of participants at each phase of the scientific process.

4.3. *Disinterestedness: the Legitimate Motives for Scientific Work*

"Disinterestedness (is) a distinctive pattern of institutional control of a wide range of motives which characterizes the behavior of scientists" (**13**). Merton precisely states that it is not an unusual or personal altruism which characterizes scientists, but "rigorous policing ... unparalleled in any other field ... (based) in the public and testable character of science." But, "For once the institution enjoins disinterested activity, it is to the interest of scientists to conform on pain of sanctions and, insofar as the norm has been internalized, on pain of psychological conflict" (**18**). Thus 'disinterest' is possible, and advisable, if not logically necessary as a personal posture for the scientist.

The counter statement to the necessity of the control of emotional involvement in scientific work and in particular ideas is the claim that men of knowledge, too, have institutional indentifications and interests, and investments in specific ideas. This proposal is most clearly identified with Marx and with the Marx-influenced sociology of knowledge, notably that stemming from Mannheim. Without detailing well worn ground, we can say that both Marx and Mannheim believed that specific class and institutional motives were expressed and interests advanced through intellectual work, and through the establishment of particular concepts as publicly credible 'knowledge'. And there is the further idea, that this is legitimate if the benefits are general; practical solutions to practical problems are the only effective basis for scholarly work.

I would argue that such assertion of tight links of interest and ideas are over simple. More accurately, individuals, institutions and classes have practical, emotional and symbolic problems. Their ideology, paradigm or theory represents past and current solutions to those problems, which of course give them an 'interest' in the conception involved, but a complex one. Another problem may lead to a search for another formulation, and sometimes to another pattern, paradigm or perspective, which will promise a potentially more adequate answer to the felt problem.

This new 'research program', or even 'central dogma', may be formulated in several ways, depending for one thing on the precise phrasing of the leading past or contemporary dogma, which normally provides an error, an adversary and a counter image, against which the metaphors of the new position can be formulated. On the other hand, clearly, not just any new formulation will do. After all, there is a specific problem to be solved, and the proposed solution will be tested. The degree of this empirical determinism of the new theoretical program will depend on the complex particulars of the case in hand, but in no case will it be a pure projective fantasy. In other words, people work on problems which come out of their own experience, that is what gives the sustained energy to work on them. They are emotionally real, but are not necessarily an entrapment because there are other determinants of what they will eventually believe: namely, the requirements of their own intellectual tradition, the appreciative and critical responses of their audience, and the observations they will make.

4.4. *Organized Skepticism: the Acceptance of Claims of Innovation vs. Established Knowledge*

"Organized skepticism (is) the suspension of judgement until the facts are at hand, and the detached scrutiny of beliefs in terms of empirical and logical criteria ... It is both a methodological and an institutional mandate." Science asks questions "concerning every aspect of nature and society" and "may come into conflict with other attitudes (of other institutions) towards these same data ... which appears to be the source of revolts against the so-called intrusion of science into other spheres" (19). Note two corollary points here. One assumes the possibility of suspended judgement in all areas without sufficient empirically based knowledge and the other the suspicion of received knowledge, of all intellectual and institutional traditions. This can be seen as the program of an insurgeant and utopian movement, the former point being applicable to areas of knowledge already incorporated into science and the latter to the margins of its expansion.

We will use here the counter statements of Polanyi, Kuhn and Mitroff. Polanyi argues that some sort of 'fiduciary program' is intrinsic to the intellectual and social life of modern man. It is "clearly indispensable: the ideal of strict objectivism is absurd" (20). Kuhn: "Like the choice between competing political institutions, that between competing paradigms proves to be a choice between incompatible modes of community life." This choice cannot be made logically compelling, "the premises and values shared by the two parties to a debate over paradigms are not sufficiently extensive for that" (21).

Clearly, a personal choice remains. Mitroff: "The scientist must believe in his own findings with utter conviction while doubting those of others with all of his worth." (22).

All three authors discount the possibility of 'suspended judgement'. Scientists, like others, are always operating on the basis of a belief, as only another paradigm and can replace a paradigm (23).

Traditional scientific philosophy insists that proof must precede belief which is countered by the view that, in the case of important scientific work at least, a degree of belief must precede the development of proof. But again as observations the statements are not truly incompatible. It is not science as a whole which is skeptical of all knowledge at once, but individuals or groups who are skeptical of one item or area of established knowledge. More important, skepticism and commitment are relevant to different phases of scientific work. Cycles, or phases, of conviction and criticism can be seen to underly the research process. I will examine this process later with Watson's autobiography of his and Crick's work on the structure of deoxyribonucleic acid (DNA) which details cycles of 'hunches', of conviction and of criticism.

5. On the Relation of Practice and Theory

This is the first of three issues regarding the relation of science and society. The other two relate science and common sense (esoteric and popular knowledge), and the intellectual (academic) or socio-political (general human welfare) legitimacy and purpose of scientific work.

With the doctrine that there is an intellectually superior and theoretically advanced 'basic' science, more worthy of social honour than 'applied' science or engineering, we come to a much newer orthodoxy. In fact, the basic/applied distinction itself was only clearly formulated in the last half of the 19th century with the development of, first, German university-based science. Ben-David links these developments both to the development of German nationalism after the defeat of the German-speaking states in the Napoleonic wars and to the particular role German universities had in offering dignified careers when business and politics did not offer sufficient opportunities for talented and ambitious young Germans (24).

Paulsen gives a vivid account of the conversion of German universities to the scientific philosophy during the 19th century (25). During the late 18th and the 19th centuries the philosophy faculties became converted from the general preparation of students for professional study in the 'higher' professional faculties – theology, medicine, law – to become "the real exponent of purely scientific research in all departments" (**26**). University education was converted (before 1900) from "the practical-dogmatic to the theoretic-academic", by (a) "... the independent acquisition of and augmentation of knowledge (becoming) the ideal for professors and for students", (b) the increasing specialization of subjects, (c) the near abandonment of any "active (professional) practice for the pursuit of pure science even in professional faculties" (excepting medicine), and (d) further innovations to aid the student "to learn how to do independent work". These were the seminar system, an extended period of residence, exams aimed "almost exclusively at theoretical competence and taking the form of special reseach, and a special period or preparation between theoretical training and professional practice" (**27**).

In sum: the assumption would seem to be that purely theoretically directed, inventive creativity is valuable in its own right, and will eventually find its own way to practical applicability and general social benefit. It was especially the former that would be to the glory of the German states which supported universities.

The counter to this thesis was launched by the noted British physical chemist and active Marxist, J. D. Bernal. Bernal argued that historically, in 17th century Britain and elsewhere, theoretical invention had been rooted in technical problems and informed by specific industrial techniques and instruments. Urgent practical problems – of navigation, mining, mechanical power, chemical dyes, etc. – and every day craft technique was the real ground of theoretic invention (**28**).

Perhaps this 'contradiction' is the most easily resolved. Ben-David has already persuasively argued, and in detail, that basic and applied science are in intimate interaction, certainly in the example of the United States, the most scientifically creative and industrially advanced country. Further, Ben-David argues that there are many steps of articulation between basic science, applied science and technical application, and that this articulation of concept, information and technique runs in both directions.

I find it difficult to improve on that, except to say that perhaps the concepts themselves have outlived their usefulness. Operatively, it may be more useful to think of investigatory and specialty-determined (defined) problems, and those to which attention is invited by people in any relevant occupation or activity. The former are more likely to be theory determined, although not necessarily. Witness the picking up of the highly practical problems of pollution, population growth, energy conservation and reduplication from renewable resources, nutrition, and 'organic' or 'ecological' gardening and agriculture, taken up by increasing numbers of academic scientists (30). And the latter – research problems on the invitation of people outside professional science – need not be theoretically uninformed.

In any case, it would seem a safe investigative assumption that problems resulting in scientific innovation can be theoretically or practically occasioned. More interesting is the possibility that it is peculiarly the people who are forcefully presented with a practical-empirical problem, and who are theoretically well-informed, who are especially prone to discoveries involving important conceptual reformulations. The research on creativity of 'role hybrids' (Ben-David) and 'marginal academic situations' (Gordon *et al.*) would seem to support this (31). Thus, theoretical creativity already has its origin in someone's practical or specific 'sense of problem' and the reason he sees for the failure of current interpretations to allow a solution (32). To systematically divide 'practice' from 'theory', as in 'applied' and 'basic' science, can only force an implicit traffic in problems and ideas, cut down these occasions for innovation, or lead to innovation primarily at the margin of the academic disciplines, as Ben-David's, Gordon's, and other data indicate.

6. On the Relation of Science and 'Common Sense' (and Other Areas of High Culture, e.g. Religion, Politics, etc.)

The academic ideology of science assumes, or at least the idea has developed during its academic phase, that scientific knowledge is esoteric, and that the more developed theoretically a specialty is, the less comprehensible it is. But not only is it asserted that laymen do not understand physics, but also that they are intellectually incapable of it. And there is the further assumption that physics is valuable-creative because it is esoteric.

The counter-statement to the radical separation of science and every day knowledge has not come directly from people attempting to make scientific knowledge popularly accessible, for example from a Gamow or an Asimov, who have taken on the role of translating esoteric knowledge into popular form. Nor has it come from science teachers or editors. Rather, the point has been raised by movements of political protest against the use and abuse of science, such as Science For The People. SFTP makes the point that science should not only serve the peoples' purposes but also speak the people's language. This is also Maoist China's point (33).

An integrating position between science as inevitably as esoteric as it is successful and the insistence that anything 'the people' cannot understand must be mystified or in error can only be outlined, because it has hardly been attempted. But we could envision a situation where scientifically qualified people had the socially legitimate and regular task of communicating new scientific work to their relevant publics, as opposed to relying on the occasional populizer, or scientific 'great' with a popular style (e.g. René Dubos) (34). At the same time the science side of public education could be improved so that the task of translation from technical to popular form would be less difficult; there would be less of a gap to bridge.

But more basically, we need to see that science is as much involved in changing our culture as in adding to it, and that what appears as the most esoteric and difficult to comprehend — for example, physical relativity theory — actually returns to common sense, or rather goes below common sense to the assumptions within which we interpret our experience. If we see spatial and temporal coordinates as only conventions of experience — although very basic ones — the mode of presenting them — that is through technical physics — can be seen as part, a major part, of the problem. In social science, one continually has the experience of reading through sometimes abstruse and difficult authors — Marx, Weber, Freud, Durkheim — only to find that the most valuable aspects of their thinking are very basic and very simple. They only seem difficult and abstruse because they are approached by the route of indirect technical argument. The arguments may be resisted because they involve change in basic and comfortable assumptions — that market economy is not natural, not linked to the fixed traits of human nature — that motives and ideas from non-economic areas of activity influence economic activity — that early and emotionally powerful experience affects future and adult behavior — that erroneous but powerful social symbols, such as those in primitive religion, can be efficient guides to the social life of a people — and so on. Why should it take decades to digest these insights? Because they have been presented through the veil of 'high culture', resisted because of vested and emotional interests, and then the ideological shadow boxing resulting from both is blamed on intellectual difficulty! We (academics) never gave the average man a change.

In sum, the separation of science and every day life is probably as much social and institutional — cultivated by another intellectual priesthood with an interest in obscurity and in prestige — as it is intellectual. And the avoidance and search for change can be conducted in simple or in complex language.

7. The Socio-Political Relevance and Purpose of Intellectual Activity and the Legitimate Basis of Its Support

The academic philosophy is that knowledge is a value in its own right. It is more valid, more objective, if it is supported not only for particular purposes but for its theoretical interests and importance alone. It is also more likely to be creative, because original insight is cramped by links to practical problems, by the conventional categories carried with them, and by even implied control. Thus, theoretically motivated research is prior both in logic and in time; innovation normally proceeds from basic to applied research rather than the reverse. Basic research must be supported and scientists must be free to define their own problems to permit this originality to flourish; freedom is originality's prime condition (35).

Again the counter principle has come from left political writers who maintain that political commitment and social purpose necessarily inform all intellectual efforts including the scientific. Bernal precipitated a continually reverberating debate by insisting in 1939 that it was only a general social purpose and intended human welfare that made science the legitimate object of public support (36).

Again, a third position is not difficult to formulate, although I'm not aware of where it has been done systematically. It would take the line that the political responsibility and social purpose of all research is important, but that it can be and often is indirect and is in any case highly variable.

A general but tolerant check on the social relevance of research, to purposes external to itself, would not do any harm even to the areas of most 'basic' — i.e. paradigm directed — research. At the local level of the research organization, we do have some results showing that interested supervision but not control contributes to scientific creativity, including theoretical (37). Whether in the local research organization or in science generally, the assumption is that people will like to be relevant to other peoples' welfare when given the opportunity. In fact, many are stimulated to great exertions by that awareness, as is again evidenced in the recent scientific concern with local and global ecology.

8. The Vocabulary of the Scientific Enterprise

The second phase of the development of new perspectives on science has been much less obtrusive. Many students working on the front lines of the new mode have become uncomfortable with one or more of the traditional terms of self-description of the scientific enterprise.

'Genius' takes its current sense from its use in Renaissance Italy. A 'genius' was someone whose accomplishment was beyond that of even talented people — extraordinary, like that of Leonardo da Vinci, Michaelangelo or Brunelleschi — so as to be incomprehensible in ordinary terms. "... there developed a conception of the individual genius whose knowledge did not stem from books but from his personal intuition ... and his contact with nature ..." (38).

As a second stage in the analysis of individual talent and contribution, we can cite Merton's "sociological theory of genius in science", first published in 1961 (39). Merton sees no necessary opposition between the concept of genius and a sociological — or 'environmental' — explanation of extraordinary scientific achievement. In his view, the genius' work is not indispensable — that is the fallacy of the 'great man' theory; his work would eventually be rediscovered, "but by an entire corps of scientists', not by an individual. The great men of science have been involved in a great number of multiple discoveries (the same discovery made independently by two or more people) both because they have made many discoveries and because a considerable number of other scientists would have been required to make the equivalent contribution. But that even a Kelvin or a Freud was not "individually indispensible ... is indicated by the many multiples in which he (Freud) was in fact engaged (more than 30 by Freud's own count) and the many others which, presumably, he forestalled by his individually incomparable genius" (40).

The key point here is that Merton did not ask *why* some individuals make such large contributions, and that is the question that the concept of genius allowed him to beg. Merton's later work (1968) on 'the Matthew Effect' would seem to give a more deeply sociological interpretation of high achievement in science, of the person who fully uses himself and is stimulated to high production by a reputation he must maintain, by resources of support and information, as the centre of networks of communication. Still here the explanation is motivational and organizational, and doesn't say anything about how an individual was intellectually able to create that range of specific ideas, which would seem to be the core question.

Kuhn, to show a further step in a social interpretation of extraordinary achievement, would locate this in the process of paradigm shift, the person formulating the shift to some extent being the beneficiary of the time and place when his science was ready because of the 'exhaustion' or completion of the existing paradigm, its failure to provide significant further problems, and the buildup of anomalous date, for another separate interpretation (40a).

Mulkay and Crane also give a contextual explanation of the apparent significance of particular authors by their writing useful articles at an early and key phase of the development of a research specialty, and then being cited repeatedly as precedent and authority for all further work in the developing communications network or specialty (41).

Futher than this, I could only suggest that the person of apparently most original achievement is the person who experiences and senses another problem, one different from the current dominant problem set in his area of work. Naturally, the person who first develops a problem and the elements of a framework addressed to it has every advantage in learning a very great deal about it. Combining this with his sensitivity to new observations and relations among new and old observations, his advantages of precedent described by Mulkay, of network position, etc. described by Merton, and we begin to have a sociological explanation of extraordinary achievement by, after all, ordinary if talented men.

'Theory' is a second concept coming under criticism and shift. Obviously, this is a most condensed and multiplex code word, key in the symbolic structure of science. I will just discuss one implication: that theory is the product, goal or purpose of intellectual and scientific activity.

The history of 'theory' can be briefly traced in English through the entry in the Oxford Universal Dictionary (42).

In ancient Greek: (Θεωπιτα), 'viewing, a sight, spectacle'. (Θεωπός), 'a spectator'.

In English in 1597: "A conception or mental scheme of something to be done, or of the method of doing it; a systematic statement of rules or principles to be followed".

1613: "That department of an area or technical subject which consists in the knowledge or statement of the facts on which it depends, or of its principles or methods, as distinct from the practice of it."

1624: "(without the article) ... abstract knowledge or the formulation of it: often used as implying more or less unsupported hypothesis: distinct from opposed to practice."

1638: "A scheme or system of ideas or statements held as an explanation or account of a group of facts or phenomena: a hypothesis that has been confirmed or established by observation or experiment ..."

1792: "In loose or general sense: A hypothesis proposed as an explanation; hence a mere hypothesis, speculation, conjecture ..."

1799: "A systematic statement of the general principles of laws or some branch of mathematics; a set of theorems forming a connected system: as the theory of equations, of numbers."

I would like to note two points here. The first is the shift from a visual, practical emphasis through a core meaning of conceptual scheme to a meaning almost opposite from the Greek origin, as principle 'distinct from practice', 'unsupported' or 'mere hypothesis'. An 1850 useage is given, "Were a theory open to no objection it would cease to be theory and become a law." Here, a new concept is introduced to point to the 1597 to 1638 core meanings, this time on a verbal and legal metaphor rather than a visual, practical one.

Second, note the shift from present and future tenses in the Greek and the early English usages: 'viewing', 'something to be done', 'principles to be followed', to the past tense from 1638 forward, 'statements held', 'hypothesis that has been confirmed'.

'Scheme' and 'system' are invoked by the O.U.D. for the 1597 usage. 'Scheme' in turn is traced to the Greek root (σχŷμα) for 'form, figure, diagram', and 'system' to the Greek root (σμστημα) for 'an organized whole', 'to set up', hence, 'a group of objects'. In this historical context it is interesting that Kuhn wanted to leave 'theory', now a learned, verbal, and institutional term, for one more direct, visual, and concrete in 'paradigm'. Paradigm' is from a Greek noun (Παράδειχμα) for pattern, with a verb form 'to show side by side'. Hence the English meaning since 1483 of 'pattern, exemplar, example'. (O.U.D.).

Kuhn states that the paradigm precedes its relevant research program rather than concludes it. Thus his 'paradigm', as the conceptual artifact of scientific work, is direct and visual rather than removed and verbal, is temporary and programmatic rather than permanent, the origin and tool rather than the final goal of the research process.

To improve on this, I suspect we will have to go back to Gestalt psychology and look again at the generic processes of pattern recognition, apperception. and the further refinement, articulation and elaboration of dimly or incompletely perceived but suggestive-informative patterns, at the uses of metaphor in speech and in thought, and the various forms of patterned expresssion in music and the visual arts.

A third term only currently queried is 'discovery', as an individual and isolated event, independent and attributable to one person at one time and place.

Woolgar has found it necessary, in order to create a history of the discovery of pulsars by radio-astronomy methods, to expand the concept itself (43). In attempting to reconcile the discovery accounts of Hewish, the chief investigator, and Bell, his research assistant and the actual primary observer, Woolgar found it necessary to give 'discovery' a temporal dimension – to see it as a months long process, not as an event. He also found it necessary to see it as a product of the interaction of Hewish and Bell (parallel to Priestly and Lavoisier, or to Maxwell, Lorenz, and Einstein), and to see 'discovery' as having both an observational and interpretive dimension. Thus in the case of pulsars, the 'scruff' of ink lines on the chart record registering radio signals was 'observed' first in August-September, 1967, by Bell, while Hewish and Bell don't appear to have firmly interpreted them until late November or December 1967. This was not reported until February 1968, in *Nature*.

Much discussion and some controversy surrounded the assumed date of the Hewish-Bell discovery, and the presumed delayed publication. Woolgar writes: (44)

Differing perceptions of the date of the discovery seem to arise from the use of the term 'discovery' itself. Commonly, the notion of discovery is associated with instantaneous revelation or sudden perception. Participants who use the term in this metaphorical sense appear to become committed to discussion of a point occurrence in time rather than of a process.

'Method' is a fourth concept which has occasioned certain problems for people trying to develop a social account of science. Circumlocutions have included research 'strategy', 'process', 'orientation', 'program', etc. The authors of these terms have variously tried to break out of the logical, deliberate, sequential assumptions of 'method' to suggest emergent rather than pre-calculated research strategies, and the generation of suggestions, leads, interpretations, rather than 'proof'. 'Investigation', however, suggests improvised, open-ended, and multi-formed procedures, as opposed to a 'research method' predesigned and rigid in format.

'Data' has not yet been systematically questioned as a descriptive term in the sociology of science. Yet, 'data', like 'method', has certain limitations of truncated meaning, as though objects 'gave' information to receptive subjects. The older term, 'observations' allows an activity and participation for the subject-observor. No doubt more of the language of self description of institutional science will have to be shifted, enriched, specified in order to create its sociology.

It strikes me that the older concept, 'investigation', which dates from 1510 according to the Oxford Universal Dictionary, is a richer and more descriptive concept than 'research'. For 'investigation' the O.U.D. gives 'to search or to inquire into', 'to examine systematically or in detail' as original usages. And in 1610, 'minute and careful research', 'tracking a beast', and as a sample usage' "characters which require a long investigation to unfold (Burke)" (45). I want to seize on 'tracking' and 'hunting' as special, significant nuances of meaning here.

The words were then as now nearly interchangeable and one was sometimes used to define the other. But there is a difference: research is 'searching, closely or carefully for or after something' (1577), 'careful study of a subject', 'a course of critical or scientific inquiry' (1609). But the allusion to tracking or hunting is missing. The reader of Watson's *The Double Helix* will be struck by the appropriateness of the older term.

The questioning of basic concepts begins to accumulate: if method becomes pragmatic procedure and theory becomes suggestive program, they no longer relate as means and ends. If no longer as means and ends, then how do acts and concepts relate in a scientific investigation? If observations are sought rather than given and 'discoveries' are invented and not just found we can better understand that the more basic the invention the more likely it involves a change in, and not a mere addition to, our thinking. Then scientific investigation becomes an exercise in deliberate cultural change. This leaves us with the question of what the actual patterns of these investigations might be.

9. An Investigative Program

Without attempting to summarize the research programs being formulated out of this new orientation to science, one can say that a major thrust is to relate science, in specific ways, to its larger social context, both organizationally and culturally (**46**). Another is to see social processes within science, and to focus on research itself more than publication, citations, and the credit-stratification system. There are still few studies of the actual processes of research, although those are most informative (**47**). An initial survey of various 'self-reports' by scientists of elements of their own work, such as Beveridge, Bronowski, Ziman, Heisenberg, Polanyi, shows that these are useful but overlain with theoretical-philosophical considerations that make actual events and experiences difficult to discern and omit much personal and social context. As one step toward formulating an investigation of research process I will look in some detail at a unique source on research, James Watson's *The Double Helix*, both rich in observation and without theoretical pretention (**48**).

Although Watson's "personal account of the discovery of the structure of DNA" (subtitle) is non-theoretical, it does show a non-romantic view of science: "... science seldom proceeds in the straightforward logical manner imagined by outsiders. Instead, its steps forward (and sometimes backward) are often very human events in which personalities and cultural traditions play major roles " (**49**). His implied question is "How did this piece of science actually happen?" at least in the experience of one major participant (**50**). I believe that one can accept Watson's cautions of a 'personal account' and the major strictures of its critics (see especially Olby and Sayre (**51**)) and still suggest the main interpretative themes set out below; they are meant to be suggestive rather than conclusive.

Being autobiographical, Watson's account contains observations at several levels, from impressions of whole disciplines, to aphorisms invoked by Crick or himself. The structure of DNA was, "too pretty not to be true", and, "Crick knew that the evidence never seemed to be clear cut" (52). Like all folksayings, these aphorisms are invoked by situation and context; to what degree do they channel, facilitate, or block work and insight? Perhaps more interesting, Watson's account is replete with metaphor that would seem to come right out of his and Crick's thinking process: 'chain', 'backbone', 'template', 'bond', and 'cozy corner'. The simple physical and everyday suggestibility of these terms seemed to especially play a key role when Watson and Crick were groping for an image at the forefront of their thinking.

But the most important contribution of Watson is an insight into the intellectual dynamics of problem solving, both individual and collective. He had taken a very specific problem, the chemical structure of the gene and the relation of this structure to its ability of self-replication. This specificity allowed his active and pointed search, and a sorting of relevant and irrelevant information, which appeared as one of its great efficiencies. In reading or hearing a paper he was inclined to sort out its 'take home lesson', even though some of its technical content was beyond him (53). On a larger scale, he could not bring himself to study bio-chemistry, even though he had a biochemical problem, until he saw its direct relation to his problem. On the positive side, after he saw Maurice Wilkins' X-ray photo slide in Naples he was determined to study X-ray chrystallography because it suggested a structure in DNA. I would like to link Watson's confidence in the soluability of a difficult problem to his specific direction of search.

His confidence was strong, and the problem was in the forefront of conscious attention when it was yielding, but when the work seemed blocked, it receded to unconsciousness and conscious attention and shifted to otherwise more peripheral matters. Watson seemed to recognize and to play along with that, coming back after diversion for a fresh attack. In a recurrent pattern, confidence in a direction of search or interest in a hunch or interpretation was succeeded by a phase of apparent failure, of skepticism and self and external criticism. Enthusiasm and energetic work was succeeded by a more passive, receptive, and even a depressed phase.

This cycle of confidence and skepticism affected the whole process of the investigation, both observation and communication. While confident of their direction, their already focused sense of relevance on their problem became intense, with a powerful screening, even closing off of information outside of this narrow focus. During the blockages the search for information in the literature became more open, and they were more receptive to outside comment and criticism. Again this was partly articulated: Watson notes that it is important to be able to "make the right choice and to stick by its consequences", even against current scientific opinion (54). During periods of doubt and confusion Watson and Crick looked about them for any available 'hard' (credible) data for clues to their next effort.

These phases of confidence or skepticism gave their work a collective intellectual dynamic and also at each of at least eight decision points to be described shortly. During the confidence-conviction phase they sought support, specific information and self re-enforcing colleagues. Sources in disagreement seemed irrelevant. During their own skepticism however, they received criticism, considered contradictory information, turned to different people within their problem area and in outside specialties; they considered redirection and reformulation of the research. For example, after the false alarm trip of Wilkins and Franklin to view their supposed three chain internal backbone model, it was clear that, "A fresh start would be necessary", but failing new access to the King's College data at London, Watson was left to use "the dark and chilly days to learn more theoretical chemistry or to leaf through journals, hoping that possibly there existed a forgotten clue to DNA" (55).

I would like to expand this to suggest that these phases of confidence and skepticism reflect one of the basic dilemmas of science. Although skepticism and criticism have been the focus of positivist philosphy, basic innovation, as in this case, would seem to come from long term and repeated thrusts of exploration based on faith and supposition. Attending also to the prior phase of confidence and of search, we can see the regular reconciliation of the contrary requirements of conviction and criticism within the phase moods of one investigator, between the collaborating pair, with Watson and Crick alternating roles as advocate and as critic, and in the roles played by sympathetic (e.g. Lwoff) and critical by-standers (e.g. Pirie) (56). These contrasting attitudes not only characterize investigation and publication as the major phases of science, but also occur in a dynamic interaction during the investigation itself.

At the most basic level, we can see the phases of confidence and skepticism linked to each major decision point of investigative strategy. At least eleven such decisions can be identified in Watson's account. Three had already been made by the time Watson entered the 'phage group' working on genes and DNA. The most basic was to seek a physical interpretation of the transferral of life from generation to generation in a coding process, that it was information that was passed on rather than a 'vital principle'. The second was to focus on simple viruses, the bacteriophages ('phages') to study genes, the viruses being viewed as 'a form of naked genes' (57). The third was to search for the basic structure of life not in the complex proteins but in deoxyribonuleic acid (DNA), known to occur in the chromosomes of all cells. These three decisions, now working assumptions, made Watson and Crick part of a 'research orientation', people with a shared problem and common major lines of approach to it.

We are one step ahead of the story in that Watson's own first decision, the one which brought him to Cambridge, was to look for a regular, simple structure in DNA. This inclination was confirmed when he heard Wilkins talk and saw his X-ray photo of DNA in Naples in the spring of 1951. "Before Maurice's talk I had worried about the possibility that the gene might be fantastically irregular. Now, however, I knew that genes could crystallize; hence they must have a regular structure" (58).

The next decisions were taken at the suggestion of Crick, whom Watson started to work with immediately after he arrived, exchanging 'phage lore' for 'crystallographic facts, (especially) the exact arguments needed to understand how Linus Pauling had discovered the a-helix" (as a model for the structure of the protein, Collagen) (59). In deciding to imitate Pauling, they were in effect making two decisions at the same time: (2) to construct a set of (physical) molecular models and (3) to look for the helix structure.

Watson and Crick's first wrong decision (4) was to postulate an internal suger-phosphate backbone rather than having the bases on the inside of the molecule. This was in spite of Watson having heard the correct interpretation and the supporting data in a seminar given by Franklin in November, 1951 (60). Here Watson's simplicity criterion lead him astray, Wilkins and Franklin were right, being based on much better data and being more patient with complexity (61). Watson and Crick were later corrected by criticism (the false alarm trip) and indirectly by data to which they had incomplete access.

Another closely related decision (5) was whether the helix had 2, 3, or 4 chains, since the Franklin photo, along with the Cochrane-Crick theory of the

relation of molecular structure to X-ray photos, dicated multiple chains. Here
a second exposure to Rosalind Franklin's data was crucial. The B form
(hydrated) of the DNA molecule was shown to Watson by Wilkins, without
Franklin's knowledge, in early February, 1953.

The real puzzle that remained – hitherto avoided – was how to fit
together the bases in the center of the molecule, a puzzle without any strong
leading clues. Watson became preoccupied with the puzzle of the bases,
"Even during good films, I found it almost impossible to forget the bases"
(62).

The three final features of the DNA model fell together almost at the
same time, consequences of Donahue's advice to use the keto rather than the
enol form of the bases. Using the enol forms had lead Watson to try to pair
'like with like' bases and to an irregular helix (63). Using guanine and
thymine in the keto form (6) lead Watson, through trial and error shifting
the base model pieces around, to discover the correct pairs. "I became aware
that an adenine-thymine pair held together by two hydrogen bonds was identical in shape to a guanine-cytosine pair held together by at least two
hydrogen bonds" (64). These became the steps in the 'spiral staircase' made
of sugar-phosphates. Thus, decision (7) was directly implied, the chains were
held together by hydrogen bonds and not salt (Mg^{++}) linkages, which had
been Watson's second major erroneous hunch (65). Decision (8) satisfactorily
followed, was in fact the beauty of the model: gene replication occurred not
by cell division or a chemical transformation, but by the alternative formation of complimentary surfaces, by 'complementary replication' as in the
image of a template. It was the long-sought information theory.

Even more exciting (than satisfying Chargaff's rules), this type of double helix suggested
a replication scheme much more satisfactory than my briefly considered like-with-like
pairing ... the base sequences of the two intertwined chains were complementary to each
other ... Conceptually, it was thus very easy to visualize how a single chain could be the
template for the synthesis of a chain with the complementary sequence (66).

At each stage of decision about the direction of search for a model the con-
fidence-skepticism process was in play. Sometimes the blockage came, in
cases of bad guesses, from 'data', and at others from colleagues' criticism, as
in the case of Franklin's and Wilkins' point that their three chain internal
backbone model underestimated the water content by a factor of ten (67). In
sum, in Watson's account, on three of the eight basic decisions they were

wrong; expecting an internal backbone, salt linkages, and enol base forms. On the backbone location and the enol form they were corrected by colleagues and colleagues' data, and the hydrogen bonds fell out as part of the overall solution. Crick was also wrong in his momentary enthusiasm for 'the perfect biological principle' of self-replication by cell division (68).

Their communication was also structured by their judgments of the credibility of other peoples' information and criticism, depending again on their own level of self-confidence. And it was structured by competition with people working directly on the same problem (Pauling, Wilkins and Franklin), and the possibilities for exchange. Within specialties exchange is a serious matter, as evidenced in Watson's and Crick's repeated urging of collaboration and Wilkins' and Franklin's refusals. But between specialties, normally within the same university, sometimes very crucial information is given freely, as by Griffith and Donahue. I cannot follow-up here an analysis on the basis of credibility, competition and exchange, but only suggest them as aspects affecting research along with the confidence-narrow focus and skepticism-broad search pattern.

10. Concluding Comment

Science is a peculiar institution — as it has always taken itself to be — but perhaps in a different sense.

Science is an open system intellectually, deliberately seeking innovation and accommodating basic change (Bacon). Yet any system has to work towards intellectual coherence, or it would fall into anarchy and confusion (Polanyi). This has never been programmatically reconciled in science, which can lead to trouble cases, as in the case of the 'Velikovsky affair'.

Perhaps science avoided having to live through and being forced to reconcile the contradiction of openness and coherence primarily because it was utopian. The belief that science would discover the whole truth — which would *have* to be coherent — one day in the future, postponed the requirement of coherence and the consequent intellectual closure. Both anarchy — giving up the *search* for coherence — and coherence itself would have been the death of science. Perhaps today we need a safer ground, or will 'evolution away from the primitive' be an adequate formulation?

Bacon was conscious of that already in the *Novum Organum* (69). The opening few pages contrast the two enemies of science — skepticism and belief. In the case of the study of nature, he optimistically believed one needed merely to discover the truth. However, in the study of man (politics), it remained necessary to convince others — always a difficult task. Perhaps we are ready to see that contrast as less clear, and therefore the study of man as more possible.

The natural history of the three stages suggests comparisons between the natural and the social sciences. Where, why, and how does this natural process of intellectual innovation abort? It may be more common in social science to get caught in a long term dialectical argument — as in the cases idealism-realism, mind-body, rationalism-empiricism, political economy-socialism, etc. But such 'schools' also form in natural science as in organism-mechanism, atomism-wholism, etc. We need case analyses of where the sequence — programmatic debate, terminological shift, and research program — gets interrupted, and where does it run to completion, regardless of, or across contrasting cases of topical content.

Thus, all science is dialectical and positive, both a process of argument in counter-concepts and images, and one of purposive experience and observation. The dialectic by itself is a recipe for persistent error, and empiricism by itself is directionless and a-theoretical.

Notes and References

1. Juan E. Corradi, 'Textures: Approaching Society, Ideology and Literature', Occasional Papers No. 19. Ibero-American Language and Area Center, New York University, New York, N.Y., March, 1976.
2. Joseph Ben-David, 'Is there a Sociology of Knowledge?' Working Paper No. 136, The Hebrew University of Jerusalem and the University of Chicago, mimeo, 1969; *The Scientist's Role in Society, A Comparative Study*, Englewood Cliffs, New Jersey: Prentice-Hall Inc., 1971, pp. 7–11.
3. Michael Polanyi, *Personal Knowledge*, New York: Harper & Row, 2nd ed., 1964, p. x.
4. *Ibid.*, p. x.
5. M. J. Mulkay, ' Three Models of Scientific Development', *The Sociological Review* 23, 3. August, 1975, pp 509–526.
   W. O. Hagstrom, *The Scientific Community*, New York, N.Y.: Basic Books, 1975, pp. 224–225.
   Nicholas Mullins, 'The Development of a Scientific Specialty: The Phage Group and the Origin of Molecular Biology', *Minerva* 10, January, 1972, pp. 51–82.
6. Ian I. Mitroff, *The Subjective Side of Science*, Amsterdam: Elsevier Scientific Publishing Company, 1974.
7. Peter Buck, 'Orientations Toward Occidental Knowledge: Comparative Perspectives on the Science Society of China, 1914–1937', unpub. Ph.D. diss. Harvard Uni-

versity, 1972; and 'Science, Revolution, and Imperialism: Current Chinese and Western Views of Scientific Development', *Proceedings of the XIV Congress of the History of Science*, Tokyo, 1974; and 'Order and Control: The Scientific Method in China and the United States', *Social Studies of Science* 5, 1975, pp. 237–267; and E. Mendelsohn, 'Physical Models and Physiological Concepts: Explanation in Nineteenth Century Biology', *'The British Journal for the History of Science* 2, 7, 1965; and 'Revolution and Reduction: The Sociology of Methodological and Philosophy Concerns in 19th Century Biology', mimeo, January 1972; and E. Mendelsohn and A. Thackray, (eds.) *Science and Human Values*, New York, N.Y.: Humanities Press, 1974 and Lewis Feuer, *Einstein and the Generations of Science*, New York: Basic Books, 1974.

8. Ian I. Mitroff, 'Norms and Counter-Norms in a Select Group of the Apollo Moon Scientists: A Case Study of the Ambivalence of Scientists', *American Sociological Review* 39, 1974, pp. 579–595.

9. Robert K. Merton, *The Sociology of Science*, Chicago: University of Chicago Press, 1973, p. 270.

10. Joseph Needham, 'History and Human Values: A Chinese Perspective for World Science and Technology', a paper given at the Canadian Association of Asian Studies Annual Conference, Montreal, Quebec, May 1975, p. 31.

11. T. S. Kuhn, *The Structure of Scientific Revolutions*, Chicago: University of Chicago Press, 2nd ed., 1970, p. 171.

12. R. K. Merton, *The Sociology of Science*; *op. cit.*, 1973, Note 9, p. 273.

13. Roger G. Krohn, 'Patterns of the Institutionalization of Research', in S. A. Nagi and R. G. Corwin (eds.) *Social Context of Research*, New York: John Wiley and Sons, 1972.

14. R. K. Merton, *The Sociology of Knowledge*; *op. cit.*, p. 273.

15. Ian I. Mitroff, 'Norms and Counternorms ...'; *op. cit.*

16. Marcel Mauss, *The Gift: forms and Functions of Exchange in Archaic Societies*, London: Cohen and West Ltd., 1954, pp. 37–40.

17. R. K. Merton, *The Sociology of Science*; *op. cit.* p. 276.

18. *ibid.*, p. 276.

19. *ibid.*, p. 278.

20. Michael Polanyi, *Personal Knowledge*; *op. cit.*, p. X.

21. T. S. Kuhn, *The Structure of Scientific Revolutions*; *op. cit.*, p. 94.

22. Ian I. Mitroff, 'Norms and Counter-Norms', *op. cit.*, p. 592.

23. T. S. Kuhn, *The Structure of Scientific Revolutions*; *op. cit.*, p. 77.

24. Joseph Ben-David, *The Scientist's Role in Society*, *op. cit.*, ch. 7.

25. Friedrich Paulsen, *The German University and University Study* (translated by F. Thilly and W. Elang), New York: Longman-Green, 1906, pp. 50–61.

26. *ibid.*, p. 53.

27. *ibid.*, pp. 65–66.

28. J. D. Bernal, *The Social Functions of Science*, New York: Macmillan Co., 1939; and *Science in History*, London: C.A. Watts & Co., 1954; and B. Hessen, 'The Social and Economic Roots of Newton's Principia', in *Science and the Crossroads*, London, 1931; republished by Cass, 1975.

29. Ben-David, *The Scientist's Role in Society*; *op. cit.*, pp. 158ff.

30. For example see: Jim Hightower, *Hard Tomatoes, Hard Times: A Report of the Agribusiness Accountability Project on the Failure of America's Land Grant College Complex*, Cambridge, Mass.: Schenkman, 1973; Andre Mayer and Jean Mayer, 'Agriculture, the Island Empire', *Daedalus* 103, 1974, p. 3.

31. Joseph Ben-David, *The Scientist's Role in Society*; *op. cit.*, 1971, Note 2. Gerald Gordon, 'Freedom, Visibility, and Scientific Innovation', *American Journal of*

Sociology 70, 1966, pp. 195–204.
32. I was first drawn to this interpretation by a study of the sociological classics, especially A. Smith, St. Simon, Marx, Durkheim, and Weber. Each can be seen to have devoted his working life to a single major national or European social problem of his time. But this is the topic of another paper.
33. Peter Buck, 'Science, Revolution, and Imperialism', *op. cit.*, 1974, Note 7.
   Science for the People, a periodical, Boston, Mass., 1970 and forward.
34. Rene Dubos, *So Human An Animal*, New York: Charles Scribner's Sons, 1968.
35. The Society for Freedom in Science strongly articulated this faith in response to Bernal's position below: See *The Society for Freedom in Sciences, Its Origins, Objects, and Constitution*, Oxford, England: Potter Press, 2nd Ed., 1953, and Society for Freedom in Science, *Occasional Pamphlets*, Nos. 1–13. 1945–1952.
36. J. D. Bernal, *The Social Functions of Science*; *op, cit.*, 1939, Note 28.
37. Gerald Gordon, 'Freedom, Visibility, and Scientific Innovation', *op. cit.*, 1966, Note 31, pp. 195–204; and 'Preconceptions and Reconceptions in the Administration of Science', Proceedings of the Second Conference on Research Program Effectiveness, Department of the Navy, Office of Naval Research, New York: Gordon and Breach Publishers, 1965.
38. Joseph Ben-David, *The Scientist's Role in Society*; *op. cit.*, 1971, Note 2. p. 57.
39. Robert K. Merton, *The Sociology of Science*; *op. cit.*, 1973, Note 9, p. 366. (first published in 1961.)
40. *ibid.*, p. 368.
40a. T. Kuhn, *The Structure of Scientific Revolutions*; *op. cit.*, 1970, Note 11.
41. M. J. Mulkay, 'Three Models of Scientific Development', *op. cit.*, 1975, Note 5, p. 521; and Diana Crane, *Invisible Colleges: Diffusion of Knowledge in Scientific Communities*, Chicago: University of Chicago Press, 1972.
42. *The Oxford Universal Dictionary* (ed. by C. T. Onions), Oxford: Clarendon Press, 3rd ed., 1955.
43. S. W. Woolgar, 'Writing an Intellectual History of Scientific Development: the Use of Discovery Accounts', *Social Studies of Science* 6, 1976, pp. 395–422.
44. *ibid.*, p. 32.
45. *The Oxford Universal Dictionary*; *op. cit.*
46. See for example L. Sklair, *Organized Knowledge, A Sociological View of Science and Technology*, London: Hart-Davis, MacGibbon, 1973; and S. Blume, *Towards a Political Sociology of Science*, New York: The Free Press, 1974; and J. Ravetz, *Scientific Knowledge and Its Social Problems*, Oxford: Clarendon Press, 1971.
47. See for example, M. J. Mulkay *et al.*, 'Problem Areas and Research Networks in Science', *Sociology* 9, May 1975, p. 2; and Ian I. Mitroff, *The Subjective Side of Science*; *op. cit.*, 1974, Note 6.
48. J. D. Watson, *The Double Helix*, New York: Athenaeum Publishers, 1968.
49. *ibid.*, p. ix.
50. *ibid.*, p. 208.
51. Robert Olby, *The Path to the Double Helix*, Seattle: The University of Washington Press, 1974; Anne Sayre, *Rosalind Franklin and DNA*, New York: W.W. Norton & Co., 1975.
52. James D. Watson, *The Double Helix*; *op. cit.*, 1968, Note 48, p. 208.
53. *ibid.*, p. 111.
54. *ibid.*, p. 208.
55. *ibid.*, pp. 100–101.
56. *ibid.*, p. 121.
57. *ibid.*, p. 22.
58. *ibid.*, p. 33.

59. *ibid.*, pp. 36—38.
60. Anne Sayre, *Rosalind Franklin and DNA*; *op. cit.*, pp. 125—128.
61. James D. Watson, *The Double Helix*; *op. cit.*, 1968, Note 48, pp. 51—52.
62. *ibid.*, p 181.
63. *ibid.*, pp. 190ff.
64. *ibid.*, p. 194.
65. *ibid.*, p. 51.
66. *ibid.*, p. 196.
67. *ibid.*, p. 94.
68. *ibid.*, pp. 126—128.
69. Thanks to the suggestion of Peter Buck, and for several other unfootnoted suggestions.

PART II

SOCIAL RELATIONS OF COGNITIVE STRUCTURES
IN THE SCIENCES

ONTOLOGICAL AND EPISTEMOLOGICAL COMMITMENTS AND SOCIAL RELATIONS IN THE SCIENCES:
The Case of the Arithmomorphic System of Scientific Production*

PHYLLIS COLVIN

Manchester University

1. Scientific Products and the System of Scientific Production

The description of science as a socially mediated work process yielding scientific products which are themselves defined by the social processes of their generation is gaining broader currency (1). Such a description asserts that scientific products are indeed social relations of the system of scientific production, and hence should be understood as embodying and, at times, concretizing the nature, the potentialities and contradictions of the system of scientific production and reproduction in which they are embedded. The task of the sociologist of science is thus, in part, to investigate the nature and context of scientific products in order to assess what these products as social relations may reveal about the larger productive system, the larger work process, which permitted their definition and formulation. In this paper I shall attempt to articulate in a preliminary way some of the features of a system of social relations of scientific production as they are implied by the nature of a specific group of scientific products to which the terms 'closed' and 'arithmomorphic' have been applied in recent descriptions (2).

Scientific products may assume many forms. They may be differentiated according to the directness of their relations to the divisions of activity and orientation that distinguish the theorist from the experimentalist, and both from the analyst, which have emerged in many areas of science. Alternatively, they may be differentiated according to the degree that they reflect detailed, technical, precisely elaborated commitments in theory, experiment or analysis,

---

* I am grateful for comments from Nicholas Georgescu-Roegen, Helga Nowotny, Peter Weingart, and Richard Whitley on an earlier draft of this paper.

Mendelsohn/Weingart/Whitley (eds.), The Social Production of Scientific Knowledge. Sociology of the Sciences, Volume I, 1977. 103–128. All Rights Reserved.
Copyright © 1977 by D. Reidel Publishing Company, Dordrecht-Holland.

as opposed to more metaphysical commitments implying adherences to systems of rationality, world views or norms of 'truth', but little else, within the same domains (3).

Scientific products may also be differentiated according to their specific ontological, epistemological and social implications; this form of differentiation is the broad basis for disciplinary, sub-disciplinary and specialty differentiation. It is also the foundation which the sociologist requires for distinguishing different systems of scientific production, although the boundaries of such systems need not correspond with traditional disciplinary or other cognitive boundaries (4). A high degree of general cognitive consistency across ontological, epistemological and social commitments and relations is necessary for the very definition of a system of scientific production, although such consistency will never be total (5). Analysis should be concerned with the differentiation of the various commitments and relations characteristic of a particular system and with the subsequent grouping of these commitments and relations into categories (5a). Such a process should reveal the degree of interpenetration among the ontological, epistemological and social categories of the system, and hence, the degree to which consistency is maintained throughout the system. As well, analysis should be concerned with the limitations of the system as defined by the properties of the system in juxtaposition with larger or different conceptual realms and values. But it is first necessary to distinguish the various commitments internal to the system, to detail the nature of the relations mediating the system, and to outline the categories which are to be employed in further analysis.

In this paper I have taken advantage of two accounts of ontological and epistemological commitments relating to broadly similar groups of scientific products, and have asked the question, what do these accounts reveal about the nature of social commitments and relations in the system of scientific production that embraces these ontological and epistemological commitments? The two accounts are those of Roy Bhaskar and Nicholas Georgescu-Roegen (6); 'closure' and 'arithmomorphism' are respectively the terms they apply to describe a broadly similar set of ontological and epistemological commitments. Each of these accounts is generally philosophical in tone, and it is the intention of this paper to employ these philosophical accounts as starting points for the description of a system of scientific production in which ontological and epistemological commitments are sufficiently clarified as to assist in the description of social commitments and relations within the same system. Thus the project is to complement Bhaskar's general question, 'what must the world be like in order for science to be possible?' (7), which lends itself to what have traditionally been termed 'philosophical' forms of resolution implying specific ontologies and epistemologies, with the question, 'what must society and social relations be like in a system which generates and reproduces the forms and relations characteristic of specific scientific products?'

It is this latter question which yields to sociological resolution, but only as long as sociology is conceived in a wide enough manner as to embrace a concern with scientific products, with ontological and epistemological commitments, and hence with the full range of the social or transitive dimensions of the world which is at the centre of Bhaskar's understanding of scientific discourse. In the following pages I shall present brief descriptions of the ontological and epistemological commitments detailed by Bhaskar and Georgescu-Roegen. I shall concentrate, in particular, on those artefacts such as the closure problematic, the discreteness of scientific products within arithmomorphism, and the arithmomorphic paradoxes, which form the basis of a discussion, in the second half of the paper, of the social commitments and relations which relate to such cognitive phenomena as the distinction between theoretical and experimental work in various sciences, paradox proliferation within theoretical development, and the enlargement of the scientific field.

2. The Closure Problematic

Let us initially examine the case of the generally (or, at least, apparently) dominant, mechanistic world view concerning scientific 'reality' and practice as it existed toward the end of the nineteenth century and into the early years of the twentieth century. R. Bhaskar has performed a considerable service in broadly characterizing the nature of certain cognitive objects which pre-quantum science generated and found legitimacy for in the approbation of scientists and their lay audiences. Bhaskar informs us that scientific experimentation, understood in terms of the dominant experimental philosophy of the nineteenth century, demanded what he describes as an experimental 'closure'. In defining closure, he employs the characteristically

Humean designation: experimental closure is effected when an investigator operates upon a system which is restricted in time and place and in which a constant conjunction of events obtains. Indeed, Bhaskar argues that the dominant tradition in nineteenth century experimental philosophy was largely Humean in nature. He denotes this tradition with the term 'empirical realism' which refers to the whole post-Humean tradition and notably its positivist and neo-Kantian wings (8). Bhaskar is intrinsically dissatisfied with the Humean characterization of experimental activity, and proceeds to demonstrate that it fails to account for the behaviour of scientists in experimental situations because it lends 'reality' to events as they are appropriated in Humean sensations, rather than to transcendental structures of the material world. From this point, he articulates a philosophical outline of the transcendental realism which he believes is the basis of scientific practice. But for the purposes of this paper, his description of the ontological basis of Hume's doctrine, and hence of certain areas of classical science, is far more interesting. He notes that the 'closure' mode of experimentation requires the fulfilment of three conditions in order to maintain its internal coherence as a methodology: at the level of the experimental system, closure demands isolation, both in the material and relational senses; at the level of individuals, atomicity, in the sense of internal neutrality and rigidity, is required; finally, as a principle of organization, only additivity, implying a strict prohibition against novelty by combination, is acceptable (9). These three conditions arise from a vision of matter as composed of rigid, neutral corpuscles in motion under the influence of external, non-discriminatory forces which possess no transformative potential. Various degrees of internal organization, including structural and hierarchical differentiation, cannot be accommodated by this ontological system. Qualitative change, growth and decay also cannot be accommodated in this format.

While Bhaskar's description of the ontological implications of Humean closure is a cogent introduction to some of the ontological commitments characteristic of classical science, we are forced by the very simplicity of this presentation to inquire, with Feyerabend (10), as to the universality and comprehensiveness of Humean thought as *the* nineteenth century doctrine of experimental philosophy. In spite of Hume, nineteenth century science cannot be reduced to corpuscular models. In physics alone, the study of electric and magnetic fields, and eventually of light as a form of electromagnetic radiation, the study of probability, the study of materials with 'historical' properties (as in the case of magnetic hysteresis) (11), the study of phenomena such as friction connected with molecular forces, are but a few of the more dramatic areas of nineteenth century interest which cannot be constrained to the theoretical confines of corpuscularism. Indeed, it is possible to argue that Hume's doctrine only represents a particularly cogent ritualization of the ontological capacities of Newtonian physics – a ritualization which certainly served philosophical interests and met some of the requirements for dogma in the scientific system of production with which it was associated (12) – but which may have also restricted the creative potential of science by attempting to legislate as to 'appropriate' scientific fields of interest and hence scientific products.

The ritual potentialities and the limitations of Humean closure are revealed by the epistemologizing of ontology under Hume. The Humean interpretation of epistemology absorbed the atomistic ontology of the classical paradigm of corpuscular action by positing that scientific experience (and hence ultimately experimentation and closure) rests in a technical sense on the basis of the perception of simple, atomistic qualities in sense experience. These qualities impinge upon the observer in the form of discrete events. At the metaphysical level of epistemology, Hume's descriptions presuppose the cognitive absorption of atomistic impulses by a mechanistic mental mechanism designed specifically to receive such impulses. It is possible to describe the development of such epistemological commitments as the epistemologizing of ontology (13), for this conception of mental process retains its adequacy only as a function of the durability of a very specific ontological world view. Alternatively, so long as that world view retains its plausibility, the Humean doctrine retains great ritualizing potential. Later in this paper such a juxtaposition of ontological and epistemological categories will be employed to illustrate the social relations of a larger productive system in science – that of arithmomorphism.

If Hume's doctrine and Bhaskar's derivative description of the ontological commitments inherent to closure are to be understood as limited, perhaps ritualized, presentations of the ontological and epistemological potentialities of pre-quantum science, it is natural to inquire as to a more generalized epistemological format which might be conducive to the decisive overthrow of long established mental habits. Bhaskar perceives science to be mediated by transcendental realism; but as this understanding remains ontologically and epistemologically undifferentiated in his presentation (14), it is difficult to relate this option to specific scientific products or specific systems of production. It is perhaps premature to search for the enlarged epistemological options which the history of science has presented, or for the epistemological potentialities of the future, without a careful examination of the ontological commitments and relations which science has found legitimacy for in the past.

3. Arithmomorphism: An Ontological System and Its Paradoxes

In fact, in the context of other work which has been performed recently to identify the ontological properties of nineteenth century science, Bhaskar's closure problematic may be enlarged and redefined beyond the Humean context. Nicholas Georgescu-Roegen, in his preliminary description of theoretical science, proceeds some way past Bhaskar in summarizing the ontological basis of historical and current physical science with the term 'arithmomorphism' (15). In this section of the paper the capacities and some of the limitations of the arithmomorphic system will be described in preparation for a discussion of the social implications of the same in the second half of the paper.

For Georgescu-Roegen, theoretical science, and hence the term, arithmomorphism, refers to the extremely potent synthesis of Aristotelian Logic as a mode of discourse and "the idea of causality as a two-way algorithm" (16) introduced by Greek philosophy (except for the First Cause everything has a cause as well as an effect). Not all science, of course, comes under this rubric; chemistry, biology, geology, meteorology are all sciences in which this synthesis displays distinct limitations in the appropriation of scientific products because these sciences concern themselves with qualitative material differentation, temporal change and other issues which do not find accommodation in this synthesis. But nevertheless, arithmomorphism has historically been, and remains, the dominant ontological framework for scientific statement – to the degree that other modes of appropriating scientific products have often either been ignored or neglected in theoretical cases where the full application of arithmomorphism has presented tremendous difficulties. This has been apparent, for instance, in the theoretical treatment of time — particularly in the context of the evolution of biological systems (17).

In the wake of the development of the causal nexus as a two-way algorithm, the Greeks launched a search for proximate causes which culminated in Aristotle's famous categorization of cause involving the *causa materialis,* the *causa formalis*, the *causa efficiens* and the *causa finalis*. And yet, in Greek thought, and in the later Renaissance development of theoretical science, two of the forms of cause advanced by Aristotle were reduced in importance: these were the *causa materialis* and the *causa finalis*. This simplification of the causal hierarchy assisted the more complete synthesis of Logic as a method of sorting propositions with the two-way causal algorithm by dispensing with problems such as qualitative change, order, and temporal evolution. But more importantly, the logical analysis of the two-way causal relations connecting various intuited conceptual products was helped by a crucial confusion between 'the why' (in the sense of the *causa efficiens*) and 'the logical ground' (in the sense of the *causa formalis*) of explanation (18). Theoretical science tends to meld these two fundamentals of explanation, concentrating far more on the *causa efficiens* than on the *causa formalis*. This rather metaphysical confusion has been highly productive as a foundation for the arithmomorphic problematic. It allows the theoretical scientist to remain reasonably unconcerned about the ground distinctions between an 'electric field' and a 'magnetic field' or between the 'velocity of a particle' and the 'temporal and spatial position of the same particle' as long as these concepts belong to that "... very restricted class of concepts, to which [we] shall refer as *arithmomorphic* for the good reason that every one of them is as discretely distinct as a single number in relation to the infinity of all others." (19). It is with concepts which possess this property of discrete distinctness that we are able to compute, to syllogize and to construct a theoretical science (20). Moreover, as Ronchi has noted in the case of the development of geometrical optics, this understanding of what scientific products are, and should be, allows us to project the vast majority of our concerns in physical science upon finite, external entities, and to ignore most of the physiological and mental problems of perception, observation and conceptualization (21).

The arithmomorphic nature of concepts such as the 'velocity of a particle' or the 'strength of a magnetic field' does not imply that the theoretical scientist fails to make important qualitative distinctions between the various arithmomorphisms. It does imply that such qualitative distinctions are not *primary* to the theoretical efficacy of such concepts. Rather, the theoretical authority of arithmomorphic concepts rests with the following properties of these constructions: their individuality or discreteness, which permits the theorist to manipulate them as entirely distinct entities; their potential for reduction, resulting from the availability or the potentiality of a set of relatively simple, discretionary relations to serve as a common denominator for reasoning (the Newtonian relations for mechanical problems; the set of relations arising from Coulomb's law for problems involving charge and electric field; the fundamental probability relations for problems concerned with random variables); and their lack of symbolic material which permits the restriction of the field of 'possible' problems to a small subset of the much larger universe of problems in which questions of form, quality and substance have a place.

Thus scientific products associated with Humean closure are but a subset of the arithmomorphic universe of discrete entities. Arithmomorphic concepts are discrete and internally neutral. They can convey neither form nor quality, except in the restricted sense of their definition in terms of other arithmomorphic concepts. They are characterized by magnitude, and sometimes by orientation relative to other arithmomorphic concepts and arithmomorphic frames of reference. Their single most important property is that they do not overlap in any sense. One is never in doubt about their individuality with reference to other arithmomorphisms. The classic form of the arithmomorphic entity, as the name implies, is the real number; in spite of the fact that we often designate the range of real numbers as an arithmetic continuum, in actuality, for theoretical purposes each element of the continuum is entirely distinct from each other element. In a similar manner, "... the concept of 'circle' [is distinct] from '10 ^{100}-gon' or from 'square', and 'election' from 'proton'. In Logic 'is' and 'is not', 'belongs' and 'does not belong', 'some' and 'all', too, are *discretely* distinct." (22).

In Georgescu-Roegen's terms every theoretical construct within theoretical science is arithmomorphically representative. The most comprehensive arithmomorphic constructs are the arithmetic continuum and its conceptual branches, the spatial and temporal continua. In each case the 'continuum' is conceptually composed of discrete entities − of real numbers, in the case of the arithmetic continuum, and of discrete points in space and instants in time in the cases of the spatial and temporal continua respectively. The arithmetic and spatial continua have been associated with material continua as in the case of the familiar material metre stick employed to define a segment of the spatial continuum. But matter has always presented more logical problems than space, time or the number system — primarily because theoretical science has not succeeded in discovering the fully discrete, qualityless, elementary particle, and because the concept of matter implies volume through dimension, although not necessarily any measure of order interior to the material continuum. However, whether one is dealing with number, space, time, or the more elusive matter, the arithmomorphic quest is for the rigorous definition and manipulation of absolutely neutral arithmomorphic concepts. Furthermore, it is with the conceptual yardsticks of the arithmetic, spatial and temporal continua that the experimental closures of theoretical science are made possible.

But it is as we pursue the ontological framework of classical science to this level of technical precision that the limitations of the enlarged closure problematic denoted as arithmomorphism become apparent in the form of paradoxes. Historically, Émile Borel, one of Georgescu-Roegen's mentors, cited a fundamental contradiction between the arithmetic continuum as an aggregate which is everywhere dense, yet is composed of countable (enumerable) elements, and the conceptual results of certain mental experiments concerned with continuity and topology. He posited the problem of what happens when we set up an arithmetic continuum in conjunction with a material continuum and attempt to "... remove a piece of the straight line round each of these infinitely numerous points [of the arithmetic continuum], points which, to use the suggestive expression of the theory of aggregates, are *dense* over the whole line" (23). He concluded that, while one may set up an arithmetical process of removal with a definite fractional limit, over an infinite number of removals such an arithmetical process is geometrically and materially absurd. Thus the confusion of 'the why' and 'the logical ground' of explanation rears its head in a 'number versus matter' paradox. This type of problem is apparent again in the inability of the arithmomorphic framework to account for the notion of sense in geometry (24), or the qualitative differentiation characteristic of the simplest chemical reaction (arithmomorphism which operates with neutral species cannot accommodate novelty by combination).

At a higher level of conceptualization Borel, and later Georgescu-Roegen, were to investigate the relational paradox embodied in the statement that 'random' as a concept is beyond the range of analytical or arithmomorphic definition (25). In an examination of the ontological basis of the Second Law of Thermodynamics Georgescu-Roegen was to discover that this gap between arithmomorphic expectations and arithmomorphic potentialities in the investigation of the concept of 'random' is centrally related to the more general concept of 'order' — another material relation which transcends the conceptual neutrality of arithmomorphism. Similarly, Georgescu-Roegen has felt obliged in reinterpreting the Entropy Law to restate the problem of temporal relations in modified Bergsonian terms in view of the fact that the clock-time of arithmomorphism is not adequate to deal with qualitative, material change — a realm which the classical Entropy Law explicitly treats (26). This particular observation has a history dating back to Zeno's Paradoxes, which treat the various properties of material existence in time and space. Finally, the Entropy Law itself is materially paradoxical in the context of arithmomorphism because it is under its influence that living organisms, which remain outside the arithmomorphic spectrum, are able to appropriate low entropy in forms such as heat and light which have conventionally been seen as arithmomorphically describable. Thus the fundamental paradoxes of arithmomorphism seem inseparable from the 'number, matter' dichotomy inherent to the arithmomorphic system's definition. In the next sections of this paper, the arithmomorphic paradoxes will be reinterpreted in terms of the social relations which mediate the system.

4. Social Commitments and Relations in Arithmomorphic Sciences

The preceding description of the closure problematic in an enlarged form allows us greater freedom to speculate concerning the nature of the social relations associated with the appropriation of scientific products. The epistemological ramifications of the arithmomorphic ontological range are undoubtedly diverse. The epistemological category of Humean thought has already been briefly mentioned; but, in order to describe the full range of epistemological categories associated with arithmomorphism, the investigator would be obliged to discriminate among the various forms of positivism, realism and neo-Kantianism which have appropriated aspects of the arithmomorphic ontological framework to varying degrees, and which have either enlarged or ritualized the potentialities characteristic of closure (27). Distinctions would have to be drawn between epistemologies that have been scientifically institutionalized and those that have been philosophically institutionalized in order to clarify the nature of the division of labour which has emerged between science and philosophy in the maintenance and reproduction of scientifically relevant epistemological categories. It is likely that the rather monistic concept of empirical realism mentioned earlier would disintegrate rapidly if such an analysis were undertaken.

The task of fully defining and analyzing the epistemological categories associated with arithmomorphism is beyond the scope of this paper. Instead, in the following pages I shall suggest the outlines of a broader system of social relations in science into which the arithmomorphic ontology is integrated. I shall concentrate, in particular, on the social commitments and relations which contribute to the definition of a system of scientific production in which the confusion between 'the why' and 'the logical ground' of arithmomorphic explanation is maintained and reproduced. In the next section I shall present a brief case study of the manner in which arithmomorphic paradoxes have been of importance in delimiting areas of cognitive capacity and ignorance within the arithmomorphic system of scientific production.

If the autonomy and authority of certain areas of the scientific field rest with the closure problematic at the ontological level, what type of social arrangements would allow the appropriation of scientific products in the arithmomorphic sense? If theoretical and experimental activity within an arithmomorphic area are oriented to the elucidation of discrete scientific products, then the above question may be answered by positing that the scientific area will display features of increased rationalization permitting the careful delineation of packages of enclosed work so as to maximize the delimiting and finitist properties of closure. Arithmomorphism embodies the conviction that analysis is most rigorous when ontological individuation is pursued as far as possible. Hence, areas in which arithmomorphic commitments are particularly plausible at the ontological level will be especially susceptible to rigorous social differentiation in line with the inclination to emphasize the discreteness and individuality of cognitive systems and products. This tendency is manifest at various organizational levels.

At lower levels of disciplinary organization, the closure imperative may be displayed in the tight prepackaging of Ph.D. topics by instructors for consumption and completion in a set period of time. This appears to be particularly characteristic of physics — the paradigmatic case of a discipline operating under closure — in which rather rigid principles of Ph.D. and research organization can be enforced (28). This situation may be contrasted with the much looser approach to Ph.D. training characteristic of some of the biological sciences. In this disciplinary context a high degree of interpersonal contact for purposes of transmitting craft knowledge and a low degree of intricate advance planning of the work schedule may be manifest (29). These features of Ph.D. training, and research in general, in some of the biological sciences relate to the necessity of conveying through practice the complex, non-arithmomorphic grounds of the study area. In these sciences, students and researchers are concerned with configurational products (30), the complexity of which may be such as to prevent the isolation of discrete 'individuals', and hence, the ready division of labour in the study area. Similarly, knowledge assimilation involving the grounds of theoretical and experimental activity cannot be rationalized easily in advance in disciplines in which closure is not a strict systemic norm. But in cases where such a norm is applicable, the division of labour in study, teaching and research may be intricately articulated in association with the detailed description of arithmomorphic cognitive systems and products. In disciplines where closure applies the 'industrialization' (31) of the research field is more feasible than in disciplines where closure is not totally normic.

At higher levels of scientific organization, the delimiting and finitist properties of closure are associated with the clear cognitive and social definition of sub-disciplinary and even disciplinary units. Divisions among the various arithmomorphic, or semi-arithmomorphic, disciplines and among sub-disciplinary units of closure oriented disciplines appear to be conceptually sharper than those characteristic of, for instance, the range of biological and geological sciences where the concern is to investigate systems of aggregates which often cannot be fully isolated from their environments or conceptually 'sliced' without some damage to the conceptual integrity of the larger entity (32). Thus, within the non-arithmomorphic sphere, 'bridging disciplines' such as, perhaps, ecology have acquired a certain status because they fulfill a requirement to unite (rather than, in the closure tradition, to separate) areas of detailed study in order to assist a larger understanding of larger systems. Superficially, general system theory would appear to be a nascent 'bridging discipline' with relevance to the arithmomorphic sphere. But in actuality, this development has emerged from insights derived from cybernetics, statistics, engineering, information theory and other areas which treat ontological aggregates. Although general system theory does embrace arithmomorphic constructs as a base for its conceptual pyramid, it is unlikely that its cognitive structure will generate new meanings in the arithmomorphic domains. General system theory will not overcome the division, the clear division, between statics and dynamics in physics, but it may contribute insights as to the biological significance of properties of aggregates like entropy (**33**).

In a similar manner, certain specialties which appear superficially to be within the arithmomorphic range display, because of the aggregate nature of the cognitive objects that are their concern, some of the features more characteristic of the richer cognitive areas of science (**34**). Thus, plasma physics, for example, while remaining largely within the arithmomorphic sphere is very much an 'interdisciplinary' specialty, as judged by physicists (**35**), because of the specific nature of its subject matter. The fact that plasmas are characterized by collective modes of behaviour not found in ordinary gases (because of the long range nature of the Coulomb forces among charged particles in a plasma) has necessitated a richer cognitive frame-work for the specialty than is characteristic of many physical specialties. Development of the specialty has demanded at least the partial integration in theory and experiment of cognitive concerns ranging from statistical mechanical concepts through to the constructs derived from radiation physics that are required to handle a new class of radiation problems thrown up by the specialty.

If closure is primary to practice in certain scientific disciplines, then not only the patterns of the division of labour, but also the nature of labour within these disciplines will reflect this fact. In disciplines operating closure, there will exist a high premium on the ability to pose scientific problems at higher levels of complexity in such a way as to ensure that closure will be achieved (**36**). This is a skilled undertaking demanding a detailed familiarity with a wide body of theoretical literature which provides a delimited context for the location of the problem at hand. Indeed, scientists aspiring to the elite strata of their area will have to acquire this ability to frame delimited problems. In the long run, this skill may be perceived to be more important within disciplines operating closure than the performance of experimental work addressed to the same problems — and this for the following reasons. If a problem is 'correctly' posed in a closure context the usually small amount of theoretical effort required to describe, or assume, the discrete, relatively simple, logical grounds of the problem has already been performed. In addition, the much more difficult task of describing the arithmomorphic theoretical base for experiment has usually also been accomplished with the aid of previous theoretical work in the mathematical disciplines and associated disciplines or specialties. Relative to the theorist, the experimentalist in a closure oriented discipline is left with the reasonably straightforward tasks of situation design for experiment and experiment performance (given certain levels of technical knowledge) — ensuring at all times, of course, that the theoretical conditions of closure are maintained to the greatest degree possible.

Thus, closure within a discipline may facilitate not only the ready division of discrete tasks among groups and individuals within the discipline, but also the strong differentiation of theoretical and experimental work in the investigation of a single conceptual realm. In his type of work differentiation, it is the theorist, rather than the experimentalist, who projects the capacities of arithmomorphism to their hilt, in that he is able to slide fairly casually over the domain of the grounds of reality, where the experimentalist might ordinarily hold sway, in order to reinforce the theoretical position of the arithmomorphic norm. It is in this context that von Bertalanffy's remarks concerning the importance of homological argument in the arithmomorphic science of physics acquire particular importance (37). He cites the case of the description of heat flow in physics in which equations suitable for the analysis of the fluid behaviour of a heat substance are used, although it has long been recognized that no such substance exists. Nevertheless, such homologies, in which the efficient factors of a problem have been ignored in order to stipulate laws which are formally correct, play a large role in the closure-oriented sciences (38). Logical homology, involving the projection of isomorphisms in science, is symptomatic of an arithmomorphic ontological framework that allows the theorist a range of tasks which is not dependent on the cognitive capacity of the experimentalist. Within this framework the theorist's role is rapidly distinguished from that of the experimentalist, and the class of theorists as a whole acquires great prestige on the basis of its problem delineating and problem framing functions (**39**).

The above situation may be contrasted with that characteristic of cognitively richer disciplines in which the scientist, because he is often as much concerned with establishing the cognitive grounds of his subject as in establishing the relations mediating those grounds, finds himself frequently acting as both theorist and experimentalist. Often in disciplines where cognitive novelty is central, or in which the evolution of scientific objects is marked, the scientist is unable to completely separate out for isolation even one stage of the process he is studying. Hence he is unable to reduce his understanding of a system to a limited number of relatively simple equations in the arithmomorphic style. Moreover, the scientist in a cognitively richer discipline is usually unable to clearly articulate theoretical relations without constant reference to the scientific grounds of his study. For example, Paul Weiss' discussion of systems concepts in his article 'The Living System: Determinism Stratified' would retain little validity and less coherence without his references to the mitochondrial systems with which these conceptual insights are associated (**40**). The very fluidity of the connections among scientific grounds which are more complex than the discrete forms of arithmomorphism, and of the relations which these more complex material aggretates bear, may militate against any discrete separation between the tasks of theorist and experimentalist in these disciplines. The biologist, the geologist, the meteorologist and others often devote much of their time simply to the task of identifying the systems that are the subject of their scientific concern. As Georgescu-Roegen has noted:

Had Logic by chance been applied first to constructing a theoretical science in a different field from geometry – where things neither move nor change, but merely are – the war now fought between logical positivists and realists would have very likely exploded soon after the first *Elements* (**41**).

Issues of change and existence as they relate to the grounds of scientific argument often force the biologist, the geologist and others to move in cognitive areas well beyond the bounds of conceptual closure and to forgo the 'efficient' division of labour between theorist and experimentalist so characteristic of closure-oriented disciplines like physics.

5. Change and Paradox Within Arithmomorphic Systems: the Mach-Boltzmann Episode

Finally, in this survey of some of the implications of the closure problematic for the description of a system of productive relations in science, it is necessary to note the type of social relations which may accompany change within a closure dominated scientific field. In the following paragraphs I shall discuss some of the more general propositions governing change in closure-oriented areas of science. There will then follow a brief case study illustrating the manner in which the study of arithmomorphic paradoxes can illuminate the nature of the processes of scientific change within arithmomorphic fields.

A number of propositions seem to govern and limit change in situations where closure is normic. First, scientific change, interpreted as the incorporation of new conceptual realms into the scientific field, is desirable in closure-oriented fields, as in all others, for the continued legitimation of the field of study, in this case in large part defined by the closure norm (42). The tendency towards reduction inherent to arithmomorphism has meant that certain arithmomorphic fields (i.e. those of physics) could be relatively easily broadened, without undue concern for the violation of symbolic realms associated with matter in bulk, as long as more and more micro universes remained for exploration. Second, all change is, at the same time, potentially threatening to the structure of the closed field, which must be continually stabilized in forms suitable for teaching purposes, for the initiation of younger scientists, and hence for the reproduction of the system of relations within which the conditions of 'objectivity' and the reputation of the field of study have been erected. Third, change in the context of normic closure is usually oriented towards conceptual realms which superficially, at least, appear suitable for appropriation in the arithmomorphic format. Having begun with, and being rooted in, an intuition of reality which is highly specific, the closure problematic has acquired an autonomy, and also a dynamic, which tend to lead its advocates to reproduce as far as possible the conditions of their own past success. Fourth, given the strong biases in situations of change and upheaval to choose for investigation 'realities' which may be appropriate to closure, and given the characteristics of the closure ethic itself, the closure system tends to display a low toleration for debate which does not appear to be evolving rapidly towards any form of consolidation about a number of researchable topics in the closed sense (43). Alternatively, research consolidation about a set of issues which yield an arithmomorphic pattern, and yet retain even a touch of ground novelty, may be very rapid indeed. However, it is because the maintenance of closure requires the appropriation of conceptual products with highly restricted properties that the closure system is subjected to frequent challenges in the form of intuitions of conceptual realms for which closure is not central. These conceptual realms are usually associated with the configurational diversity of matter in the bulk.

Georgescu-Roegen's description of the properties of arithmomorphism as a generalized ontological framework for certain regions of the scientific field introduces a basic schema for examining the nature of scientific change in closure-oriented disciplines. As is apparent from the preceding paragraph, it is essential to portray the processes of scientific change as involving a fundamental tension between the desirability of extending the ontological framework within which basic cognitive commitments may be seen to have validity, and the necessity of maintaining the cognitive structure intact for purposes of system reproduction in the face of uncertainties and possible dichotomies associated with the scientific unknown. Georgescu-Roegen's detailed examination of ontological categories permits the identification of the commitments which constitute the framework of the arithmomorphic cognitive structure. This description makes us aware of the cognitive stakes which are central to the renewal-reproduction tension which forms one dimension of scientific change. But beyond this, his work admits a consideration of the limitations of arithmomorphism, notably of the arithmomorphic paradoxes. The examination of the concept of paradox reveals that there is another dimension, another tension, inherent to scientific change.

This other dimension of scientific change may be interpreted as involving a set of relations between the cognitive capacities of a particular system of scientific production and the cognitive weaknesses of the same. The study of the growth and differentiation of the sciences, accompanied by the differentiated appropriation of scientific products and by differentiated social relations, is also a study of the manner in which science defines its domains of cognitive capacity. Alternatively, the process of delineating domains of cognitive capacity necessarily results in the outlining of the domains of cognitive ignorance (44). The dynamic interface between the domains of our apparent cognitive capacity and those of our, sometimes acknowledged, sometimes unacknowledged, ignorance is characterized by a set of cognitive phenomena which reflect choices implicit to the system of scientific production. These phenomena may reveal much concerning both the nature and limitations of scientific theorizing and scientific change. They include the phenomenon of the 'lapsed controversy' — the controversy which has been abandoned as normatively 'unproductive' without the benefit of resolution. They also include the phenomenon of the 'sudden acceleration of metaphysical debate' in science which often characterizes periods of cognitive uncertainty, transition or enlargement of interest. As a last example, it is not possible to ignore the phenomenon of 'paradox' at all levels of theoretical and experimental practice — that explosion of cognitive dissonance which reveals a gap between intuitive anticipations given a specific theoretical context and the results of attempts to demonstrate these intuitive anticipations (45).

The definition of paradox as a cognitive phenomenon relating to a tension between the cognitive capacities and weaknesses of a system of scientific production accords well with the earlier observation that arithmomorphic paradoxes are generally related to the 'number, matter' contradiction inherent to the deepest structure of arithmomorphism. Each paradox seems to reflect a central weakness in the very definition of the arithmomorphic system. Thus a case study of massive paradox proliferation in the historical development of an apparently closure bound theory should reveal some of the more important capacities and weaknesses of arithmomorphism.

This is indeed the case with one particular historical episode — that involving Ernst Mach and Ludwig Boltzmann in the famous nineteenth century controversy over the ontological basis of the classical kinetic theory of gases (46). This controversy was characterized by the highlighting and, for Boltzmann's part, the attempted resolution of a series of paradoxes which were apparently fundamental to the clarification of the Second Law of Thermodynamics as it applies to gaseous systems. These paradoxes have historically been reified in many terms such as the Loschmidt Reversibility Paradox, the Zermelo Recurrence Paradox, the probability-determinism paradox, the time elimination paradox, and others. But for purposes of this paper the most important observation to be made about this collectivity of contradictions is that each paradox reflects a particular aspect of a central dichotomy. That dichotomy is between the micro theoretical description of a mechanically governed ensemble as presented in the materially neutral, time independent format of arithmomorphism, and the macro description of classical entropic processes which necessitate some place for such arithmomorphically absurd concepts as temporal dependence, material order and progressive randomization (47). The details of the controversy are beyond the scope of this paper; what follows instead are a number of interrelated observations concerning the more general sociological insights to be derived from the interpretation of such controversies for an understanding of arithmomorphism.

In general arithmomorphism, it is recognized that the concepts of the simple particle under external forces, of the single throw of dice, and of the intensity of a magnetic field are not by any means identical, but that because these scientific products are discrete, single and reasonably neutral they can be treated in similar ways. In Humean ritualization, on the other hand, the more general capacities of arithmomorphism are reduced ontologically and epistemologically to the simple, even the simplest, image of the material particle under the influence of centrally directed forces.

This distinction between the general potentialities of arithmomorphism and those of Humean ritualization is reflected in the Mach-Boltzmann controversy. Boltzmann was essentially a Humean with a very strong, although highly sophisticated, commitment to corpuscular models and their development. Mach's central point against Boltzmann's strong commitment to atomism was that it restricted the scientific field to the consideration of a single arithmomorphic image. He argued with force that the paradoxes of the mechanistic presentation of the behaviour of gases were too serious to be neglected. His own approach to scientific argument, which Feyerabend describes as "general methodology" (48), overcame the ritualizing potential of Humean orientations by incorporating a certain agnosticism as to the nature of all scientific objects. Mach's ontologically abstruse, and yet still arithmomorphic, methodology based on the discrete concept of the 'element' and a functionalist understanding of scientific theorizing allowed him greater philosophical and scientific flexibility in this transitional period than Boltzmann was able to command. Essentially, Mach believed that the description of gaseous behaviour might be accomodated by any number of arithmomorphic images (49), and lacking demonstration of the validity of any one, he argued for the virtues of agnosticism.

In the sense that the existence of 'atoms' was eventually demonstrated, Mach lost the battle with Boltzmann over the issue of atomism and corpuscular models as Blackmore documents **(50)**. But in the sense that new probabilistic theories of the behaviour of gases and sub-atomic species emerged in the wake of the kinetic controversy, Mach won the war for an enlarged interpretation of arithmomorphism within science — and hence, extended the cognitive capacity of the productive system both scientifically and philosophically. This is particularly reflected in Boltzmann's gradual relinquishment, under strong pressure from the Machians, of the corpuscular images of his early work in gas theory in favour of varying, and increasingly articulated, probabilistic formats for the description of the evolution of gaseous systems. This was accomplished as every 'number-matter' paradox was argued to its limit by Boltzmann's opponents, and as he was gradually forced to implicitly concede that mechanical descriptions were not adequate to the purposes he has set himself (the explanation of entropic phenomena).

The theoretical tension between Mach and Boltzman is representative of the tension inherent in scientific growth and change between the necessity to accomodate novel ontological structures — in this case by loosening the arithmorophic context — and the tendency to retain, even to ritualize, the structural aspects of well established theories in order to stabilize the legitimacy of past science and, by extension, current science in flux. But this development also displays the limitations of the whole arithmomorphic framework. For Boltzmann's number-matter paradoxes were never adequately resolved in the classical context. They were only ontologically reduced. Paradox proliferation at the mechanistic level forced Boltzmann to shift his ontological basis from mechanism to forms of probabilistic argument. In the process, mechanistic determinism, and models involving collision mechanisms, were theoretically sacrificed for a description based on random choice **(51)**. Ontologically, the introduction of random arguments into the presentation of kinetic systems opened the scientific field up to a wide number of arithmomorphic appropriations — particularly the various interpretations of probability characteristic of the quantum theories **(52)**. But this development did not resolve the contradiction at the heart of theory associated with the Second Law between a ritualized mechanistic rationalization of system evolution and the actuality of randomized theoretical accomodations for the same phenomenon.

Thus, in this historical instance of the evolution of an arithmomorphic theory, paradox proliferation in the mechanistic context assisted in the broadening of the arithmomorphic spectrum. Novel conceptual realms were introduced into the system, and the capacities of the system were demonstrated without seriously threatening the integrity of the closed framework. But nevertheless, the resolution of the tension between the needs for renewal and reproduction within the productive system was only possible in this instance because the level of ontological debate was subtly shifted from the mechanistic level characteristic of classical corpuscular theorizing to the probabilistic, randomized level suitable for quantum development. The paradoxes of the mechanistic format were not resolved, only bypassed. They remain to delineate an interface between scientific areas of cognitive capacity in the arithmomorphic sense and areas of cognitive ignorance. In essence, the Boltzmann paradoxes represent the slackening of the tension between capacity and ignorance at the classical level of explanation. They are no longer thriving as centres of debate. In this instance, it appears that the vitality of these paradoxes and the dynamism of this capacity-ignorance interface have been sacrificed in order to stabilize a system with apparent productive capacity at other arithmomorphic levels.

In the case of paradox proliferation at the mechanistic level, where the deep weaknesses of arithmomorphism were encountered, this historical episode has yielded an interesting social development, the ritualization of ignorance. Over the twentieth century, in the interests of system maintenance, we appear to have witnessed the cognitive atomization of the Boltzmann paradoxes.

The Boltzmann paradoxes are seldom mentioned in modern discussions of kinetic theory, although most scientists are aware of them, at least superficially, usually from a brief perusal of the history of science. As Yourgrau has demonstrated, the Boltzmann paradoxes are but a subset of 'a budget of paradoxes' (53) in physics, including a multitude in kinetic theory. As regards paradoxes in general, two tendencies of a seemingly contradictory nature are noted by Yourgrau: on the one hand, there is a tendency to cultivate the growth of paradoxes apparently as an aid to theory elaboration – this seemingly representing a creative, extensional capacity of the theoretical system; on the other hand, there is a tendency to evade paradoxes without solving them, apparently in an effort to minimize their importance and to blend them in with the theoretical background. This appears to be a tendency to ritualize existing systems, and would explain why many of the paradoxes of Yourgrau's budget are seen as unimportant and remain neglected within science. Such paradoxes delineate frontiers of cognitive capacity and may be ignored as curious outposts describing a field which, after many years of controversy, has failed to yield to the arithmomorphic battering ram. Boltzmann paradoxes would appear to be of this type. And as is the case with other artefacts of arithmomorphism, their articulation and treatment have been a function of the system in which they have emerged.

The Boltzmann paradoxes are symbolic of the failure of arithmomorphism to appropriate scientific products with any inherent structure or containing any symbolic material prior to elaboration at the predicative level (54). As such, these paradoxes have been arithmomorphized even in the processes of their conceptual immobilization in order to conceal their awkward implications. There has been a tendency to atomize the paradoxes of kinetic theory, to discuss them only as discrete, historical curiosities without reference to theoretical potentialities. Seldom are they discussed in the text books, or even in the histories of science. When they are discussed, they are not treated in sequence or in parallel. More often, they are neglected, ignored and hence forced out of the cognitive spectrum. One might describe this process as a cognitive 'hiving' off', as the arithmomorphizing of ignorance. The Boltzmann paradoxes have been ritualized in the atomistic mode such that their internal dynamic is now stultified (55).

6. Conclusion

This discussion of some of the arithmomorphic characteristics of the borders of ignorance concludes this survey of closure and arithmomorphism as descriptions of a particular system of scientific production. This has been a preliminary attempt to demonstrate the nature of the issues and problems which might arise if the sociological understanding of science were enlarged so as to embrace the full discussion of scientific products as social relations within a system of scientific production. Much effort will be required in the future to describe adequately the detailed structure of the arithmomorphic system of scientific production. Further, the elaboration of productive systems beyond the arithmomorphic will require a careful and critical analysis of the structure and content of the non-arithmomorphic sciences and of such critiques of arithmomorphism as are beginning to emerge **(56)**. Such an investigation will undoubtedly lead backward in time to intellectual and social developments which may have been overwhelmed historically by the ideological capacities of arithmomorphism. An excellent starting point for such an exercise would be the artefacts of ignorance briefly discussed in this paper. This process should aid the development of a critical conceptual vocabulary with regard to scientific theorizing and a richer perspective on the growth and development of the sciences.

Notes

1. R. D. Whitley (ed.), *Social Processes of Scientific Development*, London: Routledge and Kegan Paul, 1974; R. D. Whitley, 'The Sociology of Scientific Work and the History of Scientific Developments', Manchester Business School, 1975, to be published shortly in S. S. Blume (ed.), *New Perspectives in the Sociology of Science*, New York: J. Wiley, 1977; Pierre Bourdieu, 'La spécificité du champ scientifique et les conditions sociales du progrès de la raison', *Sociologie et sociétés* VII, 1975, pp. 91–118.
2. Roy Bhaskar, *A Realist Theory of Science*, Leeds: Leeds Books, 1975; and Nicholas Georgescu-Roegen, *The Entropy Law and the Economic Process*, Cambridge, Mass.: Harvard University Press, 1971, respectively.
3. R. D. Whitley, 'Components of Scientific Activities, Their Characteristics and Institutionalization in Specialties and Research Areas', in Karin Knorr, Hermann Strasser and H. G. Zilian (eds.) *Determinants and Controls of Scientific Development*, Dordrecht: Reidel, 1975.
4. Traditional cognitive distinctions are problematic in the definition of scientific systems of production.
5. Ontological, epistemological and social commitments and relations will not reduce to each other. Further, analysis should reveal the contradictions inherent to the system which at once represent system inconsistencies and properties of the system.
5a. Systems of production thus consist of these three types of categories – which are imputed by the analyst – together with commitments to them which must be reproduced for the system to continue.
6. Bhaskar, *op. cit.*, 1975, Note 2; Georgescu-Roegen, *op. cit.*, 1971, Note 2.
7. Bhaskar, *op. cit.*, 1975, Note 2, pp. 239–250.
8. *ibid.*, pp. 63–65; for an illustration of a nineteenth century epistemological format which does not fall under this categorization, see Hirst's discussion of the epistemological commitments of Claude Bernard, the nineteenth century physiologist, in P. Q. Hirst, *Durkheim, Bernard and Epistemology*, London: Routledge and Kegan Paul, 1975.
9. Bhaskar, *op. cit.*, 1975, Note 2, pp. 73–77.
10. P. K. Feyerabend, 'Philosophy of Science: A Subject with a Great Past', in R. H. Stuewer (ed.), *Historical and Philosophical Perspectives of Science*, Vol. V, Minnesota Studies in the Philosophy of Science, Minneapolis: University of Minnesota Press, 1970, p. 173.
11. See Georgescu-Roegen, *op. cit.*, 1971, Note 2, pp. 124–126; see also Edward

Purcell's 'Parts and Wholes in Physics', in Daniel Lerner (ed.), *Parts and Wholes*, New York: The Free Press of Glencoe, 1963.

12. T. S. Kuhn, 'The Function of Dogma in Scientific Research', in A. C. Crombie (ed.), *Scientific Change*, London: Heinemann, 1963.

13. Bhaskar, *op. cit.*, 1975, Note 2, pp. 80−81; see also Trevor Pinch, *Paradoxes and Impossibilities: A Study of the Cognitive and Social Roles Played by Paradoxes and 'Impossibility Proofs' in Non-Relativistic Quantum Theory*, unpubl. M. Sc. diss. University of Manchester, 1976.

14. To argue, as Bhaskar does, that closure as an experimental system is incapable of handling individuals with any degree of internal structure or self motivation is true. But the closure system also does not appear to bear any specific relation in its social evolution to the problem of examining individuals with internal structure, and thus the previous observation does not serve a specific purpose in sociological terms (although, as Whitley notes in this volume, the 'arithmetic' ideal has been important in a variety of sciences, particularly in connection with the professionalization of the sciences). Transcendental realism does offer opportunities for development in a sociological context, but, to date, it remains a rather monistic ontological and epistemological construct yielding few insights into cognitive alternatives to closure at the level of specific products and processes of production. See Richard Whitley, 'Changes in the Social and Intellectual Organization of the Sciences: Professionalization and the Arithmetic Ideal', in this volume, pp. 143−169.

15. Georgescu-Roegen, *op. cit.*, 1971, Note 2.

16. *ibid.*, 31. The two-way algorithm signifies a bi-directional understanding of cause, such that each identified component of nature arises out of something and shall impinge upon something. This understanding allows the elaboration of a causal hierarchy.

17. *ibid.*, Ch. V; reference is also made to my dissertation: Phyllis Jenkin (née Colvin), *Structure and Contradiction in Scientific Development: The Case of Nicholas Georgescu-Roegen and the Entropy Law*, unpubl. M. Sc. diss. University of Manchester, 1975, Ch. 2; Thomas Gold, 'Cosmic Processes and the Nature of Time', in R. G. Colodny (ed.), *Mind and Cosmos*, Pittsburgh: University of Pittsburgh Press, 1966.

18. Georgescu-Roegen, *op. cit.*, 1971, Note 2, p. 31.

19. *ibid.*, p. 14.

20. *ibid.*, p. 45.

21. Vasco Ronchi, 'Complexities, Advances and Misconceptions in the Development of the Science of Vision: What is Being Discovered?', in A. C. Crombie (ed.), *Scientific Change*; *op. cit.*, 1963, Note 12.

22. Georgescu-Roegen, *op. cit.*, 1971, Note 2, p. 45.

23. Émile Borel, *Space and Time*, London: Blackie and Son Ltd., 1926, p. 104. See also Georgescu-Roegen's discussion of the arithmetical continuum, Georgescu-Roegen, *op. cit.*, 1971, Note 2, Ch. III and Appendix A.

24. Borel, *op. cit.*, 1926, Note 23, p. 88.

25. Émile Borel, 'Sur l'imitation du hasard', *Comptes Rendus*, CCIV, 1937, pp. 203−205; Georgescu-Roegen, *op. cit.*, 1971, Note 2, pp. 55−59; Jenkin, *op. cit.*, 1975, Note 17, pp. 40, 57−63.

26. Georgescu-Roegen, *op. cit.*, pp. 1971, Note 2, pp. 69ff.; Jenkin, *op. cit.*, 1975., Note 17, pp. 63−70.

27. For some mention of this problem, see Roy Bhaskar, 'Philosophies as Ideologies of Science: A contribution to a Critique of Positivism', a paper presented at a British Sociological Association, Sociology of Science Study Group meeting, in London, February, 1976.

28. Kuhn, *op. cit.*, 1963. Note 12, pp. 363ff. Kuhn speaks of "restricted vision" (363) in research and the anticipation of results in advance (364). It is my contention that these characteristics of the research process are more marked in arithmomorphic areas, and that Kuhn is speaking of physics (from which he draws all of his examples) rather than science as a whole in this excerpt.

29. Whitley, *op. cit.*, 1975, Note 1, pp. 13–15, 22–23.

30. Norbert Elias, 'The Sciences: Towards a Theory', in R. D. Whitley (ed.), *Social Processes of Scientific Development, op. cit.*, 1974, Note 1; also R. D. Whitley, 'Types of Science, Organizational Strategies and Patterns of Work in Research Laboratories of Different Scientific Fields', presented at a conference on 'The Role of Research Organizations in Orienting Scientific Activities', Vienna, July 5–6, 1976. Manchester Business School, May 1976. See also Whitley, *op. cit.* in this volume, Note 14.

31. J. R. Ravetz, *Scientific Knowledge and its Social Problems,* Oxford: University Press, 1971.

32. Although, of necessity, analysis requires some form of differentiation.

33. Ludwig von Bertalanffy, *General System Theory*, London: Penguin, 1971. The arithmomorphic nature of scientific products also permits the easy export of concepts between subject areas with arithmomorphic commitments.

34. C. F. A. Pantin, *The Relations between the Sciences*, Cambridge: University Press, 1968.

35. W. B. Kunkel (ed.), *Plasma Physics in Theory and Application*, New York: McGraw-Hill, 1966, pp. 2–19; J. G. Linhart, *Plasma Physics*, Amsterdam: North Holland Pub. Co., 1960, pp. 1–5; E. J. Hellund, *The Plasma State*, New York: Reinhold Pub. Co., 1961.

36. For a discussion of 'simplicity' as it relates to the general problem of isolating problems for investigation, see Peter Alexander, *Sensationalism and Scientific Explanation*, London: Routledge and Kegan Paul, 1963, pp. 45–46.

37. von Bertalanffy, *op. cit.*, 1971, Note 33, pp. 85–86.

38. For discussions of the role of models and analogies, see Rom Harré, *The Principles of Scientific Thinking*, London: Macmillan, 1970; M. B. Hesse, *Models and Analogies in Science*, Indianapolis: University of Notre Dame Press, 1966. In speaking of homologies in arithmomorphic areas, it is important to remember that these homologies may have applications in superficially 'richer' cognitive domains. Thus, the differential equation associated with the harmonic oscillator may have applications in areas as diverse as the study of electrical circuits and the study of animal population dynamics. In the latter case, however, the application of homological argument depends upon the possibility of defining discrete populations. Thus, population dynamics is an area with arithmomorphic potential, which must be differentiated from other areas with richer, more systemic, more quality centred cognitive potential. The limitations of the arithmomorphic are likely to be revealed more fully as the pressure upon science to reflect a concern with external (economic, military, infrastructural) goals increases. See Gernot Boehme, W. v. d. Daele, and W. Krohn, 'Die Finalisierung der Wissenschaft', *Zeitschrift für Soziologie* 2, 1973, pp. 128–144.

39. Jerry Gaston, *Originality and Competition in Science*, Chicago: Chicago University Press, 1973, pp. 59–68.

40. P. A. Weiss, 'The Living System: Determinism Stratified', in Arthur Koestler and J. R. Smythies (eds.), *Beyond Reductionism*, London: Hutchinson, 1969.

41. Georgescu-Roegen, *op. cit.*, 1971, Note 2, p. 31.

42. It is possible, however, to occupy a great amount of time in simply manipulating a formalism, as is the case with much theorizing in economics – perhaps the most 'arithmomorphic' of the social sciences.

43. As in the case of the paradox proliferation associated with the development of the H-theorem in gas theory.
44. Bourdieu, *op. cit.*, 1975, Note 1. This designation owes much to Bourdieu's understanding of the scientific field.
45. For discussions of specific controveries in a sociological vein see, Harry Collins, 'The Seven Sexes: A Study in the Sociology of Scientific Phenomena', *Sociology* 9, 1975, pp. 205–224; Helga Nowotny, 'Controversies in Science: Remarks on the Different Modes of Production of Knowledge and Their Use', *Zeitschrift für Soziologie* 4 1975, pp. 34–45; Trevor Pinch, 'What Does a Proof Do if It Does Not Prove? A Study of the Social Conditions and Metaphysical Divisions Leading to David Bohm and John von Neumann failing to communicate in Quantum Physics', in this volume. For discussions of the phenomenon of paradox, see Pinch, *op. cit.*, 1976, Note 13, Ch. 6; and Jenkin, *op. cit.*, 1975, Note 17, Ch. 3.
46. J. T. Blackmore, *Ernst Mach: His Work, Life, and Influence*, Berkeley: University of California Press, 1972.
47. Jenkin, *op. cit.*, 1975, Note 17, pp. 117ff.
48. Feyerabend, *op. cit.*, 1970, Note 10, p. 175.
49. Jenkin, *op. cit.*, 1975, Note 17, Ch. 1; also Feyerabend, *op. cit.*, Note 10, p. 176.
50. Blackmore, *op. cit.*, 1972, Note 46, pp. 214–216.
51. S. G. Brush, 'The Development of the Kinetic Theory of Gases VIII. Randomness and Irreversibility', *Archive for History of Exact Sciences* 12, 1974, pp. 1–88; see especially pp. 55–56 and 80–86.
52. *ibid.*, Max Jammer, *The Conceptual Development of Quantum Mechanics*, New York: McGraw-Hill, 1966, pp. 1–61; Of necessity, the Boltzmann conception(s) of probability was not introduced into the quantum domain without modification (pp. 22, 285–286). See also Jammer's *The Philosophy of Quantum Mechanics*, New York: J. Wiley, 1974, p. 7.
53. Wolfgang Yourgrau, 'A Budget of Paradoxes in Physics', in Imre Lakatos and Alan Musgrave (eds.), *Problems in the Philosophy of Science*, Amsterdam: North Holland Pub. Co., 1968, pp. 178–209;
54. J. W. Alexander, *Bergson, Philosopher of Reflection*, London: Bowes and Bowes, 1957, p. 72.
55. Jenkin, *op. cit.*, 1975, Note 17, Ch. 3; Georgescu-Roegen, *op cit.*, 1971, Note 2, Ch. VI. Even in cases where the Boltzmann paradoxes are treated, the tendency seems to be to view them as rather 'academic' issues, although it is sometimes acknowledged that genuine theoretical difficulties are associated with the paradoxes, See Raymond Jancel, *Foundations of Classical and Quantum Statistical Mechanics*, Vol. 19 in D. ter Haar (ed.), International Series of Monographs in Natural Philosophy, Oxford and London: Pergamon Press, 1969.
56. Georgescu-Roegen's work represents a critique of arithmomorphism as it has been extended to areas of investigation like gas thory, information theory, certain aspects of economics, certain aspects of biology, and other areas where, Georgescu-Roegen believes, constructs beyond arithmomorphism ('dialectic' constructs in his presentation) require development.

COGNITIVE NORMS, KNOWLEDGE-INTERESTS AND THE CONSTITUTION OF THE SCIENTIFIC OBJECT:
A Case Study in the Functioning of Rules for Experimentation

GERNOT BÖHME

Max-Planck-Institut, Starnberg

1. Introduction

When the role of the scientist first became a focus of sociological analysis this social phenomenon was characterised by a particular set of norms: the well known Mertonian Norms of universality, communism (communality), disinterestedness, organized scepticism. From the very beginning, however, there could be no doubt that this conceptualization of the scientific community would not be appropriate to determine the fine structure of social organization in science. But even as a global concept of science as a profession it came under criticism. Subsequent authors (1) pointed to cases in which these norms were offended, while others, at most, conceded a historically limited validity to them (2). To be sure, the violation of a norm is no objection to its validity. But, within sociology, the unsanctioned violation is. For, in contrast to Ethics, the sociological concept of a norm is an empirical one: the 'existence' of a norm (3) sociologically depends on the fact that its offence is negatively sanctioned. From this point of view, Mulkay's 'Some Aspects of Cultural Growth in Natural Science' (4) was a notable stroke against the claim for particular social norms of the scientific community. Taking the Velikovsky affair as an example Mulkay has shown to what degree the supposed Mertonian norms are offended, and what is more: are offended without punishment. But he did not end with this critique. He demonstrated that the 'professional norms' are offended in favour of, and in defence of another set of norms, namely the so-called cognitive or theoretical-methodological norms. Velikovsky had been treated in an 'unfair' way, because his ideas offended some cognitive norms, the guidance of which was the concern of the scien-

Mendelsohn/Weingart/Whitley (eds.), The Social Production of Scientific Knowledge.
Sociology of the Sciences, Volume I, 1977. 129–141. All Rights Reserved.
Copyright © 1977 by D. Reidel Publishing Company, Dordrecht-Holland.

tific community. This position of Mulkay accords very well with certain concepts developed within the philosophy and historiography of science. Kuhn had described normal science as characterized by a certain degree of dogmatic adherence to theoretical ideas, experimental procedures, to types of problems and solutions (5). He suggested that the particular social groups within the large scientific community maintain their identity through the adherence to certain ideas and methods and that they reproduce themselves through their transmission by scientific education. Later he proposed to study particular scientific communities by way of their 'disciplinary matrices' (6); that is the accepted ideas of 'symbolic generalizations', 'heuristics', and 'paradigms'.

But, unfortunately, this Mulkay/Kuhnian approach too has turned out unsatisfactorily for the sociologist. Some authors even deny that the Kuhnian paradigm communities can be identified empirically (7). The essential problem follows from the fact that cognitive norms, too, may be violated without any sanction − a fact which, again for the sociologist, implies that they do not 'exist'. To be sure there is rejection of articles, polemics and neglect. However, on the one hand the productive overcoming of established ideas belongs to the essence of science. On the other hand any scientist whose ideas do not fit in the dogma of a certain scientific community may get acceptance within another or initiate a new one (8). So, the 'anything-goes-methodology' seems to make also the social validity of cognitive norms a relative one. As a consequence of this situation, sociology of science − if it does not, under the concept of science as labour, follow another strategy altogether − has confined itself to the investigation of the formal organization of science (processes of social institutionalization of science via scientific societies, departments, chairs, degrees), and to the investigation of informal group formation via networks of communications.

Thus the drive towards a cognitive sociology of science has weakened rather quickly. But there is no reason to drop the enterprise completely. Until now there has not been a distinct idea of how to conceive of 'cognitive' norms. The hope of obtaining an immediate answer from the philosophy of science turns out to be illusive since the relation of the philosophy of science to the everyday reality of science is obscure. On the other hand empirical investigations in the cognitive norms of science do not seem to be very promising considering the predominantly 'tacit' character of cognitive norms. So progress will be very slow. First of all, a theoretical discussion of what types of cognitive norms are to be expected is necessary. Then their function for the process of knowledge generation and confirmation is to be studied. And last, but not least, the particular type of commitment to cognitive norms is to be specified.

In the following pages I approach the answer to such questions by concentrating on one type of cognitive norms, namely 'rules for experimentation'. This is based on the more general approach developed elsewhere (9), where two general classes of cognitive norms are specified. First, norms which regulate the empirical approach to the subject matter of a science, and second, norms which regulate the discourse about the subject matter of a science. My aim here is to analyse cognitive norms within a context, which may be called the intellectual culture or the intellectual framework of a science, a discipline, a particular school. This context comprises the knowledge-interests which guide the particular scientific specialty, as well as the general anticipation of what the subject matter essentially is. If the connection between the interest in knowledge, the cognitive norms and the constitution of the particular subject matter can be established, we shall be able to understand the particular type of 'commitment' to cognitive norms through the identification of a scientist with the intellectual culture of his discipline. Then the functions of cognitive norms for the formation of social subsystems in science may again come under scrutiny.

2. Titchener/Baldwin: A Controversy about Rules for Experimentation at the Beginnings of a Segmentation of Psychology

The kind of rules for experimentation so far stipulated by the philosophy of science have been derived not so much from investigations of experimental behaviour itself but rather from inquiries into the function of the experiment within the experimental method (10). In addition these rules operate at a high level of generality and characterize scientificity as such rather than any particular discipline. So philosophy of science does not provide much help here. Nor will exploration of textbooks bring us much illumination, for the way of how to design and how to perform experiments in a particular discipline or specialty is not laid down by explicit prescriptions (11) but is acquired within the scientific process. As the apprentice learns his trade by imitating the master craftsman, so the young scientist learns science by imitation and by intercourse with his teacher or his fellow scientists. How, then, can we say anything more about the rules governing scientific practice?

My answer to questions of this kind is: to discover the rules we must explore scientific controversies. The scrutiny of scientific controversies can have a similar function within the study of science as do twin studies in certain fields of medicine and biology. This is because scientific controversy reveals and makes explicit the rules and standards which normally only inconspicuously direct the steady operation of science. The exploration of controversies will at the same time show us to what extent such rules are binding and offer distinctions between related specialties.

Now, without trying to formulate any further assumptions, I shall turn to the analysis of an example. It is the controversy between the psychologists Titchener (a representative of the Leipzig School) and Baldwin regarding simple reactions (12).

Interest in the study of reaction times can be traced back to the first half of the nineteenth century. It originated in the astronomers' observation of a personal difference between individual astronomers in their observation of the times of stellar events and their attempts to improve astronomical observations by taking into account what came to be referred to as a 'personal equation'. When the psychologists took up the problem in the 1880's it was from the first informed by the concerns of the new experimental psychology. Experimental psychology had endeavoured to achieve scientific status by holding narrowly to the image of the natural sciences. The primary aim of experimental psychology at the time was to find the 'elements' of the life of the mind (13). And it is within this frame that psychological experimentation on human reactive behaviour was started (14).

Compound reactions were distinguished from simple reactions. Simple reactions are reactions in which a subject reacts to given predetermined stimulus by a given predetermined movement. In compound reactions the subject has to discriminate a specific stimulus from others and to make a choice among a set of possible reactions. The scientific endeavour now was to determine the periods of certain elements — say that of the act of choice — by applying a subtractive procedure which consisted in subtracting the period of a simple reaction from that of a compound reaction.

The controversy which arose around the question of simple reactions was first set off by attempts to determine with the simple reaction the time of one element within the range of attention, namely that of apperception. In Wundt's theory simple reaction comprised five elements (*Teilakte*): one each for the physical transmission of both stimulus and reaction, one element for the perception of stimulus, one for the apperception of stimulus, and one for the excitement of voluntary movement (15). If there were grounds for holding that a particular reaction process was reflexlike and automatic this would be taken to mean that it lacked an element, that in other words apperception was not involved, according to the above approach. By comparison with the corresponding non-automatic or non-reflexlike reaction process it should be possible to find out how much time apperception took. Now, Lange in 1888 (16) had found a pair of reaction processes which were susceptible to this interpretation. He distinguished two types of simple reaction, the sensorial and the muscular. He called a reaction sensorial in which the reagent directed his attention exclusively upon the sense-impression, the stimulus, and he called a reaction muscular where the reagent directed his attention upon the movement to be made in response to the stimulus. His experiments had shown that, as a rule, the muscular reaction was shorter and this with a fair constancy of about 100 m/sec. It was the muscular reaction, that is the reaction with attention not on the stimulus, which was held to be an automatic one.

Bringing the stimulus within the focus of consciousness, it was argued with some justification, gives rise to a hiatus between stimulus and the reaction itself, slowing down the latter. On this interpretation, then, the muscular reaction should be shorter than the sensorial precisely by the time taken by 'apperception' (17).

The experimenters therefore focussed on the determination of what came to be called 'the sensorial-muscular difference'. Efforts where made to measure it as precisely as possible, to exclude all other influences, to be sure that this difference could be ascribed to apperception. This account covers the genesis, the purpose and the findings of reaction experiments up to the point when Baldwin joined the discussion.

The experiments carried out by Baldwin gave sometimes a shorter muscular reaction time in line with the theory and findings of the Leipzig School and sometimes a shorter sensorial reaction time and in some cases no substantial distinction between the two. Baldwin explained his results by a type-theory of reaction. Earlier research of another kind had shown that variations are to be found in individual speech, memory or association behaviour. In each particular exercise of speech, memory· or in forming mental images different people required either a 'motor' or a 'sensory' cue. Thus in the performance of speech, for some the cue was to think, or to have in mind, the movements of the vocal organs, lips, tongue, etc., involved in speech, and for others to think of the sounds of the words as heard or the image of the words as written.

Baldwin then argued that the man who gave relatively shorter muscular reactions was of the 'motor' type and the man who gave relatively shorter sensory (auditory, visual) reactions was a 'sensory' in his type. According to Baldwin, therefore, not the direction given to the reagent's attention, but rather the individual disposition of the reagent himself, was the primary cause of variations in reaction times (18).

Obviously Baldwin had formed an entirely different theory of human reactions to explain the contradictory results reached by him as compared with those of the Leipzig School. Yet the first question that comes to mind and that is also most relevant to our topic is *why* the outcome of the experiments of the Leipzig School varied so greatly from Baldwin's. The answer can only be that in each case the experiments were differently designed. Baldwin's main charge against the Leipzig School was that for their experiments they selected individuals who had a certain mental *Anlage* or attitude or who were able to acquire it by training. Evidently the difference in the findings of the Leipzig School on the one side and Baldwin's on the other are attributable to *the kind of rules they applied in the selection, treatment and assessment of their subjects.*

I shall now examine the position of the two contending parties a little more closely in this respect. When one reads the works of the Wundtian school today one is surprised to discover that the individuals, who in the current terminology would be called the test subjects, are frequently referred to as the 'observers'. Another thing the reader may well find surprising is that these observers are at the same time the investigators and the authors of the respective reports. This will be better understood if it is called to mind that Wundt's principle was that "all psychology begins with introspection (*Selbstbeobachtung*)" and that for this there are two aids (*Hilfsmittel*): "experiment and *Geschichte*, the natural history of mankind" (19). In this view man could never merely be the object but was always also the subject of an experiment – he was the observer. It follows from this that the individual never came under scrutiny in his totality. Rather, the point of interest was the inquiry into the functioning of the inner psychological apparatus which was held to be a natural object of investigation, as any other object, except that it could only be an object before the *inner*, not the *outer* sense (speaking with Kant).

The scientific interest addressed itself to the general laws of the inner psychic processes and it was assumed that these laws applied to all men with the same validity so that eventual differences between reagents were attributable above all to their competence as scientific instruments. This seems to be the reason why it was emphasized time and again that the reagents must have the necessary psychological disposition (20). Now an instrument is expected to function smoothly and to be reliable. Here the scientists of the Leipzig School in their capacity as reagents did not in any way feel biased, on the contrary: they insisted that outsiders brought into the laboratory must first be well trained in introspection. Furthermore, for particular experiments, account would have to be taken of the suitability of the reagent in the light of the phenomenon being investigated. Thus, when measuring the difference between muscular and sensorial reactions, reagents whose reactions were irregular or who did not unequivocally give this distinction were to be excluded. And persons who turned out differences in the other direction, that is with whom the sensorial reaction was the shorter one, were not cited as counter-examples to the theory but were simply excluded on the ground of incompetency or unsuitability for measuring the given phenomenon.

It is this conception of the test subjects as psychological instruments which explains why so small a number of reagents was actually tested in the Leipzig laboratory. To be sure, for each experiment a large test series was made to be able to statistically rule out any deviations. But these were not expected to accrue from the individual dispositions, the individual differences of the subjects, but from fluctuations in the stream of consciousness. It was held that persons with individual differences were unsuitable for experimentation or had at least to practice long enough to become accepted as competent, neutral observers of their inner apparatus.

It was an entirely different case with Baldwin. Admittedly, in his experiments as well the reagents were in many cases identical with the authors and the number of the reagents small. But with Baldwin this was a consequence of being still rooted in the Leipzig tradition. In the rules he had himself formulated his stipulation was "to test everybody". and "to take persons just as they come" (21). He emphatically rejected the procedure of allowing only persons with the necessary mental disposition to participate in the experiments. For him, on the contrary, variances in disposition became the object of his inquiry. Nor did he accept the idea that more practice should serve to diminish differences between individuals; as he saw it, individual differences themselves were fruitful data for theory.

Only under these conditions did reagents become test subjects in the usual sense of the term. Their mind and its reactions as a whole came under experimental analysis. Yet once this became the accepted practice the experimenter could no longer appeal to the reliability of a part of the reagent's psychic functions as the yardstick for the assessment of his findings. Introspection could no longer hold good as a quasi-standardized instrument for psychological experimentation. Instead new independent methods of investigation had to be developed to establish correlations on the basis of which data could be validated.

Thus for instance, independent methods had to be found to elucidate the memory and mental image types of the subjects in Baldwin's reaction time experiments. Introspection was not adequate to the task since the aptitude for introspection capable of producing constant and regular results, after all, was itself a disposition and practising it might well have modified the psychological type of the reagent. Training was to be altogether avoided in reaction time work since, according to Baldwin's theory, variations in type, that is in disposition, were not innate but were acquired by habit. A little later Angell and Moore (22) had shown that in a longer sequence of reaction time experiments the reagent's forms of reaction were indeed changed by practice.

Before we now try to discover the real meaning of these differences in the experimental rules as applied by the Leipzig School and by Baldwin let us once more state the crux of the problem in a simple formula. The Leipzig School tried as far as possible to make the test subjects objective and 'standardized' observers of a pure and laboratory psychic phenomenon. For Baldwin the test subjects were to be influenced as little as possible by the experimental conditions and in this sense to remain 'natural' objects of the inquiry.

That divergent norms for the conduct of experiments can yield different data is self-evident. If we now ask what implications such divergencies carry for science the answer will be that:

(1) in each case the research rules articulated a different research interest;

(2) that through the experimental rules the researchers in each case had a different object in view; and

(3) that the divergent rules for experimentation marked off different schools.

(1) For the Leipzig School the sensorial-muscular difference was a particular natural phenomenon − as is electrical induction or magnetism − and therefore a phenomenon which should be presented in its purest form to infer from it the laws of its underlying nature − in this case the nature of the mind. In this view reagents incapable of constant and regular reaction seemed to be unsuitable observers. Those who on the other hand reacted regularly but not in the sensorial-muscle relation had to be excluded from the tests because their reaction times were influenced by education, by habit or by abnormality of mental constitution (23).

Baldwin's interest, on the other hand, laid precisely in the individual differences of man. He was searching for regularities precisely here: the objection he made to the Leipzig School was that they were looking exclusively for results which were *regularly regular.* His case, he argued, was the contrary: results might be *regularly irregular* (24). His concern was no longer the nature of man's psyche as such but much more to develop methods which could be of value in the treatment of school children and in the diagnosis of mental diseases. For him, the reaction experiment was no longer a means to find what elements constituted the psyche but more a method to develop tests for determining the psychological type of individuals (25).

(2) As a result, Baldwin was dealing with a different object of inquiry from the Leipzig School. This has been well formulated by Krantz (26) when he says that the Leipzig School was investigating the human mind, Baldwin human minds. Or perhaps, more exactly, for Leipzig the object was the mind to the extent that it was describable in its general structure, that is as a psychic apparatus identical in all men as members of the species homo sapiens, or perhaps, going even beyond that, as animality. Baldwin, on the other hand, was investigating psychic processes in a particular context, in

that of particular intentions, contents and social life complexes. It is for this reason that with Baldwin mental acts appeared as functions bearing the imprint of disposition, education and habit.

(3) This difference as to the objects of research was only a little later interpreted as a difference of schools or disciplines in psychology by Titchener (27). Titchener made this distinction clear by an analogy with biology. Biology comprises morphology concerned with the structures of living organisms, physiology concerned with the functions of various organs and processes, and genetics which deals with the evolution of living beings. Employing the same principle of division, modern psychology could be represented as structural, functional, and genetic psychology. True, loyal to the Leipzig tradition Titchener still insisted that structural psychology must be developed first before there was any prospect that functional and genetic psychology could establish itself. Nonetheless, this scheme, or as he termed it 'working' classification (28), recognized that an entirely different kind of psychology had emerged in America in the 1890's. The functional psychology developed by Cattel, Baldwin, Dewey, Angell and others was informed by the programs of the more specifically applied psychologies: child, educational and developmental psychology on the one side, and by certain new fields, such as animal psychology, on the other (29).

In its choice of methods the new school felt itself to be in opposition to the continental model, first and foremost to the Leipzig School. Its relation to the empirical was informed by the principles enounced by Baldwin: the need to make individual differences explicit, to eliminate introspection, to collect data from large samples, including group testing, to determine correlations of variables, to develop mental tests. It would seem then that in the rules for experimentation developed by Baldwin we have found what Kuhn's 'disciplinary matrix' suggests: a body of rules accepted as binding by a particular discipline or school in its practice of science, rules which mark off a particular community of specialists from related disciplines.

3. Conclusion

With this my analysis of one scientific controversy is concluded. It was intended to show that to try and uncover the commitments implicit in a discipline, which are usually obscured by the scientists' absorption by their subject matter, that is to try and bring out the discipline's underlying assumptions, is not a futile venture; that the attempt to articulate these commitments explicitly is not necessarily 'a source of continual and deep frustration' (30). In scientific controversies this process of explication is accomplished by the scientists themselves. And second, the analysis was intended to give a preliminary notion of what a more extended study of the rules for experimentation might bring. There appears on the one hand to be a close connection between the research interest and the empirical approach. On the other hand, what is the particular object of research is determined in turn by the manner in which the scientist empirically approaches the subject matter of his inquiry, that is by the rules which govern the experimental procedures. These rules account for:

— the manner in which the object is isolated;
— the idealizations which are presupposed within the experiment, i.e. the separation of the phenomena from systematic irregularities;
— the manner in which dispositional properties manifest themselves;
— the manner in which conditions are ordered operationally according to cause and effect;
— what in the experiment counts as simple and what as complex;
— the type of quantification procedures adopted (31).

We may then conclude that the rules of experimentation do what we had assumed them to do: they guarantee to members of a scientific community that the object of their research is identical and that their experiments become controllable and reproducible.

If we have thus presented the scientific effect of the rules for experimentation as both a cognitive and social constellation there is still one thing we should never forget: in no case is it the experimental rules alone which determine the nature of a discipline or a specialty. A paradigm, as defined by Kuhn, a disciplinary matrix, is a complex within which the rules for experimentation, theories, heuristics, symbolic generalizations and the research goal function together.

Finally, one other misunderstanding must be avoided. To demonstrate that particular social groups within the science system (scientific communities) are constituted on the basis of specific shared commitments — for instance of experimental rules — and that these give the community its character distinguishing it from the practice of other groups cannot be taken to signify that the scientific achievements of the group only have a regional validity. The effect of such a tribalization of scientific truth would be self-destructive. Here the relationship between regional method and universal validity, we would say, corresponds more to the relationship familiar to us from the use of lemmas. A scientist working in a mathematical discipline, say a topologist, to prove a theorem sometimes will have to introduce 'lemmas' from other disciplines (e.g. functional analysis). These are propositions he often cannot prove by the means offered by his own discipline. However, this does not imply that in so doing he is assigning these theorems only a regional validity. On the contrary, that he has 'borrowed' them indicates that he is, in using them, relying for proof on the methods of the related field.

It is precisely the 'rule-directed' behaviour of scientists which guarantees that any other man, if he observed the same rules, would get the same results – this even if the rules in question are accepted only by the practitioners of some particular scientific community who by this fact constitute a specific group within the science system.

Notes and References

1. Cf. e.g. M. J. Mulkay, 'Some Aspects of Cultural Growth in the Natural Sciences', *Social Research* **36**, 1969, pp. 22–52; R. A. Rothman, 'A Dissenting View on the Scientific Ethos', *British Journal of Sociology* **23**, 1972, pp. 102–108.
2. E.g. S. B. Barnes and R. G. A. Dolby, 'The Scientific Ethos: A Deviant Viewpoint', *European Journal of Sociology* **11**, 1970, pp. 3–25.
3. Mulkay, *op. cit.*, 1969, Note 1, p. 35.
4. *ibid.*
5. T. S. Kuhn, 'The Function of Dogma in Scientific Research', in A. C. Crombie, (ed.), *Scientific Change*, London: Heinemann. 1963, pp. 347–369; T. S. Kuhn, *The Structure of Scientific Revolutions*, Chicago: Chicago University Press, 2nd. ed., 1970.
6. Kuhn, *op. cit.*, 1970, Note 5.
7. For a general review of such investigations see: Joseph Ben-David, 'Probleme einer soziologischen Theorie der Wissenschaft', in Peter Weingart (ed.), *Wissenschaftsforschung*, Frankfurt and New York: Campus, 1975, pp. 133–161.
8. There are classical examples of this possibility such as Virchow's foundation of 'Pathologische Anatomie' and Galton's foundation of 'Biometrics', both results of their papers being rejected.
9. See: Gernot Böhme, 'The Social Function of Cognitive Structures: a Concept of the Scientific Community within a Theory of Action', in Karin Knorr, Hermann Strasser, and H. G. Zilian (eds.), *Determinants and Controls of Scientific Development*, Dordrecht and Boston: Reidel, 1975, pp. 202–225.
10. This distinction has been made very clear by: H. Parthey and D. Wahl, *Die experi-*

mentelle Methode in Natur- und Gesellschaftswissenschaften, Berlin, 1966. For an overview of the rules for experimentation from the standpoint of the philosophy of science see: Gernot Böhme, 'Die Bedeutung von Experimentalregeln für die Wissenschaft', *Zeitschrift für Soziologie* 3, 1974, pp. 5–17.

11. Hence the difficulty of replicating experiments, especially in developing specialties; cf. H. M. Collins, 'The Seven Sexes: A Study in the Sociology of a Phenomenon', *Sociology* 9, 1975, pp. 205–224.

12. The main stages of the controversy are marked by the following publications. J. M. Baldwin, 'Types of Reaction', *Psychological Review* 2, 1895, pp. 259–273; E. B. Titchener, 'The Type Theory of Simple Reactions', *Mind* 4, 1895, pp. 506–514; J. M. Baldwin, 'The Type Theory of Reactions', *Mind* 5, 1896, pp. 81–90; E. B. Titchener, 'The Type Theory of Simple Reactions', *Mind* 5, 1896, pp. 236–241. Another account of the controversy, from a different standpoint, has been provided by Krantz. See: D. L. Krantz, 'The Baldwin-Titchener Controversy', in D. L. Krantz (ed.), *Schools of Psychology*, New York: Appleton Century Crofts, 1965.

13. W. Wundt, *Grundzüge der physiologischen Psychology*, 2 volumes, Leipzig: Engelmann, 3rd edition, 1887.

14. Regarding the historical background, see: E. G. Boring, *A History of Experimental Psychology*, New York: Appleton Century Crofts, 2nd edition, 1950, pp. 147ff.

15. Wundt, *op. cit.*, 1887, Note 13.

16. See Wundt's report in Wundt, *op. cit.*, 1887, Note 13, Vol. 2, pp. 265ff.

17. Regarding the subtractive procedure see: Boring, *op. cit.*, 1950, Note 14, pp. 14f. How cautious Wundt himself was in his conclusion regarding this point is made evident in Wundt, *op. cit.*, 1887, Note 13, Vol. 2. He not only expected particular elements (Teilakte) to be eliminated but also anticipated changes in physiological conditions.

18. Baldwin, *op. cit.*, 1895, Note 12.

19. Boring, *op. cit.*, 1950, Note 14, p. 320.

20. See Titchener, *op. cit.*, 1895, Note 12, p. 50, "endowed with the gifts requisite for psychological experimentation".

21. Baldwin, *op. cit.*, 1896, Note 12, p. 89.

22. R. J. Angell and A. Moore, 'Reaction-Time: A Study in Attention and Habit', *Psychological Review* 3, 1896, pp. 245–258.

23. Titchener, *op. cit.*, 1895, Note 12, p. 54.

24. Baldwin, *op. cit.*, 1896, Note 12, p. 83.

25. Baldwin, *op. cit.*, 1895, Note 12, p. 271.

26. Krantz, *op. cit.*, 1965, Note 12, pp. 8f.

27. E. B. Titchener, 'The Postulates of a Structural Psychology', *Philosophical Review*, 7, 1898, pp. 449–465.

28. *ibid.*, p. 450.

29. Boring, *op. cit.*, 1950, Note 14, pp. 550–578.

30. Kuhn, *op. cit.*, 1970, Note 5, p. 106.

31. The evidence for this list of rule determinations obviously cannot be drawn only from the analysis of the Titchener-Baldwin controversy. But there are other case studies such as the Goethe-Newton and Stumpf-Wundt controversies, and others should be undertaken. See: Gernot Böhme, 'Die Kontroverse zwischen Stumpf und Wundt über Vergleichungen von Tondistanzen: ein Streit über Regeln der Datenerzeugung in der Psychophysik', unpublished paper, Max-Planck-Institut, Starnberg, 1973. Regarding the problem of dispositional properties and relations with experiment and causality, see: Albrecht Wellmer, *Erklärung und Kausalität; zur Kritik des Hempel-Oppenheim Modells der Erklärung*, Frankfurt: Habilitationsschrift, 1971.

CHANGES IN THE SOCIAL AND INTELLECTUAL ORGANISATION OF THE SCIENCES:
Professionalisation and the Arithmetic Ideal

RICHARD WHITLEY

Manchester Business School, Manchester University

1. Introduction

The ontological and sociological corollaries of epistemological stances have recently been emphasised by Bhaskar in his critique of phenomenalism (1). Views as to the nature of scientific knowledge, he points out, involve certain assumptions about the nature of the world and the nature of a society which produces that knowledge. While logically necessary connections between ontological, epistemological and sociological commitments such as those traced by Bhaskar need not occur empirically, in the sense that particular groups adhere to a logically coherent set of beliefs, there are certain combinations of commitments, types of knowledge and patterns of social organisation which are more empirically likely than alternative combinations. The institutionalisation of a particular theoretical ideal in the sciences has sociological consequences which affect the future production of knowledge. Furthermore, that institutionalisation itself occurs under particular social circumstances which might not be so favourable to alternative theoretical ideals. While, then, not being directly concerned with the mutual relations of aspects of philosophical doctrines and systems, a major focus of the sociology of the sciences should, I suggest, be to consider how particular social arrangements are consonant with particular theoretical ideals and lead to the production of particular types of knowledge. The development and institutionalisation of certain epistemological principles as courts of appeal in scientific disputes, as justifications for particular authority structures in the sciences and as exemplary instances of 'scientificity' are of considerable importance to an understanding of scientific development. In particular, the reasons for, and

*Mendelsohn/Weingart/Whitley (eds.), The Social Production of Scientific Knowledge.
Sociology of the Sciences, Volume I, 1977. 143–169. All Rights Reserved.
Copyright © 1977 by D. Reidel Publishing Company, Dordrecht-Holland.*

consequences of, adopting the 'arithmetic' ideal (2) as a major component of professionalised science seem to me to be an important topic in the sociological study of modern science.

In seeking to account for differences in organisation between the sciences and changes in the forms of organisation, both the dominance of physics as the paradigmatic science and, within physics, the high status of mathematical analysis and modes of expression are of major significance. In many respects formalisation has come to be seen as the most 'scientific' of activities in science and the fully formalised or axiomatised science as the most acceptable type of science. A science which institutionalises this ideal in its textbooks, courses and assessment procedures is likely to develop a particular form of social organisation which, if it is taken to be the exemplar of scientificity, will have considerable influence on other sciences and relations between the sciences.

The success of arithmetic reasoning in achieving what Bhaskar terms 'closure' in some parts of physics is undeniable but this alone is not sufficient explanation of why arithmeticism has become institutionalised as one of the most important exemplars of scientificity in other fields (2a). Nor does it justify the assumption that when sciences can be represented by relatively coherent mathematical formalisms they are then 'finalised' and their internal theoretical dynamic decays (2b). The sociological problem is to account for the way in which a particular scientific strategy has become elevated to a superior position as a general criterion across the sciences and to trace the consequences of such elevation. This problem is only meaningful in the context of a belief in the plurality of the sciences and the concomitant refusal to reduce all scientific developments to a single linear model derived from certain areas of physics (3). The cognitive imperialism of a certain type of intellectual production system is thus called into question by the approach adopted here.

In this paper, I shall outline the sort of social organisation which seems to me characteristic of restricted sciences which institutionalise the arithmetic ideal, in comparison with what Elias (3a) terms 'configurational' science, as a preliminary to exploring the impact of the former upon the latter. A key aspect of social organisation is competition for authority in the science (4) and this differs between restricted and configurational sciences although the prestige of the former has affected the form of competition and basis of authority in the latter. Generally, though, the professionalisation of scientific work itself has altered the nature of competition for authority (5) and this needs to be briefly considered before discussing particular sciences.

2. Professionalisation and the Organisation of Competition for Scientific Authority

There is, of course, a large literature on the professions and processes of professionalisation (6) and I do not intend to discuss the concept in detail here but rather to indicate how changes in scientific work and authority have taken place during the professionalisation of the sciences. The development of formal training structures for neophyte scientists, of organisations which employ scientists on full time research, of a career structure in scientific bureaucracies and universities, of administrative systems for allocating and controlling research facilities and resources are all important parts of the professionalisation of scientific work. A further major aspect of professionalisation is, of course, the claim to specialised expertise and knowledge which justifies the institutional separation of an activity and its practitioners from everyday, lay activities and concepts and the concomitant establishment of relative social and normative autonomy. The separate control of training, recruitment and reward allocation is commonly regarded as a crucial component of professionalisation. However, autonomy without resources – and some control over the extent and size of those resources – will not establish a profession and it is a peculiarity of scientific work that the celebration of 'purity' and 'uselessness' and 'freedom' from lay control is associated with claims for more money and staff.

Science has managed to develop an institutional identity which at once proclaims its autonomy and independence while demonstrating its economic utility through agricultural and inorganic chemistry and its military utility in two world wars. It did this by successfully distinguishing itself as 'pure' science from technological developments but at the same time insisting on the dependence of the latter upon its own development. Utility was proven but only at second hand, thus insulating 'basic' science from everyday economic considerations and control while ensuring continued economic support for a self proclaimed 'useless' activity. Purity was often exhibited by emphasising mathematical formalism which had the added advantage of clearly demonstrating cognitive distance from lay knowledge and excluding the bulk of the population from participation in scientific activity.

As well as effectively excluding lay competition, the professionalisation of the sciences changed the basis of intellectual and social challenges within them. The more there is an apparatus to be organised, the more important administrative authority becomes. Whereas previously prestige based on past achievements was the main form of 'capital' in science (7), the development of a professional hierarchy and elaborate training facilities meant that control over resources used in scientific production constitutes an additional major form of capital. While prestige may be a necessary condition of obtaining such control — or at least of denying resources to deviants — it is not always sufficient and, correspondingly, administrative control need not imply scientific authority in terms of current work and approaches. Competition for recognition and authority (8) in professional sciences is premised upon the possession of the correct educational background and minimal resources necessary for contributing to the field as currently understood (9). While technical facilities have always been needed for experiments or other forms of scientific work and self sustenance during them, these were readily obtainable by 'amateur' scientists provided sufficient money was available. Nowadays, this is no longer the case and access to scientific apparatus — itself growing more and more complex and expensive — is controlled by the professional hierarchy. Competent competition, therefore, implies professional membership and organisational employment which, in turn, suggests that the distribution of all forms of capital and hence scientific 'chances' is reflected in the relations between employing organisations. The type and location of employment becomes a major factor in stratifying scientists and available resources in professionalised sciences. Without the right educational experience and organisational identity the neophyte scientist will find it difficult to compete effectively. Indeed, scientists at low prestige institutions may not even conceive of undertaking daring innovations or seeking major rewards. This tendency will be reinforced if they are, in addition, socially upwardly mobile. By contrast, scientists who have been educated at scientifically and socially authoritative institutions will consider it natural to make inspired guesses, to attack major problems and obtain and organise resources for work in new areas, especially if they are also from a high status stratum (10).

In pre-professional sciences, prestige and authority was a personal possession which could not really be reproduced, except perhaps through a few
disciples, and provided one lived long enough it was possible, at any rate in
principle, to successfully challenge the orthodoxy. Indeed, it is not clear
whether an orthodoxy existed in the sense we use the term to-day. Contrarily,
in professional sciences, authority becomes institutionalised in employing
organisations which educate neophytes, provide resources and generally
control the conditions of scientific work. Orthodoxies become reified in
textbooks, courses and organisational commitments; the death of an eminent
individual no longer opens up new possibilities and challenges from outsiders.
Innovation, if it occurs, is much more likely to come from within prestigious
organisations and is unlikely to severely attack the foundations of that
prestige. Authority develops into an organisational form of property. Professionalisation, then, has important consequences for competition and controversies in the sciences and for the type, and operation, of authority structures.

3. Restricted Sciences and the Arithmetic Ideal

In contrasting 'restricted' with 'configurational' sciences, both the nature of
objects dealt with and the preferred ways of dealing with them are relevant.
Pantin's distinction between 'restricted' and 'unrestricted' sciences and Elias'
suggestion that the sciences can be ordered according to the degree of struc-
turedness or integration of their objects refer primarily to differences in the
way objects are conceived while Georgescu-Roegen's discussion of arithmomorphism in the sciences focusses on the way they are to be understood (11).
However, in practice these two aspects are closely associated in that only if
objects are delineated in particular ways are they amenable to arithmetic
analysis although not all 'restricted' sciences are necessarily arithmomorphic.
As a theoretical ideal both aspects are important, and it is the combination
of epistemic and ontological commitments in a relatively undifferentiated
doctrine which seems to have been a crucial feature of successfully institutionalised ideals. Because the relations between these two sets of commitments are rarely specified and classified, and this has been assisted by the institutional separation of philosophy and science, difficulties arising from one
set can be glossed over by invoking immutable truths from the other (12).

While the ontological commitments originally associated with epistemological atomism may no longer direct the everyday practices of physicists, the ideal of science represented in what Bhaskar calls the 'corpuscularian/mechanical world view' remains authoritative within physics and across the sciences. The institutionalisation of this ideal as a major aspect of professional science has had important consequences for the organisation of the sciences. The term 'arithmetic ideal' is used here to highlight some of the main features of this ideal and indicate the sort of science it suggests as a preparatory step to discussing some of the organisational implications of its institutionalisation.

Pantin separated the 'restricted' from the 'unrestricted' sciences largely by comparing the richness and complexity of the phenomena they deal with (13). Generally, the more unrestricted the science the more complex are its objects and the more open is the research process in the sense that problems may necessitate scientists following "the analysis of their problems into every other kind of science" (14). In restricted ones, contrarily, relevant features of objects are severely circumscribed and scientists restrict themselves to a very small number of properties which can be quantitatively interrelated. As Georgescu-Roegen puts it (15): "physics studies only those properties of matter that are uniform, that is, independent of novelty by combination and of time as well".

This distinction can be clarified with the help of Harré's (16) discussion of the corpuscularian philosophy. The reduction of the primary qualities of matter to extension, figure, motion and solidity and the concomitant assertion that secondary qualities are only "various combinations, collocations and resultants of primary qualities" (17) enabled distinctions between the nominal and the real to be justified and focussed attention on a very limited set of properties which could be mechanically interrelated. The understanding of matter was thus restricted to the quantitative exploration of these interrelations and other properties, such as colour, relegated to the psychology of perception (18). Simple Newtonian dynamics took this process of reduction a step futher by expressing the fundamental relations of motion as a simple 'reticular' theory of axiomatic laws which can be made to look like a string of tautologies (19). The distinction made by Harré here between reticular theories, defined as: "a set of relationships between refined observational concepts, mediated by one or more theoretical concepts which are to be understood wholly in terms of a complex of the refined observational concepts of the theory" (20) and explanatory theories, which involve notions of causation between different sets of facts, is a useful one because it indicates that arithmetisation of relations need not imply the sort of closed conceptual system exemplified by Newtonian dynamics and apparently adopted in General Equilibrium theory in economics (21).

Restricted sciences need not therefore necessarily be axiomatically closed systems although they do seem to tend towards arithmetisation of basic relations and it is this aspect which Georgescu-Roegen focusses on in his discussion of statistical mechanics. He contrasts sciences which are based on concepts which are logically discrete and additive — hence 'arithmomorphic' (22) from those which use concepts that focus on forms and qualities and so overlap with their opposites — hence 'dialectical'. The former, he suggests, cannot deal with qualitative change or novelty and hence, if constituted as a theoretically closed system, excludes all sciences which examine phenomena with novel properties produced by combination. Chemistry may be largely arithmetised but as long as it remains interested in novel properties of compounds it will not form a 'reticular' theoretical system (23).

However, it is precisely the logical closure of axiomatic systems which has received much attention from philosophers and quantum logicians, as well as imitative efforts in the social sciences (24), and which may be seen as the key aspect of the institutionalised definition of science. The elevation of highly abstract, logically closed conceptual systems to definitive status as science results in attention being focussed on purely formal properties of concepts and relations and the exclusion of all those which are not susceptible to treatment by the current most 'elegant' and 'simple' formalism. It also directs attention away from substantive problems towards esoteric manipulations which may or may not have any physical meaning. Abstraction and mathematical complexity come to be seen as the hallmark of scientificity thus increasing the distance between science and everyday experience, indeed devaluing the latter for its untidyness and lack of logical coherence. If a science deals with phenomena that are not amenable to representation by such formalism then it is that much less of a science. Similarly, within restricted sciences this view implies there is a hierarchy of prestige and authority resting on abstraction and formality (25). A further implication of this emphasis is the stress on static completeness. Knowledge is 'finalised' (26) when it is expressed in a coherent, closed formalism. Knowledge production is hence directed towards the goal of logical closure which guarantees its validity and permanence and so science is not a transitive·(27) process but rather a progression towards the finality of a closed logical system. In the last resort, then, all the sciences will be expressed as derivatives of a central set of logically interdependent axioms and knowledge production will stop. Given enough resources and autonomy a complete representation of certain knowledge will be obtained, hence the powerful attraction of this idea for scientific elites. This view is reductionist and non historical, knowledge production inevitably leading towards the final state of completeness. Radical changes in knowledges are therefore ruled out as is the rationality of any substantive challenge to established authority and beliefs.

Arithmetisation of restrictedly defined phenomena need not, though, imply logical closure in this sense. It does, however, have similar effects in terms of the fetishisation of mathematical formalisms. The apparent success of quantitative representations of relations between properties in restricted sciences leads to their extension to other fields and the elevation of arithmetisation as one of the most important criteria of scientificity. Similarly, the restriction of salient properties to those amenable to arithmetical manipulation leads to a restriction of phenomena considered scientific objects. Discreteness and additivity become the hallmark of scientific properties and arithmetic relations the guarantee of scientific knowledge.

4. Configurational and Unrestricted Sciences

Before continuing to discuss the sociological implications of arithmetisation in the restricted sciences some comments about unrestricted sciences are necessary. In restricted sciences, "processes of integration and disintegration are reversible" (28) while they are irreversible in highly structured fields. In these latter, the "interdependence of the constituent parts is so high that the independence of these parts, though not entirely lacking, is very small" (29). This irreversibility and integration means that lawlike theories of universal regularities which ignore time are not possible in configurational sciences. As Elias says: "The fit of a lawlike, an ideal type representation of the connection of part events of a nexus, one might say, increases or diminishes in inverse ratio to the degree of integration of the nexus" (30). This view is, of course, close to Georgescu-Roegen's emphasis on quality and novelty in non arithmomorphic sciences and Elias' attack on the atomistic fallacy could easily be expressed in similar terms. The movement away from relations between discrete, qualityless parts expressed as quantitative laws to more structured phenomena exhibiting distinct qualities by virtue of the particular connections of the parts emphasises the particular and the qualitative at the expense of the universal and the quantitative. It also leads to the consideration of richness and complexity in Pantin's sense because attention is focussed on qualitative properties of complex wholes which cannot be reduced to agglomerations of simple properties of basic constituents. Unrestricted sciences deal with structures and integrated phenomena because they do not restrict their objects to a small number of highly general relations of basic particles or events but consider qualities of phenomena as legitimate scientific objects without reducing them to formal relations of component parts.

There are two important aspects of configurational sciences which become more noticeable as integration increases. First, the number of classes of individuals is relatively large and the number of individuals in each class is small (31). While electrons and protons exist in vast numbers, the number of biological macromolecules is less and the number of societies much less. Similarly, there are more classes of men and animals than there are of elementary particles and chemical compounds. This is because the increased complexity of individuals results in more qualities and properties and hence more classes to accommodate them. It also means that variations among individuals increase because structural differences can occur along an increased number of dimensions and so qualities vary. The more structurally complex are objects the more variability they exhibit and the richer is their set of properties. Richness of objects is, in this sense, a corollary of complexity. Consequently, the highly configurational sciences deal with a relatively small number of individuals exhibiting a high degree of structure and a large number of properties.

The second important aspect is the crucial role of taxonomy in these sciences. The complexity of objects and multitude of properties require ordering in a way that restricted sciences could ignore precisely because they limit the relevant set of features for consideration. Classification is important in all sciences (32) but it assumes a crucial role in highly structured ones in ordering the multiplicity of objects and qualities in such a way that scientists do not need to unravel each individual object anew. Locating a given organism in a particular taxonomy should enable a number of predictions to be made about its properties and behaviour (33) without actually studying it in detail. It also says something about how it is to be understood, which properties are to be regarded as prior to others and so orders qualities in a way that leads to explanation. Competing classifications are therefore competing explanations. The definitive characteristics of social systems, for example, imply an explanatory account at variance to that implied in a classification of modes of production. The importance of classification here means that distinct explanatory approaches require distinct means of ordering and describing phenomena, emphasising different properties and relations so that the 'same' object can be understood and described in a number of different ways. While restricted sciences basically seek to reduce objects to a simple formal representation which is 'complete', the more structured sciences can quite legitimately incorporate a number of descriptive systems focussing on different orderings of properties. Consequently the 'polyparadigmatic' nature of the social sciences (34) can be seen as a function of their configurational nature and attempts at a monistic reduction seen as fundamentally mistaken.

Orderings of properties are rarely complete in the sense that they unequivocally order all qualities into discrete categories. As a result, they are not mutually exclusive and overlap, in some cases extensively. A configurational science does not consist of discrete, exclusive 'paradigms', each with its own explanatory principle and taxonomy but rather exhibits a number of interrelated approaches which diverge on some points but overlap on others. Similarly, the same explanatory approach may be pursued in a number of different fields without necessarily seeking to reduce the variety of structures to a simple representation. The selection of particular properties as primary, e.g., biochemical, can be used as a research strategy in studying a variety of systems so that the conceptual boundaries of configurational sciences are fluid and highly permeable. The structured complexity of objects in these sciences generates a great variety of qualities which can be approached in a number of ways which characterise the object in terms of different combinations of qualities. These overlapping approaches are not restricted to any individual science but frequently range over a number of objects and hence no single science or object can be unequivocably linked to a single explanatory approach. Sciences and approaches interpenetrate and exhibit organisational elasticity.

5. Patterns of Organisation, Competition and Authority in Minimally Structured Sciences

In considering likely social corollaries of particular types of science — i.e., arithmetical and configurational — I am not suggesting that each type can, in fact, be located within a definite and distinct mode of social organisation or that without the 'appropriate' form of social structure a type of knowledge cannot be produced. Rather, the dominance of one form of science and the institutionalisation of its associated social relations in the emergence of the scientific 'profession' has had a major effect on the social structure of all the sciences and the development of other forms of knowledge. While I think that there are aspects of the social organisation of configurational sciences which can only be understood in relation to their intellectual structures, the general development of these sciences has to take into account the dominance of the arithmetic and reticular ideal and its associated social relations. In this section, I shall outline some of the probable social corollaries of institutionalising this theoretical ideal as a major component of professional science.

The arithmetic ideal in low structured sciences leads to an emphasis on formalisms and formalisable properties which devalue qualitative distinctions in favour of quantitative continua. Even if qualities are becoming relevant in particle physics, as Georgescu-Roegen suggests (35), physics as a whole still adheres to the arithmetic ideal. As Georgescu-Roegen says: "physics, in spite of the stochastic form of its laws and the indeterminacy of the instrumental observations, is still a mechanistic science ... (in that) ... it assumes only a finite number of qualitatively different elements and ... it assumes a finite number of fundamental laws relating these elements to everything else in the same phenomenal domain' (36). These fundamental laws are usually expressed in terms of cardinal measures and it is not without significance that Kuhn himself trained as a physicist writing about physics as the paradigm science, seizes on symbolic generalisations represented as arithmetic relations as a major component of 'paradigms' (37).

Competition in such a science focusses on the successful reduction of phenomena to an arithmetic formalism. Because the ideal knowledge structure is basically reticular in Harré's sense — while it is possible to have non-reticular arithmetically formulated theories I think Georgescu-Roegen is probably right in suggesting physics is still founded on the presumption of a closed axiomatic structure being the ideal form of knowledge; certainly 'completeness' is still a powerful notion in physics however it is understood (38) — recognition tends to be awarded more on the basis of success in developing elegant formalisms than on experimentally identifying structural properties of materials. The dominance of the Oxbridge universities in Britain in theoretical physics, found by Gaston (39), and their concomitant receipt of high recognition indicates the authority of theoretical work in physics. These universities, it should be noted, also dominate — and again physicists appear to be to the fore — the British scientific advisory system (40). It is not at all unusual when talking to experimental physicists for them to say that they were not intelligent enough for work in theoretical physics and certainly this view was not rejected by theoreticians in a large department I studied.

Because the ideal of the discipline is that all physical phenomena will eventually be expressed as derivatives of a basic axiomatic structure, work on that structure and associated formalisms in principle affects all work in physics and therefore has more impact, at any rate potentially, than most experiments. If scientific authority rests on the scope of potential implications of one's work then in a discipline based on the ideal of conceptual closure and reticular theories the development of sophisticated formalisms will be seen as an authoritative practice.

The greater authority of theoretical work in restricted, arithmetised sciences is not only due to the use of mathematical formalisms *per se*, but also arises from the emphasis on completeness and coherence in such a science. Because the ideal is the reduction of all the special fields of research to a coherent formalism, work directly focussing on this goal is more central to the discipline as a whole than research in any derivative field. As long as there is the expectation that physics will be unified through some set of formalisms, mathematical work will continue to have high prestige and authority even though it may become increasingly remote from most physicists' concerns.

The dominance of the arithmetic ideal in physics and, perhaps to a slightly lesser extent, in chemistry means that competition over major theoretical issues involving challenges to this ideal is unlikely to occur very often. Where mathematisation of relations in a closed, coherent system is reified as the basic goal of a discipline in educational curricula, reward systems and career structures, any controversy over fundamental ontological problems will be short lived because it could threaten the whole structure of organisational authority and the disciplinary identity. By and large, the existence of an ordering principle embodied in journal policies, recruitment strategies and promotion criteria which fairly unambiguously ranks contributions and approaches to phenomena tends, I suggest, to restrict controversy to more technical than theoretical issues. The institutionalisation of a theoretical ideal which sets goals for the discipline and orders priorities means that fundamental issues have effectively been excluded from disputes.

While 'revolutions' cannot be ruled out — though there are major social mechanisms for coping with, and controlling, potentially threatening views in professionalised, hierarchised science, not the least being the institutionalisation of specialised, differentiated labour — I suggest that 'extensional' and 'technical' competition are more likely to occur than 'oppositional' and even these forms may be insulated by the allocation of sufficient resources (41). The separate institutionalisation of theoretical work itself reduces the likelihood of violent controversy across a range of components of scientific activity by organisationally dividing related aspects of scientific work. Disputes over one aspect become socially and cognitively removed from those over other aspects and hence controversies cannot 'crystallise'.

This differentiation of topics and foci of research can be termed 'vertical' in contrast to the 'horizontal' segmentation of disciplines discussed by Hagstrom (42). While in the latter situation, complete sets of commitments and beliefs are separated, in the former distinct components of the 'same' scientific activity are organisationally distinguished. Disciplinary segmentation refers to the institutional separation of scientific goals, models and techniques whereas vertical differentiation involves the differentiation of tasks and concerns within the same theoretical commitment. Specialisation in the study of models in particle physics, for example, results in 'phenomenologists' becoming distinct from other theoreticians and from accelerator physicists who in turn are separated from computer scientists concerned with improving the analysis of experimental results. Even when these groups are in the same employing organisation they do not appear to be members of a common enterprise although the official rhetoric so describes them (**43**). Vertical differentiation of this type may be extreme in this field, but is increasingly occurring in sciences where a distinct theoretical goal provides the basis for institutional separation of theoreticians and experimenters.

Because of the institutional separation of theoretical and experimental physics and the greater authority of the former, organisational interests of theoretical physics require the continued proclamation of the arithmetical ideal and the axiomatic method since, in the last resort, it is on this that claims to autonomy and authority rest. As Coddington points out, the axiomatic approach, by making a strict distinction between the formal aspect of a theory and a particular interpretation "greatly reinforces the scope for theoretical autonomy" (**44**). The proliferation of sub fields in all areas of physics may make theoretical unification unlikely (**45**) but this goal remains a powerful ideal and symbol of theoretical supremacy. So much so that one can order the various parts of physics according to their consonance with this ideal and more or less predict their relative prestige. Materials science, for example, as Georgescu-Roegen points out (**46**), deals with quantified qualities, such as, e.g., hardness, deformation, flexure, rather than with quantity measures and so has a 'qualitative residual' which results in relations being non linear and difficult to reduce to a simple, universal law of proportion. Indeed many relations are expressed as empirically determined graphs rather than being theoretically derived fomulae — as is also the case in many biomedical areas. An important reason for this is the existence of internal structure which is not amenable to simple arithmetical reduction (**47**) but the point here is that structural mechanics, and the science of materials in general, is not a very prestigious part of the sciences of matter.

An important aspect of this theoretical authority is its success in institutionalising mathematical ability as an exclusionary device. Given that formalisms have authority because of their key role in the disciplinary ideal, further mathematical refinement renders theoretical work beyond the comprehension of most physicists and so ensures that its authority remains immutable. Establishing mathematical formalisms as the general basis of theoretical work and training effectively excludes the bulk of researchers from rationally criticising it and so renders the authority of this sort of work practically impregnable. The professionalisation of physics allowed theoreticians to institutionalise their dominance of the field and indeed of the sciences by using their authority as guardians and developers of the disciplinary ideal to organisationally separate those with mathematical ability from those without and impose their definition of the former as 'real', 'pure' and 'brilliant' physicists. Once this was firmly established in curricula and journal policies it acquired a momentum of its own and specialisation intensified so that even if individual elite physicists decried this emphasis on formalism at the expense of physical interpretations little response on an institutional basis is to be expected.

Indeed, the attack on Bohm's 'hidden variables' theory — especially the more emotional aspects **(48)** — can be understood as a reaction against the threats to theoretical authority posed by raising ontological and physical issues in the context of quantum theory. By reopening the whole issues of the physical meaning of formalisms and threatening the authority of pure mathematics, Bohm was, perhaps, seen as a danger to the authority structure of physics. Certainly he raised important questions which highlighted some major difficulties in quantum mechanics. In contrast to Bondi and Gold **(49)**, he emphasised the physics of his position rather than deriving a physical conclusion from an epistemological stance, and so could not be ignored as a philosopher. It is interesting to note here that some of the dismissals of his 1952 paper were based on his alleged lack of mathematical rigour showing that this had become institutionalised as a dominant criterion in evaluating work and excluding deviant work **(50)**.

A similar process seems to be at work in economics as Coddington shows in his analysis of General Equilibrium theory **(51)**. This theoretical approach is regarded as useful by its practitioners because of its formal precision and syntactic explicitness. However, its utility appears in practice to be exemplified — according to Hahn, a leading exponent — by the capacity to show how other approaches are incompatible with it. A quote from Hahn's inaugural lecture at Cambridge, cited by Coddington, shows this clearly: "Debreu and others have made a significant contribution to the understanding of Keynesian economics just by describing so precisely what would have to be the case if there were no Keynesian problems" **(52)**. The fetishisation of formalism and concomitant disregarding of what Coddington terms 'semantic properties' or substantive issues seem to be almost parodied by this part of economics. The main point here is that once the leading principle of scientific authority has become institutionalised and professionalised, it is no longer simply a question of individuals and battles of ideas, but a social hierarchy of organisations is based on and legitimated by this ideal which makes any radical change unlikely.

With regard to patterns of social organisation, the focus on arithmetised relations of a highly restricted set of properties results, when institutionalised, in restrictive and exclusionist social relations. Objects are in general clearly bounded and defined because this is a key aspect of the disciplinary ideal and so social boundaries can be firmly drawn. Obviously, the further away an area is from the defining features of the science the less this will be true and social relations in, for example, parts of materials science will not be as distinct as in more central areas. Basically, then, it seems reasonable to suggest that the more an area of physics deals with arithmetic relations which can be ordered in reticular theories the more central it will be to the discipline and the clearer will be its cognitive and social boundaries. Conversely, the more configurational the phenomena and their properties, the less prestigious and authoritative will an area be and the more fluid its boundaries. As a result the latter fields will be more liable to invasion by physicists from the former ones. Exclusivity and impermeability are a feature of highly formalised areas focussing on restricted phenomena. Furthermore, once arithmetic fomalisms have become established as a dominant feature of the central area new fields will tend to imitate this aspect as means of acquiring respectability.

6. Patterns of Organisation, Competition and Authority in Highly Structured Sciences

This imitative behaviour is not, of course, confined to neophyte sciences of matter. It has been noted and described throughout the biological and social sciences (53). It seems to me that the present social and cognitive organisation of these sciences can best be understood in relation to certain features of their objects and concerns together with the dominance of intellectual ideals and modes of social organisation based on physics. The major feature of these sciences, as discussed above, is the configurational qualities of their objects. Scientific objects are not tightly defined and bounded, considerable overlap between them occurs and different approaches appropriate similar properties. Consequently, social groups focussing on particular objects or phenomena cannot easily form tight boundaries and identities; exclusionist strategies are difficult to implement when a number of approaches are possible, each giving primacy to a different set of properties. In terms of the scientific objects analysed, then, the cognitive and social map of these sciences should be fluid, permeable and overlapping on a number of dimensions. This can be seen in the variety of dimensions used by scientists to indicate their basic conceptual identity. These may be: the object studied, e.g. virology; the mechanism analysed, e.g., immunology; the technique used, e.g., radiobiology or the theoretical approach, e.g. biochemistry (**54**).

Whereas in arithmetic sciences, competition and authority are focussed on the arithmetic and reticular ideal which provides a common ordering standard and criterion for allocating recognition, there is no such similar overarching principle in configurational sciences, considered in *abstracto*, unless it be the injunction to regard each level of organisation as irreducible. Pantin's methodological principle for unrestricted sciences to pursue problems into other fields does not really constitute an adequate criterion for a reward system or for ranking theoretical approaches. The major theoretical activity in configurational sciences has probably been taxonomic and this requires considerable attention to detail and qualitative judgments. Theoretical autonomy is unlikely to develop around such an activity because of its closeness to qualitative distinctions and hence a high degree of differentiation of labour on the theory experiment dimension is unlikely to occur. Since taxonomic principles vary according to one's theoretical purpose, and there is no general system for ordering these across levels of organisation, configurational sciences will not be integrated in the same way as arithmetic ones. Theoretical models and associated classification schemes remain fairly closely tied to their relevant 'facts' and there is no clearly articulated ideal to order them.

Competition therefore will focus here on fairly immediate issues concerned with the correct ordering of facts, establishing primacy of particular relations and particular structured representations to account adequately for central phenomena. As there is no overall, integrating theoretical ideal, we would expect competition between theoretical approaches to be more common in configurational sciences and to include overtly metaphysical components. While object descriptions and explanations are not necessarily incommensurable, indeed there has to be some presumption that the same 'thing' is being studied for competition to occur, the plurality of approaches and models without .an articulated theoretical ideal to justify their mutual ordering and integration means that 'oppositional' and 'explanatory' competition (55) is more likely to occur here than in professionalised arithmetic sciences. Furthermore, the more structured phenomena are and the more qualities they exhibit the more likely these forms of competition will occur and extend into the metaphysical realm. Also the less likely components of scientific activities will be articulated and integrated (56). A plurality of problem formulations and technical approaches is probable in highly configurational sciences and these will be relevant to a number of models and theories in a variety of ways which are not unambiguous. Difficulties of obtaining conceptual closure and restricting relevant properties will lead to disputes over theoretical foundations and their relations to current research practices. Of course, where arithmetisation has become institutionalised as the dominant dogma this tendency will be mitigated though not, I suggest, entirely removed as witness the not infrequent, and often unresolved, debates over the scientificity and realism of orthodox economics (57).

7. The Institutionalisation of the Arithmetic Ideal and Relations between the Sciences

The present authority structure of configurational sciences is subject to considerable influence by the general hierarchy of the sciences and the principles on which it is based. In fact it is not entirely clear that the criteria for acquiring recognition and authority in these sciences are separate from those in less structured fields. Certainly the prestige of mathematical ecomomics would seem to indicate that in at least one social science they are not. The dominance of reductionist strategics in many biological sciences also demonstrates the power of arithmetic reasoning and ideals, even if in practice configurational representations are used (58). The success of physicists in ignoring the rich qualitative distinctions in genetics and seeking to isolate and map the essence of reproductive mechanisms (59) indicates the susceptibility of biology to one form of arithmetisation (60). It is unlikely that such strategies would have become so influential in biology if the arithmetic ideal was not regarded as authoritative. Similarly, the influx of physics into geology and subsequent development of plate tectonics has led one observer to talk of a Kuhnian revolution and increasing 'maturity' in geology (61). However, as

Elias points out (62), molecular biology in fact uses a notion of structure which is not totally reducible to arithmetical laws and it is interesting to note that a recent textbook in geology talks of concepts of 'fit' in discussing current controversies which indicates a qualitative judgment (63). The analytical ideal, though, still exercises a powerful attraction in the biological and social sciences.

In fact it may be possible to order these sciences in the same way as the subfields of physics and impute prestige accordingly. So, sciences approximating to the arithmetic ideal would be considered more 'scientific' than those exhibiting complexity and qualitative distinctions. To a certain extent this can be seen in the dismissal of some sciences as 'mere description' or 'natural history' in contrast to 'real', mathematised science. This need not mean that colonising physicists simply sweep all before them in struggles for scientific authority throughout the sciences but that the relatively high extent of institutionalisation of the arithmetic ideal as an important criterion of scientificity ensures they have substantial social and organisational support for their work. Additionally, their self confidence, which their background in the dominant discipline provided, enables physicists seriously to consider they could solve fundamental problems in other fields while geneticists and geologists pay much more attention to qualitative differentiation and the complexities of their objects. Scientific authority arising from the hierarchy of the sciences, based on approximation to the arithmetic ideal, not only means that physicists' approaches are taken seriously but leads to their own conviction that they could successfully bypass existing views and consideration of detailed descriptions to identity fundamental processes.

The institutionalisation of the arithmetic ideal as a major part of professionalised science would also affect training processes throughout the sciences. Extended periods of training for neophyte scientists would emphasise mathematical skills and arithmetic reasoning as the key to professional competence and identity. The longer the training period and the more it focusses on abstract formalisms the more a science distances itself from lay expertise and demonstrates its professional status and so can claim intellectual and social autonomy. The ability of restricted sciences to package research topics for apprentices should lead to similar imitative behaviour in other fields so that, for instance, the 3 year Ph.D. becomes the definitive feature of professional training in all the sciences and the state support system effectively institutionalises it. The division of labour implicit in such packaging of research topics would also spread so that a high degree of specialisation and narrowing of problems becomes common across the sciences. Similarly, attempts at institutionalising the theory-experiment (or field work) split and so introducing vertical differentiation could be expected once restricted arithmetic science becomes institutionalised as the paradigm of a professionalised science (64).

'Rational' ways of organising research are also implied by the ability of restricted sciences to package discrete topics and integrate the results. Once problems can be fairly clearly specified and their likely interrelations confidently predicted, in the sense that there are well articulated rules about the interpretation and acceptability of results, research becomes susceptible to formal administrative methods. By emphasising formal, discrete properties and logical coherence and rigour the arithmetic ideal at least fosters the impression of clear boundaries and hierarchical integration if not actually encouraging systematic planning and organisation. Certainly it represents a potential for the 'rational' direction of research since it posits, in some variants at least, logical closure and the derivation of all special sciences from a central set of axioms. The ordering of scientific priorities and research strategies can, therefore, incorporate administrative and political goals because once the basic structure is obtained it is simply a matter of filling in holes — or finding solutions to 'puzzles' — and from a strictly scientific viewpoint it does not make too much difference which hole is filled first.

As an ideal, then, arithmeticism offers considerable scope for the 'rational' administration of research and it is not surprising that after the success of organising one of the most recondite fields of science to make the atomic bomb similar structures have been established to solve numerous 'problems' and 'pure' science itself has become extensively subsidised by the state and by industry. Even if in practice organisational procedures and bureaucratic structures do not mean much in many laboratories — especially those working on more 'configurational' phenomena (65) — they indicate the spread and influence of administrative rituals and rhetoric. The domination of professional science by the arithmetic ideal should lead, in this view, to an emphasis on formalisms in training and reward system and increased formality and 'rationality' of work organisation throughout the sciences.

Insofar as the professionalisation of physics and chemistry has occurred around the arithmetic ideal it has had major consequences for the organisation of all the sciences by establishing on the one hand an organisationally reified image of scientificity which has had a considerable impact on struggling sciences trying to acquire respectability and on the other hand by serving as a model of how work should be organised and disciplines structured. The former effect has produced axiomatic schemes and arithmetised phenomena in many social sciences while the latter has resulted in the development of the full panoply of Ph.D. training, journals, referees, conferences, etc. throughout the sciences. The influence of this model has been increased by the celebration of professionalised physics by much work in the philosophy and sociology of science. The concentration on this field as the paradigm science and exemplar of disciplinary development in many case studies and models of scientific development shows how powerful the hierarchy of professionalised science has become (66).

8. Conclusions

In tracing the development of differentiation of sciences, considerable attention has to be paid to, on the one hand, the professionalisation of scientific work and, on the other hand, the type of theoretical ideal which dominates professional and lay views of what is scientific. The way in which a particular ideal, and its associated form of organisation, comes to dominate professionalised science has major consequences for the development of the sciences. The arithmetic ideal implies a particular type of science and suggests a particular form of social organisation, basis for authority and type of competition which are distinct from those suggested by the more pluralistic, open ideal of the configurational sciences. The institutionalisation of this ideal and its subsequent dominance of professional science, at any rate as an epistemic standard if not in everyday practices, has influenced the development of many biological and social sciences by attracting scientists to certain fields (67) and by encouraging certain styles of work and the use of physical techniques and analogies throughout the sciences. The organisation of work in the sciences has become more similar to that of professionalised, restricted areas although attempts at institutionalising the theory-experiment distinction in biology seem unsuccessful. The cult of arithmeticism in the social sciences has combined with the adoption of a professional apparatus to produce extended training systems initiating the neophyte into mathematical reasoning which then serves as a means of showing one's scientificity and superiority to lay reasoning. Generally speaking, the more arithmetised and restricted a science, the more extended is its initiation programme and the more it seeks to distance itself from everyday concerns and beliefs by emphasising professional training and arithmetic manipulations. This suggests that the more a science − or school within a science − is concerned about professionalisation the more they will emphasise arithmetic reasoning and extended periods of training in mathematical techniques.

I have not dealt with relations between the professionalisation of the sciences and that of other activities, nor the general changes in work organisation and occupational structures which constitute the broader context of professionalisation. Similarly, changes away from the ideal of the 'free' professional operating in a 'free' labour market towards the full time employment of professionals by large bureaucratic organisations have not been covered but obviously they are important in any consideration of changes in the organisation of the sciences. In some ways the development of government and industrial research laboratories could be seen as foreshadowing the organisation of accountants, lawyers and doctors into large corporate units. In any case the mythology of the free professional in what Collins terms 'cold war sociology of science' (68) was never really appropriate to scientists, whether genteel amateurs or organisational employees.

Notes and References

1. See Roy Bhaskar, *A Realist Theory of Science*, Leeds: Leeds Books, 1975, pp. 16−57.
2. This term is taken from Georgescu-Roegen's discussion of 'arithmomorphism' and Harré's analysis of the Newtonian general conceptual system. It refers to the belief that scientific knowledge is essentially arithmetic, i.e., its elements are "discretely distinct as a single number in relation to the infinity of all others". Concepts which cannot be analysed in terms of simple arithmetic continua are not considered scientific in this view. See Georgescu-Roegen, N., *The Entropy Law and the Economic Process,* Harvard University Press, 1971, pp. 14, 25−52 and Harré, R., *Matter and Method,* London: Macmillan, 1964, pp. 8−58.
2a. Bhaskar, *op. cit.*, 1975, Note 1, pp. 64−126; cf. Georgescu-Roegen, *op. cit.*, 1971, Note 2, pp. 25−59, 114−139.
2b. cf. Böhme, G., W. v. d. Daele and W. Krohn, 'Finalisation in Science', *Social Science Information* 15, 1976. See also the application of the 'finalisation thesis' to the field of cancer research by Rainer Hohlfeld: Cognitive and Institutional Determinants Directing Science, the case of Biomedical Research', paper presented at a PAREX-IAS meeting, Vienna, July, 1976.
3. For one expression of this belief see: Norbert Elias, 'The Sciences: towards a

theory', in R. D. Whitley (ed.), *Social Processes of Scientific Development*, London: Routledge and Kegan Paul, 1974. See also: Richard Whitley, 'The Sociology of Scientific Work and the History of Scientific Developments', in S. S. Blume (ed.), *New Perspectives in the Sociology of Science*, New York, and London: John Wiley, 1977.

3a. Elias, *op. cit.*, 1974, Note 3.
4. Pierre Bourdieu, 'The Specificity of the Scientific Field and the Social Conditions of the Progress of Reason', *Social Science Information* 14, 1975, pp. 19–47.
5. cf. Pierre Bourdieu, *op. cit.*, 1975, Note 4; J. R. Ravetz, *Scientific Knowledge and Its Social Problems*, Oxford: Clarendon Press, 1971, pp. 37–53. Collins has linked the development of professional and bureaucratic types of organisation in the sciences to differences in task uncertainty and co-ordination difficulties in an interesting way but does not consider how theoretical ideals can vary and affect these processes. See: Collins, R., *Conflict Sociology*, London: Academic Press, 1975, pp. 506–523.
6. cf. e.g. Terence Johnson, *Professions and Power*, London, Macmillan, 1972; H. M. Vollmer and D. L. Mills (eds.), *Professionalisation*, Englewood Cliffs, N. J.: Prentice Hall, 1966; J. A. Jackson (ed.), *Professions and Professionalisation*, Cambridge University Press, 1970. Krohn has developed a useful contrast between 'intellectuals' and professionals' as careeer types in contemporary science and emphasised the historicity of present forms of organisation. See Roger Krohn, *The Social Shaping of Science*, Westport, Conn. and London: Greenwood Press, 1971, pp. 153–161;
7. Bourdieu has distinguished cultural and social capital as well as economic capital. See Pierre Bourdieu and J.-C. Passeron, *La reproduction: éléments pour une théorie du système d'enseignement*, Paris: Editions de Minuit, 1970, pp. 90–129; Bourdieu, P., Luc Boltanski and Monique de Saint Martin, 'Les Stratégies de reconversion: les classes sociales et le système d'enseignement', *Social Science Information* 12, 1973, pp. 61–113. See also: Bourdieu, P., *op. cit.*, 1975, Note 4.
8. I should point out here that competition in the present sense incorporates cognitive structures as the basis and focus of the struggle for authority. Scientific authority rests on the dominance of particular approaches, phenomena and beliefs; it is not simply a matter of acquiring the trappings of social prestige, although these are not necessarily epiphenomenal. Competition for recognition in the sciences is competition for recognition of the importance and correctness of one's ideas and work. Additionally, competition does not occur in a 'free' market between equals. The structure of intellectual and social authority defines heterodoxy and orthodoxy in a way which stratifies the nature of controversy and opportunities to engage in disputes and conduct competent but competitive work.
9. As Bourdieu says, accumulated scientific resources increase the cost of entry to the competitive struggle, Bourdieu, *op. cit.*, 1975, Note 4, p. 33.
10. Much of this paragraph is similar to Bourdieu's views on science. However, he does not consider the nature of the sciences or their ideals in discussing scientific authority, Bourdieu, *op. cit.*, 1975, Note 4.
11. Elias, *op. cit.*, 1974, Note 3; Georgescu-Roegen, *op. cit.*, 1971, Note 2; C. F. A. Pantin, *The Relations Between the Sciences*, Cambridge University Press, 1968, Ch. 1.
12. Jenkin has suggested that some of the influence of Mach's phenomenalism on quantum physics may be due to its 'success' in assisting Boltzmann's statistical mechanics to reinstate arithmomorphism and mechanics in thermodynamics. See Phyllis Jenkin, *Structure and Contradiction in Scientific Development: the Case of Nicholas Georgescu-Roegen and the Entropy Law*, unpublished M.Sc. Thesis,

Manchester University, 1975, pp. 11–22, 100–109. See also Georgescu-Roegen, *op. cit.*, 1971, Note 2, Chs. 5, 6, 7; and P. Forman, 'Weimar Culture, Causality and Quantum Theory, 1981–1927: adaptation by German Physicists and Mathematicians to a hostile intellectual environment', *Historical Studies in the Physical Sciences* 3, 1971.

13. Pantin, *op. cit.*, 1968, Note 11, pp. 17–25.
14. *ibid.*, p. 18.
15. Georgescu-Roegen, *op. cit.*, 1971, Note 2, p. 123.
16. Rom Harré, *Matter and Method*, London: Macmillan, 1964.
17. *ibid.*, p. 97.
18. *ibid.*, p. 112.
19. *ibid.*, p. 17.
20. *ibid.*, p. 13.
21. *ibid.*, p. 35; and see Alan Coddington 'The Rationale of General Equilibrium Theory', *Economic Inquiry* 13, 1975, pp. 539–558 for a detailed discussion of General Equilibrium Theory; also Georgescu-Roegen, *op. cit.*, 1971, Note 2, passim for economics in general.
22. Georgescu-Roegen, *op. cit.*, 1971, Note 2, pp. 14–15, 44–47.
23. *ibid.*, p. 15.
24. A well known example in sociology is H. L. Zetterberg, *On Theory and Verification in Sociology*, Totowa, N. J.: Bedminster Press, 1963.
25. Trevor Pinch, 'What Does a Proof Do If It Does Not Prove? A Study of the Social Conditions and Metaphysical Devisions Leading to David Bohm and John von Neumann failing to communicate in Quantum Physics', in this volume, pp. 171–215.
26. cf. Böhme *et al.*, *op. cit.*, 1976, Note 2b.
27. Bhaskar, *op. cit.*, 1975, Note 1, pp. 21–24.
28. Elias, *op. cit.*, 1974, Note 3, p. 28.
29. *idem*.
30. *ibid.*, p. 29.
31. cf. R. W. Gerard, 'Hierarchy, Entitation and Levels', in L. L. Whyte, A. G. Wilson and D. Wilson (eds.), *Hierarchical Structures*, New York: Elsevier, 1969, p. 225.
32. Gerard, *op. cit.*, 1969, Note 31; Pantin, *op. cit.*, 1968, Note 11.
33. Michael Ruse, *The Philosophy of Biology*, London: Hutchinson, 1973, p. 162.
34. cf. C. Lammers, 'Mono- and Poly-Paradigmatic Developments in Natural and Social Sciences', in R. D. Whitley (ed.), *Social Processes of Scientific Development*, London: Routledge and Kegan Paul, 1974; Herminio Martins, 'The Kuhnian 'Revolution' and its Implications for Sociology', in T. J. Nossiter, A. H. Hanson and Stein Rokkan (eds.), *Imagination and Precision in the Social Sciences*, London: Faber and Faber, 1972.
35. Georgescu-Roegen, *op. cit.*, 1971, Note 2, p. 115.
36. *idem*.
37. T. S. Kuhn, *The Structure of Scientific Revolutions*, Chicago: Chicago University Press, 2nd ed., 1970, pp. 182–184.
38. For the role this notion played in the Einstein, Podolsky and Rosen 'paradox', see C. A. Hooker, 'The Nature of Quantum Mechanical Reality: Einstein versus Bohr', in R. G. Colodny (ed), *Paradigms and Paradoxes, the Philosophical Challenge of the Quantum Domain*, Pittsburgh University Press, 1972; and Trevor Pinch, *Hidden Variables, Impossibility Proofs and Paradoxes: a Sociological Study of Non-Relativistic Quantum Mechanics*, unpublished M.Sc. Thesis, Manchester University, 1976.
39. J. C. Gaston, *Originality and Competition in Science*, Chicago: Chicago University Press, 1974, pp. 62–66.

40. S. S. Blume, *Toward a Political Sociology of Science*, New York and London: John Wiley, 1974, pp. 193–214.
41. These types of competition are discussed in R. D. Whitley, 'Konkurrenzformen Autonomie und Entwicklungsformen wissenschaftlicher Spezialgebiete', in Nico Stehr and R. König (eds.), *Wissenschaftssoziologie*, Köln and Opladen: Westdeutscher Verlag, 1975; and in R. D. Whitley, 'Specialty Marginality and Types of Competition in the Sciences', in P. Gleichmann, Johan Goudsblom and H. Korte (eds.), *Human Configurations, Essays in Honour of Norbert Elias*, Amsterdam, 1977.
42. W. O. Hagstrom, *The Scientific Community*, New York: Basic Books, 1965.
43. See Alan Bitz, 'History, Division of Labour and the Information Process in Fundamental Particle Physics', and A. Bitz, 'Scientific Research and the Information Process in a Nuclear Physics Laboratory', both in A. Bitz, Andrew McAlpine and R. D. Whitley, *The Production, Flow and Use of Information in Different Sciences*, London: British Library Report Series, 1975.
44. Coddington, *op. cit.*, 1975, Note 21, p. 548.
45. As Bitz has suggested, see A. Bitz, 'History, Division of Labour and the Information Process in Fundamental Particle Physics', in A. Bitz *et al.*, *op. cit.*, 1975, Note 43.
46. Georgescu-Roegen, *op. cit.*, 1971, Note 2, pp. 97–113.
47. cf. C. S. Smith, 'Structural Hierarchy in Inorganic Systems', in L. L. Whyte, A. Wilson and D. Wilson (eds.), *op. cit.*, 1969.
48. cf. e.g. L. Rosenfeld, 'Physics and Metaphsics', *Nature*, 181, 1958, p. 658.
49. Bondi and Gold attempted to derive their steady state theory of the universe which posits continuous creation of matter from what they considered to be incontrovertible philosophical doctrines. In contrast to Bohm's 1952 paper, this attempt does not seem to have created much of a stir in the literature, outside a small circle in Cambridge and London, until Ryle's experiments in the 1950's claimed to disprove it. However, Dingle felt compelled to use his position as President of the Royal Astronomical Society to launch a vitriolic attack on the 'new cosmology' in 1953 which suggests Bondi and Gold had had some impact among astronomers. See: H. Bondi and T. Gold, 'The Steady State Theory of the Expanding Universe, *Monthly Notices of the Royal Astronomical Society* 108, 1948, pp. 252–270; H. Dingle, 'Science and Cosmology', *Monthly Notices of the Royal Astronomical Society* 113, 1953, pp. 393–407; J. Singh, *Modern Cosmology*, London: Penguin, 1970, pp. 192–218. For a sociological analysis of the controversy over the steady state theory see: Ben Martin, *The Development and Capitulation of Steady State Cosmology: a Sociological Study of Authority and Conflict in Science*, unpublished M.Sc. diss., Manchester University, 1976.
50. Trevor Pinch has analysed the reception to Bohm's 1952 paper and his subsequent work in some detail in his M.Sc. Thesis, see T. Pinch., *op. cit.*, 1976, Note 38. The authority of the formalisms in this dispute and some reasons for elite physicists becoming involved in the 'hidden variables' controversy are discussed in Pinch's paper in the current volume. For some of Bohm's own reconstructions see: D. Bohm, *Causality and Chance in Modern Physics*, London: Routledge and Kegan Paul, 1957; and D. Bohm, 'Science as Perception – Communication', in Suppe, F., *The Structure of Scientific Theories*, Urbana, Illinois: University of Illinois Press, 1974. See also: Hooker, *op. cit.*, 1972, Note 38.
51. Coddington, *op. cit.*, 1975, Note 21.
52. Coddington, *op. cit.*, 1975, Note 21, p. 552. The original is in: Hahn, F., *On the Notion of Equilibrium in Economics*, Cambridge University Press, 1973.
53. c.f. e.g. Elias, *op. cit.*, 1974., Note 3; Gerard, *op. cit.*, 1969, Note 31; Paul Weiss, 'The Living System: Determinism Stratified', in Arthur Koestler, and J. R. Smythies

(eds.), *Beyond Reductionism*, London: Hutchinson, 1969; David Willer and Judith Willer, *Systematic Empiricism*, Englewood Cliffs, N.J.: Prentice-Hall, 1974.

54. cf. A. Bitz, *et al.*, *op. cit.*, 1975, Note 43, passim.

55. These types of competition involve controversies over explanatory models and definitions of the central problem of specialties as well as over techniques and research practices, c.f. R. D. Whitley, *op. cit.*, 1975, Note 41.

56. Five distinct components of scientific activities can be identified. These are: metaphysical, specialty concern, explanatory model, techniques and research practice. In any given activity, these components vary in their degree of clarity and coherence or integration. See: R. Whitley, 'Components of Scientific Activities, Their Characteristics and Institutionalisation in Specialties and Research Areas', in Karin Knorr, Hermann Strasser and H. G. Zilian (eds.), *Determinants and Controls of Scientific Development*, Dordrecht: Reidel, 1975a.

57. cf. A. Coddington, 'Positive Economics', *Canadian Journal of Economics* 5, 1972, pp. 1–15; M. Friedman, 'The Methodology of Positive Economics', in *Essays in Positive Economics*, Chicago: Chicago University Press, 1953; P. D. McClelland, *Causal Explanation and Model Building in History, Economics and the New Economic History*, Ithaca, N.Y.: Cornell University Press, 1975, pp. 117–145; S. Latsis, 'Situational Determinism in Economics', *British Journal for the Philosophy of Science* 23, 1972, pp. 207–245; F. Machlup, 'Theories of the Firm: Marginalist, Behavioural, Managerial', *American Economic Review* 57, 1967, pp. 1–33.

58. cf. Steven Rose, *The Conscious Brain*, London: Weidenfeld and Nicolson, 1973; Weiss, *op. cit.*, 1969, Note 53.

59. See, among others, D. Fleming, 'Emigre Physicists and the Biological Revolution', in D. Fleming and B. Bailyn (eds.), *The Intellectual Migration*, Harvard University Press, 1969.

60. cf. Harré, *op. cit.*, 1964, Note 16, p. 35.

61. A. Hallam, *A Revolution in the Earth Sciences*, Oxford University, Oxford University Press, 1973, pp. 103–114.

62. Elias, *op. cit.*, 1974, Note 3; cf. Georgescu-Roegen, *op. cit.*, 1971, Note 2, appendix G.

63. See the comparison between the 'analytical approach' and the 'numerical approach' in constructing and evaluating models of tectonic plate motion in E. R. Oxburgh, 'Plate Tectonics', in I. G. Gass, P. J. Smith and R. C. L. Wilson (eds.), *Understanding the Earth*, Sussex: Artemis Press, 1972, especially pp. 273–285. Other articles in the same book also discuss qualitative problems of 'fit' and difficulties of assessing rival accounts.

64. This may be the case in economics where mathematical economists have become a distinct group from econometricians.

65. In some biomedical laboratories we studied, project numbers had recently been instituted by the Medical Research Council in an attempt to monitor scientific work at a more specific level but most scientists had no idea what project they were supposed to be working on and some did not know project numbers existed. Such control procedures were often discussed as 'accounting fictions'. For a discussion of how different types of science are related to organisational strategies see: R. D. Whitley, 'Types of Science, Organisational Strategies and Patterns of Work in Research Laboratories in Different Scientific Fields', paper presented to a PAREX-IAS meeting in Vienna, July, 1976.

66. cf. e.g. D. Crane, *Invisible Colleges*, Chicago: Chicago University Press, 1972; M. J. Mulkay, *The Social Process of Innovation*, London: Macmillan, 1972; M. J. Mulkay, G. N. Gilbert and S. Woolgar, 'Problem Areas and Research Networks in Science', *Sociology* 9, 1975, pp. 187–203; N. Mullins, 'The Development of a

Scientific Specialty: the Phage Group and the Origins of Molecular Biology', *Minerva* **10**, 1972, pp. 51–82.

67. cf. N. Tinbergen, 'Ethology', in R. Harré (ed.), *Scientific Thought, 1900–1960*, Oxford: Clarendon Press, 1969.
68. Collins, *op. cit.*, 1975, Note 5, p. 473.

WHAT DOES A PROOF DO IF IT DOES NOT PROVE?*

A Study of the Social Conditions and Metaphysical Divisions Leading to David Bohm and John von Neumann Failing to Communicate in Quantum Physics

TREVOR J. PINCH

Bath University

1. Introduction

One of the more interesting problems to arise from the Kuhnian (1) analysis of science is the problem of communication between scientists with differing cognitive commitments. By conceiving of scientists as being bound by monistic paradigms which change at times of scientific revolution Kuhn raised the problem of how scientists working within rival paradigms communicate. Kuhn refers to the adherents of the rival paradigms as talking 'through each other' (2) which implies that little communication between paradigms occurs.

The vagueness of the term 'paradigm' (3), the failure of sociologists to identify monistic cognitive boundaries in science (4), the emphasis by sociologists on social network analysis (5), all coupled with the philosophical problems associated with the term 'incommensurability' (6), have meant that case studies have not tended to focus specifically on the problem of communication breakdown.

Communication breakdown in this context refers not so much to the difficulties encountered by scientists in actually talking to each other (although this is part of the problem) but rather more to the difficulties encountered at the cognitive level, that is in 'conceptualising', 'understanding' or 'making sense' of the work of other scientists. I am more interested in scientists talking through each other than failing to talk at all. Although

---

* I am grateful for comments from Helga Nowotny, Richard Whitley and colleagues at the University of Bath on an earlier draft of this paper.

emphasising the cognitive aspect of scientific activity I do not see this paper as addressing itself to the philosophical problem of whether a universal theory for the growth of scientific knowledge can be found. My concern is to understand communication problems which arise in the actual development and practice of science and not in some 'third world' (6a). For the purpose of this case study there is no need to touch on wider epistemological issues. The relevance of epistemological issues to the sociology of science has been discussed by Whitley (7) and is still an issue in contemporary sociology of science as Collins and Cox (8) have recently emphasised.

Bhaskar, in his recent book (9), has drawn attention to the importance of socially constructed cognitive objects in the sciences. This paper is intended to explore a communication breakdown over a specific cognitive object, namely a proof that a certain type of theory in quantum mechanics is impossible. Apart from using the historical material in the study to establish that a communication breakdown has occurred over this proof, I will also attempt to develop the type of sociological explanation I consider appropriate for conceptualising this kind of communication breakdown.

Thus, Section 2 of this paper is devoted to developing a sociological framework for analysing communication breakdowns, Section 3 comprises a brief account of the 'hidden variables' controversy including an analysis of the social preconditions for Bohm's heterodoxy to arise, Section 4 is devoted to a brief history of the 'hidden variables impossibility proofs' and their relation to Bohm's interpretation, Section 5 is a reconstruction of aspects of the cognitive content of Bohm's interpretation and von Neumann's proof with a view to showing along which dimension they failed to communicate, and Section 6 is an attempted explanation of the failure to communicate.

2. A Sociological Framework for the Analysis of Communication Failure

The failure of scientists to communicate can be seen as stemming from the social nature of scientific activity. The type of sociological account of communication breakdown I wish to consider must have two essential elements: firstly it must be possible to conceptualise differentiated cognitive objects and secondly it must be possible to conceptualise social structures which are seen as interrelated with the cognitive objects. A differentiated cognitive object such as a particular proof, theory, experiment, interpretation or classification is an object which can be analysed along more than one dimension. The dimensions along which a particular object can be analysed are to be seen as related to social structures. The social processes which have led to a particular kind of differentiation can then be invoked to explain a failure to communicate. In other words, failure to communicate can be conceptualised as arising from scientists' adherence to different dimensions of a cognitive object.

A schema for the analysis of science along different cognitive dimensions has recently been developed in a paper by Whitley (10). In this paper he outlines five different components of scientific activity. These are (1) the research practice, which includes the norms and guidelines involved in the formulation of a specific area of concern, (2) the research technique, which consists of the procedures and techniques used in the definition of an area of uncertainty and its attempted resolution, (3) the explanatory model, which contains some idea of the appropriate explanations against which results are evaluated, (4) the specialty concern, which is some overall field of concern and interest that defines and characterises some reality, and (5) the metaphysical level, which consists of a general set of values and beliefs that define an area as "scientific" and legitimise it as such.

In considering this specific case study I will attempt to elucidate, using some of the components outlined above, the dimensions along which communication breakdown occurred. No claim is made to treat the social processes which led to this differentiation in the same manner as Whitley advocated, but by using the five components of scientific activity it is hoped that the case study can at least be placed within the domain of comparative analysis.

The type of social explanation for the cognitive differentiation which I consider to be appropriate is that which emphasises that science is a productive activity. As Whitley (11) has pointed out, the conceptualisation of scientific activity as work has not been sufficiently emphasised in the sociology of science. If scientific work is regarded as the transformation of socially produced cognitive objects then cognitive differentiation can be explained in terms of different types of transformation activity. As in other kinds of work, the products of labour in scientific work, that is the cognitive objects, can be used for the purpose of maintaining particular social structures. In analysing the breakdown of communication between Bohm and von Neumann I will attempt to show that the particular differentiation of the cognitive object arose out of the differing transformation activities or work situations of the scientists involved, and that the cognitive object produced by this transformation activity was used to maintain a particular social structure.

In order to illustrate communication breakdown in science it is not necessary to examine periods of scientific revolution. The study of any controversy in science may yield evidence of a failure to communicate. For instance, Collins' case study of the meaning of a repeatable experiment in connection with the controversy over the existence of the new physical phenomenon of gravity waves can be interpreted as showing a failure to communicate (11a). The fact that physicists interpret the 'same' gravity-wave experiment in differing ways is evidence of less than perfect communication. By showing that a repeatable experiment is not a simple test against reality, but is a multi-dimensional socially constructed cognitive object, it is possible to explain scientists' failure to communicate over the meaning of a repeatable gravity-wave experiment in terms of different dimensions of the cognitive object being emphasised by different scientists.

The value of focussing on specific cognitive objects over which scientists fail to communicate, rather than on more general communication difficulties between different groups of scientists, is that the articulation of the cognitive objects themselves can be used as the basis for the analysis of the communication breakdown, and for the analysis of controversies. The construction of a specific disputed cognitive object can be used as the defining point around which differing groups of scientists can be identified. The type of communication difficulty associated with specific cognitive objects is to be distinguished from that experienced by competing groups of scientists who, although sharing a reality concern or *doxa*, may not be in conflict over a specific object. Such competing groups, for instance, may be uninterested in, or even unaware of, the work of rival groups. It is important to consider why, in some cases, specific cognitive objects are disputed and, in the case of Bohm, I will attempt to outline some of the social preconditions for the construction of such objects. Before attempting this I will first consider the articulation of disputed objects and, in particular, I will consider two differing modes of articulation.

The two types of articulation I want to consider are what I shall call the *research-area* mode of articulation and the *official-history* mode of articulation. These two modes are to be taken as opposite poles of a spectrum of differing modes of articulation. The research-area mode of articulation occurs when the disputed object forms part of the particular area of concern of scientists involved in the controversy. When their day-to-day work actually consists of exploring the object they can be regarded as articulating it in the research-area mode. An example of such articulation would be scientists actually carrying out gravity-wave experiments. The official-history mode of articulation, by contrast, occurs when the cognitive object is referred to in some other context than the immediate area of concern. Obviously, in using the term 'official history' (12), I regard this context as being mainly the production of a cumulative history or rationalisation of how a particular field developed. For example, references by scientists to the non-existence of gravity waves because the original experiment was not repeatable can be regarded as articulations in the official-history mode.

The main differences between the two modes lie in the notions of change and differentiation of the cognitive object. By definition, the research-area mode of articulation is dynamic because the process of working on a specific object implies some attempt to transform the object, such as, for example, by the addition of *ad hoc* hypotheses. In contrast, the official-history mode is static with the object treated as if it is unchanging and closed, and hence processes such as the addition of *ad hoc* hypotheses will not occur. The amount of differentiation will also, I suggest, be different in the two modes of articulation. In general, in the research-area mode the cognitive object will be well differentiated with the possibility of scientists working on different dimensions of the object. The research-area mode of articulation contains the possibility of a variety of interpretations of the object; for example Collins found that a gravity wave experiment could be interpreted in up to sixteen different ways (13). In the official-history mode the object will be much less differentiated and often a kind of Aristotelian logic will be applied to it. For example, experiments will be regarded as either repeatable or non-repeatable, a proof will be considered to be either valid or invalid.

These two modes of articulation are analytically distinguishable but empirically they may overlap. There may, however, be different empirical ramifications of the two modes of articulation. For instance, the research-area mode of articulation is more likely to appear in scientific journals devoted to the particular specialty to which the cognitive object is closest. The official-history mode of articulation is less likely to appear in such journals because it is difficult to produce scientific papers from the articulation of a static undifferentiated object; it is more likely to appear in review articles, textbooks, Festschriften, book reviews and special lectures.

In analysing the communication breakdown between Bohm and von Neumann I will be concerned with identifying the two modes of articulation. By considering how components of scientific activity are related to the two modes I hope that some understanding of the social and cognitive processes of communication breakdown can be gained.

3. The 'Hidden Variables' Controversy and the Social Preconditions for Bohm's Heterodoxy

The 'hidden variables' controversy stemmed from a heterodox interpretation of the quantum theory, put forward by the physicist David Bohm in 1952. Reconstructions of the history of quantum theory by physicists, historians and philosophers are usually expressed in terms of two distinct cognitive objects. Firstly, the quantum *theory*, characterised by a formalism or a mathematical algorithm, and secondly, the *interpretation* which is usually characterised by doctrines as to the nature of the mathematical constructs and the nature of the reality described by them. This notion that there were two separate objects, a theory and its interpretation, was firmly institutionalised by 1952 and Bohm's heterodox paper was entitled: 'A Suggested *Interpretation* of the Quantum Theory in Terms of Hidden Variabes' (14), (my emphasis).

The social and cognitive processes which led to the development of these two objects would make a fascinating subject for sociological investigation. *Prima facie* they seem·to have involved a most extraordinary episode in the development of physics, with the physics elite holding special congresses to decide on the interpretation of a theory that was presumably already part of an active research programme (15). It not my intention to investigate this problem as my case study focusses on a period when the interpretation was a firmly established cognitive object. However, the problem is of some relevance to Bohm's work for it would seem that the construction of the cognitive object of interpretation can be a means for establishing social control. This is because static cognitive objects, which are the form which most interpretations take, may not be an effective way of challenging a continuing research programme.

Interpretations of the quantum theory tend to be static in character because they always involve the interpretation of something else, which in most cases is the formalism. The formalism is considered to be the 'essence' of the theory, with the interpretation regarded as a mere appendage which can be attached later, and which is interesting if you are philosophically inclined but otherwise is of little importance. As a result, interpretations appear to be closed packages to be picked and chosen according to philosophical biases. The interpretation is usually articulated in the official-history mode, with text-books on quantum theory usually having a section, or more often than not just a paragraph, devoted to 'the interpretation' or 'philosophical issues', which rarely implies that such issues are open problems.

There is no *a priori* reason why a philosophical approach to the quantum theory, if it involves raising basic ontological and epistemological considerations, should not be dynamic in character. Indeed some of the research-area mode articulations of specific philosophical problems by physicists, in the form of paradoxes in quantum physics, have led to research programmes which can be regarded as posing serious challenges to the quantum theory **(16)**. If attempts to establish such rival research programmes are regarded as mere rival *interpretations*, the impact of such a challenge to orthodoxy may be weakened.

An example of this is to be found in Bohm's work dating from 1952. Bohm's paper of 1952, although centering on an interpretation of the quantum theory, goes beyond constructing a static cognitive object. Outlined in the paper is the beginning of a research programme towards the development of the quantum theory by the consideration of certain basic ontological issues. This approach, initiated in Bohm's 1952 paper, was further developed by Bohm in association with other physicists such as Jean-Paul Vigier and Louis de Broglie. This aspect of Bohm's work and its subsequent development in considerable depth is almost always ignored by physicists who, in referring to the 'hidden variables' controversy, usually mention only Bohm's 1952 interpretation **(17)**.

The publication of Bohm's interpretation in *Physical Review* led to a fairly heated controversy. I think a good indication of the heat of a controversy in physics is the extent to which physicists themselves become concerned about the objective image of science being corroded. The 'hidden variables' controversy has raised such issues. For example, the physicist J. M. Jauch has written that: "... the discussions which surround the quest for hidden variables in quantum mechanics have, on both sides of the camp, often been conducted in a spirit of aggressiveness which resembles more the defence of orthodoxy of one ideology than a spirit of scientific objectivity" (18). The physicist, Ballentine, has referred to the issue as being "clouded by emotionalism" (19) and the physicist and philosopher of science, P. W. Bridgman, in 1960 remarked about the "surprising cleavage of present-day physicists into two camps, a cleavage all the more surprising when it is considered that sometimes the complete publicity and objectivity of science are incorporated into the very definition of science" (20).

As controversies in modern science are comparatively rare, with much unorthodox science simply being ignored, it is interesting to consider why Bohm's work should have resulted in controversy. In particular I wish to consider the social conditions leading to the construction of disputed cognitive objects. Bourdieu has recently developed an interesting analogy between capitalism and science and, in discussing the social preconditions for controversies to occur, I will make use of some of his ideas (21).

Bourdieu analyses scientific activity as a competitive struggle with the specific issue at stake being the monopoly of scientific authority. Scientific practices are directed towards the acquisition of scientific authority in terms of prestige, recognition and fame. It is important to realise that Bourdieu does not see scientists competing only for social rewards, but that authority encompasses cognitive authority, such as technical competence, as well as social authority. This view of authority is commensurate with the view that cognitive conflicts in science are inseparably social conflicts.

The struggle to gain scientific authority can be regarded as a struggle to gain what Bourdieu calls the social capital of recognition. In this view scientists are regarded as being engaged in competition to obtain social capital, in which they follow particular investment strategies to ensure a return on their investment. Bourdieu outlines two main investment strategies which scientists can follow to acquire capital. These are *succession strategies*, which bring a small but ever growing return on capital, by scientists producing limited innovations within authorised limits, and *subversion strategies*, which are high-risk investments which bring a large amount of profit, but will only be successful if a scientist can produce a redefinition of the field. In this view scientific revolutions are not merely cognitive redefinitions, but are inseparably social redefinitions, and, in particular, the processes of allocating recognition are redefined by the revolution.

These investment strategies vary at different stages in the development of science and require differing amounts of initial social capital for scientists to successfully follow them. In particular, Bourdieu conceives of modern physics (post Einstein) as requiring high social capital for a scientist to produce a heterodoxy by following a subversion strategy. This is because as science becomes more autonomous the social preconditions for scientific change become increasingly institutionalised within scientific activity. This means that the attempted redefinition can only be achieved by an 'insider' who has acquired the necessary capital. However, if a scientist must 'make his or her name' before producing a heterodoxy the consequences of the redefinition of the field will be weakened because the scientist will already be dependent on the institutionalised cognitive and social structures. Bourdieu's ideas are not sufficiently developed to show the details of the processes involved but I believe that the social preconditions for the 'hidden variables' controversy illustrate a part of this process.

In particular I would like to consider Bohm's own investment strategy, pre-1952, as a succession strategy, which had led Bohm to accumulate considerable social capital before launching into his subversion strategy. I would like also to further illuminate the role of interpretations of the quantum theory by suggesting that Bohm's emphasis on interpretation can be viewed as resulting from the processes of acquiring this capital. Then, if I am correct in my earlier assertion that interpretation is not a particularly effective object by which to achieve a redefinition of the field, the social preconditions for a heterodoxy to arise (social capital requirements) can in this case be seen as related to the outcome of the heterodoxy, a relationship which it is desirable for a social theory of heterodoxy to establish.

Bohm was born in 1917 in Pennsylvania and from 1935 he attended Pennsylvania State College, graduating in 1939. In 1943 he increased his social capital by obtaining a Ph.D. from the University of California, Berkeley, which has one of the most prestigious American physics departments. In 1946 he acquired more capital by his appointment to the position of assistant professor at Princeton, again in a highly prestigious physics department.

Whilst at Princeton Bohm researched into the plasma and produced several theoretical papers on it. These papers were important developments in the field and formed part of Bohm's succession strategy of investment. That Bohm's work on the plasma was a succession rather than subversion strategy is illustrated by an extract from an interview I have conducted with Professor Bohm. When commenting on his work on the plasma, Bohm remarked:

"... that was not challenging anybody, because it was just going along the lines that people generally accepted" (22).

In 1949 Bohm completed his book, *Quantum Theory* (23), which was published in 1951. This book is highly regarded as an exposition of the quantum theory and by 1960 was already in its eighth edition, having become one of the standard texts for university courses. The book adheres to the orthodox interpretation although it contains a theory of measurement which is somewhat different from Bohr's. The emphasis of the book is, unlike that of most expositions, not on the formalism. Bohm wrote in the preface that he had simplified the mathematics sufficiently "to allow the reader to follow the general lines of reasoning without spending too much time on mathematical details". Sections of the book are specifically devoted to philosphical issues and in particular the book contains a clear and novel exposition of the Einstein, Podolsky, and Rosen Paradox (E.P.R.) which is one of the main lacunae in the orthodox interpretation (24). So, although not fully commensurate with Bohr's approach, Bohm's allegiance to Copenhagen is clearly stated, and in particular he agrees with Bohr's approach to E.P.R. and rejects any interpretation in terms of 'hidden variables'. The book was liked by such founding fathers of the quantum theory as Einstein, Bohr and Pauli (25). Einstein, according to Bohm (26), particularly liked the book and thought it was the best exposition of the Copenhagen Interpretation "you could get". This book, then, provided Bohm with further capital and helped him to establish a relationship with the quantum elite.

Following the appearance of his book Bohm was invited by Einstein, who was also at Princeton, to come and discuss the quantum theory with him. Einstein, of course, had never accepted the Copenhagen Interpretation as being the last word in matters microscopic (27). Bohm acknowledges these discussions explicitly in his 1952 paper when he writes: "The author wishes to thank Dr. Einstein for several interesting and stimulating discussions" (28). Apart from Einstein, Bohm was also stimulated by attacks on the Copenhagen

Interpretation by the Soviet physicists, Blokhintsev and Terletskii, which were published in the West at this time (**29**).

Bohm then, by 1952, had accumulated considerable social capital of recognition as reflected by his reputation for 'brilliance' (**30**) and his rapport with the quantum elite over his book on quantum theory. Having followed a succession strategy, Bohm then switched to a subversion strategy with the publication of his heterodox paper (**30a**). I consider that the large amount of capital accumulated by Bohm was a prerequisite for a controversy over his work to occur. Had a physicist with a lesser social capital of recognition produced the rival interpretation it might well have been ignored, but for Bohm, who was 35 (**31**), to come out with a 27 page paper in *Physical Review* (a long paper published in the most prestigious journal, despite special refereeing used for his work (**32**)), with Einstein in the wings and soon with the support of another member of the quantum elite, Louis de Broglie, constituted a real challenge to the orthodox interpretation.

However, having gained the social capital necessary to produce a heterodoxy, Bohm chose to centre his subversion strategy around the cognitive object of interpretation. The emphasis on interpretation can be seen as part of the process whereby Bohm had been acquiring capital. That is, Bohm, by his special insider relation with the elite, had become interested in the elite's problem of interpretation. Bohm had, to a certain extent, been encouraged by the elite to focus on interpretative problems, at the same time as gaining capital from this association. As already mentioned, it is beyond the scope of this paper to show in detail that interpretations are not in general powerful objects on which to centre challenges to the quantum theory, but I think enough has been said to indicate such a possibility in this case. If this is so then it can be seen that the social preconditions for this controversy occurring constrained the possible outcomes of the controversy.

Bohm's heterodox interpretation of quantum mechanics was soon under attack. In particular, members of the quantum elite were quick to reject the interpretation. De Broglie, who had put forward similar ideas at the Solvay Congress in 1926 (**33**), published a criticism of Bohm's work after reading a preprint Bohm had sent him. De Broglie's reaction was described to me by Bohm:

"... I sent it [the preprint] to de Broglie and he wrote back saying he had already done this sort of thing and given it up for various objections" (**34**).

De Broglie had given up his interpretation soon after putting it forward, under pressure from objections by Pauli and because of the little support shown for it. In particular he had expected support from Einstein but in fact received none publicly and, as Bohm put it to me, 'felt alone' (35).

Pauli also reacted quickly to Bohm's preprint, and, as Jammer described it, "Pauli rejected the paper, saying that it was 'old stuff, dealt with long ago' " (36). Bohm, at the time of writing the preprint in 1951, was unaware of de Broglie's earlier interpretation and, on receiving de Broglie's letter, he looked up the objections and found he could answer them. He included these answers as an appendix to the published paper (37). These answers were in part enough to convince de Broglie who then took up his original interpretation again.

Pauli soon put his objections into print, and in a Festschrift dedicated to de Broglie, published in 1953, there was a paper by Pauli specifically criticising both de Broglie's and Bohm's interpretations (38). Pauli criticised Bohm for making "non-symmetrical and arbitrary eliminations" and claimed that Bohm's interpretation "introduced an asymmetry". According to Pauli, no reason for the introduction of the asymmetry could be found in "the system of our experience nor in the mathematical formalism of wave mechanics". This type of criticism was later reiterated by Heisenberg in a Festschrift dedicated to Bohr (39), and by Hanson who accused Bohm of destroying "the very symmetry which we have seen to constitute the power, and the glory, of quantum theory" (40).

Pauli further claimed that Bohm's interpretation was 'metaphysical' and that the only admissible interpretation of quantum mechanics should be based on complementarity. This preference, Pauli stated, was not based on 'philosophical prejudices' but rather on 'physical reasons'. This type of criticism was shared by Heisenberg who considered Bohm's interpretation to be 'metaphysical' as it was an 'exact repetition' of the Copenhagen Interpretation but in a different language.

A further attack on Bohm's interpretation appeared in the de Broglie Festschrift (41). This came from Leon Rosenfeld, a close colleague of Bohr, and one of Bohm's most ardent critics (42). Rosenfeld's main criticism was based on a claim that Bohm was attempting to restore determinism and Rosenfeld devoted most of his paper to showing the implausibility of such a philosophy.

These criticisms typify the sorts of objections put forward against Bohm. They are criticisms which are along the metaphysical dimension of scientific activity and do not involve the construction of a specific cognitive object onto which the dispute could crystallise.

There have been attempts to focus on specific points and one such attempt came from Einstein. Having encouraged Bohm to produce a heterodoxy, Einstein did not much like the form Bohm's interpretation took; he regarded Bohm's interpretation as 'artificial' (43) and 'too cheap' (43a). Apart from these general objections, in a Festschrift dedicated to Max Born, published in 1953 (44), Einstein raised a specific point criticising the implied relation in Bohm's interpretation between the classical and quantum levels. However, Bohm was able to reply to Einstein in the same Festschrift, claiming that Einstein's objection was based on an untenable premise (45). Einstein never replied to Bohm and, as Freistadt put it in a review of Bohm's interpretation published in 1957:

"Bohm's reply to Einstein's objections was left unanswered, without, however, any indication from Einstein whether he agrees with Bohm's reply" (46).

That Bohm was able to get his reply into the same Festschrift indicates his close relation with the quantum elite. The attacks by the quantum elite on Bohm are interesting because they have mainly appeared in Festschriften. Such publications are usually reserved for philosophising physicists and philosophers writing about particular individuals' contributions to physics, histories of particular theories, or individual approaches to general philosophical and physical topics. The contemporaneous nature of many of the attacks on Bohm in such volumes is obviously of interest here. This is a subject for further sociological investigation; such questions as the refereeing system, the amount of controversial material published, and the potential audience of such Festschriften are all pertinent questions to be investigated. Provisionally I suggest that, in this case, this rather special mechanism of social control is related to the articulation of the cognitive object of interpretation.

Apart from Einstein's specific objection (47), there have never been any criticisms of Bohm's interpretation showing it to be 'logically incoherent' or 'empirically inadequate'. In other words the normal ways of rejecting knowledge claims were not used in Bohm's case. Bohm himself has frequently stressed that his interpretation is 'logically consistent' and that it can account for the 'same data' as the orthodox interpretation (48).

Although Bohm's research programme, launched is his 1952 paper, as opposed to his interpretation, gave a possibility of a repeatable experiment (49), no such object was constructed as being in dispute in relation to his interpretation. However, there was one specific cognitive object constructed and disputed and this was a proof which claimed that any interpretation in terms of 'hidden variables' was impossible. It is on this particular cognitive object that the rest of the paper focusses.

4. 'Hidden Variables Impossibility Proofs' and Their Relation to Bohm's Interpretation

The idea of 'hidden variables' was considered in 1926 when it was first realised that the quantum theory was a statistical theory. Max Born considered such a possibility in the same paper in which he outlined his statistical interpretation of the wave function. He wrote:

"But, of course, anybody dissatisfied with these ideas [the statistical interpretation] may feel free to assume that there are additional parameters, not yet introduced into the theory, which determine the individual event" (50).

A useful analogy for understanding what 'hidden variables' were meant to do is the analogy of the causal accounts of molecular motions which were used to explain the apparently random motion of smoke particles suspended in a gas, known as Brownian Motion. Although the position co-ordinates of each smoke particle fluctuate in a random manner, it is nevertheless possible to give an explanation of the motion in terms of the motions of molecules of the gas which collide with the smoke particles. The motion of individual molecules of the gas can, in principle, be described by causal laws, that is by equations which, when the initial conditions are given, describe the motion of gas molecules over space and time. The apparently random motion at one level, that of the smoke particles, can be explained by assuming many collisions with a large number of real individual gas molecules obeying causal laws acting, as it were, at a sub-level (51). Now in quantum theory, only statistical predictions of variables can be derived and so the question arises as to whether the statistical result at one level can be explained in terms of particles acting at a sub-level, that is in a manner analogous to that in which Brownian Motion is explained. To make the assumption of 'hidden variables' is to assume that there are well defined variables acting at a sub-level which produce the randomness at the quantum level.

The possibility of a 'hidden variables' or 'hidden parameters' interpretation was considered by the German mathematician John von Neumann in 1932. In his book on the mathematical foundations of quantum theory (52) he formulated a proof that such an interpretation was impossible. Von Neumann regarded his proof as being of such importance that he devoted part of the preface to discussing it, although the proof only occupied 20 pages of the 445-page book. In introducing his proof he remarked:

"Whether or not an explanation ... by means of hidden parameters, is possible for quantum mechanics, is a much discussed question. The view that it will sometime be answered in the affirmative has at present prominent representatives" (53).

The structure of von Neumann's proof will be elaborated below when I compare it with Bohm's interpretation; all that is needed at this stage is to know that von Neumann defined 'hidden variables' in terms of various axioms, and that he defined the quantum theory by various axioms. By assuming that a 'hidden variables' theory must also obey these axioms, he showed that such a theory was inevitably in contradiction with the quantum theory and, as the quantum theory was well validated, he concluded that a 'hidden variables' theory must be impossible. Von Neumann stated this conclusion by saying "... we need not go any further into the mechanism of the 'hidden parameters', since we now know that the established results of quantum mechanics can never be re-derived with their help" (54), and he made his position absolutely clear when he stated:

"It is therefore not, as is often assumed, a question of a re-interpretation of quantum mechanics, − the present system of quantum mechanics would have to be objectively false, in order that another description of the elementary processes than the statistical one be possible" (55).

The proof was accepted and welcomed (56) by the physics elite and was not challenged for 20 years. For example, Pascual Jordan remarked in 1943 that:

"There is only one interpretation ... which is capable of conceptually ordering the ... totality of experimental results in the field of atomic physics" (57).

In the editorial of a special issue of *Dialectica* published in 1947 and devoted to the interpretation of quantum mechanics, another leading quantum physicist, Pauli, wrote on the subject of 'hidden variables':

"In this connection I may also refer to von Neumann's well known proof that the consequences of quantum mechanics cannot be amended by additional statements on the distribution of values of observables, based on the fixing of values of some hidden parameters, without changing some consequences of present quantum mechanics" (58).

Although no physicist challenged von Neumann's proof before 1952, its validity was challenged in 1935 by the philosopher Grete Hermann (59). She claimed that one of the axioms introduced by von Neumann, which the 'hidden variables' were supposed to obey, was, in fact, an axiom to which no 'hidden variables' theory could possibly adhere. She claimed, therefore, that all the proof showed was that if one assumed self-contradictory axioms one could derive self-contradictory results. Hermann's criticism has been largely ignored although, ironically, it was essentially this criticism which was later adopted by physicists as showing the proof's irrelevance to 'hidden variables' theories (60).

The validity of the proof was challenged by another philosopher, Hans Reichenbach, in 1944. He pointed out that von Neumann had not shown that 'hidden variables' were logically impossible, as the proof depended on the validity of von Neumann's conception of the quantum theory, and, of course, this theory could change. Reichenbach writes (61):

"... we cannot adduce *logical* reasons excluding such a further development of physics ... although some eminent physicists believe in such a possibility" (my emphasis).

The degree of success achieved by the proof in preventing 'hidden variables' approaches being developed can be gauged from the remarks of the physicist F. J. Belinfante in his recent review of 'hidden variables' interpretations (62). Belinfante writes that "The truth, however, happens to be that for decades nobody spoke up against von Neumann's arguments, and that his conclusions were quoted by some as the gospel" and he goes on to say that "... the authority of von Neumann's over-generalised claim for nearly two decades stifled any progress in the search for hidden-variables theories."

Von Neumann's proof was an important objection which Bohm had to overcome in 1952. Bohm has stressed to me that that one of the main reasons he put forward his interpretation was to overcome the logical objection that it could not be done (**63**). Bohm's interpretation claimed to do what von Neumann had declared to be impossible; that is it claimed to be logically consistent and to account for the same data as the quantum theory. Bohm devotes a section of his 1952 paper to von Neumann's proof claiming that the proof does not apply to his interpretation because von Neumann had not considered the possibility of 'hidden variables' in the measuring apparatus as he himself had done. This reason alone is not enough to show the invalidity of the proof as Bell was able to show in 1966 (**64**).

Bohm's interpretation can be regarded as an articulation of the disputed cognitive object of von Neumann's proof. Bohm was, in effect, disputing the proof by producing a counter-example to it. Bohm's interpretation was a challenge to von Neumann's proof for, if a 'hidden variables' theory was literally impossible, it had to be shown where Bohm's interpretation was wrong. Bohm's articulation of von Neumann's proof can be regarded as being in the research-area mode. Bohm was making a contribution to the research problem of the validity of von Neumann's proof and, more generally, to the problem of axiomatisation of the quantum theory because Bohm's counter-example could be interpreted as showing the limits of von Neumann's axiomatic approach to the quantum theory. Bohm expressed his articulation in the appropriate journal for reporting theoretical investigations, that is in *Physical Review.*

The response of the elite to Bohm's articulation was also to articulate von Neumann's proof and to dispute Bohm's challenge to it. However, I believe that much of the reponse of the elite has been in the official-history mode. That is, the elite would cite the proof as ruling out the possibility of 'hidden variables' but would not explore how Bohm's interpretation failed in relation to the proof. Their articulation seems mainly to have been of the static, undifferentiated kind such as asserting that 'hidden variables' are impossible because the proof is valid.

For example, Rosenfeld simply places his faith in von Neumann when he writes about "... the celebrated reasoning by which von Neumann earlier showed the formal incompatibility of quantum mechanics and determinism" (**65**). Another example of this type of articulation came from F. Cap, in a review article of 1956. Cap wrote:

"This speculation is known to have been refuted by Neumann; if present-day quantum theories are correct – and this can hardly be doubted in view of the fine successes achieved — such hidden parameters cannot possibly exist, for if this were the case the quantum theories would give different results" (66).

There is a problem in finding evidence of the use of von Neumann's proof in relation to Bohm's work because articulation in the official-history mode cannot normally be expressed in scientific papers reserved for expressing the results of research-area mode articulation of cognitive objects. That is to say it would be difficult to get a paper published simply asserting that Bohm was wrong and von Neumann was correct. It would also be difficult to integrate such articulation with other arguments against Bohm's interpretation for if it is believed that Bohm's interpretation is logically impossible there would be little point in producing other criticisms of the interpretation. If, as seems likely, articulation in the official-history mode occurs mainly at the informal level, then evidence of it can best be recaptured from accounts of the informal activity of scientists. Unfortunately there were no contemporaneous sociologists of science interested in the problem who could have conducted interviews with scientists to obtain details of the informal articulation process. However, some details of the use of von Neumann's proof can be obtained from accounts by philosophers, especially philosophers who actually talked to scientists.

One such account comes from the physicist turned philosopher, P. W. Bridgman, who remarked in 1960:

"Now the mere mention of concealed variables is sufficient to automatically elicit from the elect the remark that John von Neumann gave absolute proof that this way out is not possible. To me it is a curious spectacle to see the unanimity with which the members of a certain circle accept the rigor of von Neumann's proof" (67).

Further evidence on who comprised the membership of the 'certain circle' can be gained from the account of N. Hanson who had many personal contacts with physicists. Hanson wrote in 1958:

"... Bohm tries to meet von Neumann's formidable proof of the impossibility of such an interpretation of quantum theory. Whether he succeeds cannot be examined here; in conversation Heisenberg, Oppenheimer, Dirac and Bethe have expressed to me their strongest doubts" (68).

It seems clear from both Hanson's and Bridgman's remarks that it was mainly the quantum elite who used the proof against Bohm.

Further evidence on the mode of articulation of those using the proof comes from Dr. E. W. Bastin, a well known critic of the orthodox interpretation of the quantum theory. He has told me that those physicists who used von Neumann's proof against Bohm, in his experience, did so without 'ever going into' the proof (**69**).

The failure to explore in detail the relationship between the proof and Bohm's work was, to a certain extent, shared by those who considered the proof to be irrelevant to the assessment of Bohm's interpretation. For instance Pauli, unlike most of the elite, considered that "This manner of avoiding von Neumann's theory ... is indeed without contradiction" (**70**), but he did not show how Bohm managed to avoid the proof. Similarly de Broglie (**71**) reached the conclusion that the proof was fairly trivial in the context of 'hidden variables' and "did not greatly add to what was already known, since the conclusion is already implied in the uncertainty relations", but, like Bohm himself, he was not able to show in detail why the proof was invalid. I think it is generally true that much of the articulation of the proof in the context of Bohm's interpretation has been in the official-history mode.

Von Neumann's proof has, in the 1950's and early 1960's, been examined by physicists, philosophers and mathematicians, but not specifically in the context of Bohm's work. I do not intend to go into the details of these papers here and accounts of them can be found elsewhere (**72**). These papers were possibly stimulated by Bohm's 1952 paper but they did not play a direct part in the 'hidden variables' controversy. The situation over the validity of the proof seems to have been characterised by confusion as Bohm (**73**), Ballentine (**74**) and Jammer (**75**) have asserted. This confusion is expressed in a paper published by H. Nabl in 1959 (**76**). He pointed out how greatly ten different physicists differed in their evaluation of the proof. He complained that no clear-cut answer existed as to whether the proof had ever been refuted and he appealed to all physicists and mathematicians to attempt to clarify the issue and to provide an unambiguous answer to the question.

With the validity of the proof in question there was, in 1957, an attempt to formulate a new proof against the possibility of 'hidden variables'. This proof was formulated by two physicists, J. M. Jauch and his student, C. Piron (**77**). Jauch, who had been a colleague of Pauli, belonged to that group of physicists who, like von Neumann, favoured an axiomatic approach to the quantum theory. Jauch and Piron, in the introduction to their proof, claimed that full justice had not been done to von Neumann and they remarked that "Bohm ... even goes so far as to accuse von Neumann of circular reasoning." They continue by saying that "If this were true, this 'proof' would mean, of course, exactly nothing and would leave all doors for speculations on a 'sub-quantum mechanical level' and a 'deeper reality'." Jauch and Piron, although obviously addressing their proof against Bohm's work, made no attempt to show how Bohm's interpretation escaped von Neumann's proof or what its relation was to their own proof.

The situation as regards von Neumann's proof and the further proof of Jauch and Piron was not clarified until the appearance of a paper written by J. S. Bell in 1964, lost in the editorial office of the journal, *Reviews of Modern Physics*, for two years (78), and thus finally appearing in that journal in 1966. In this paper Bell claimed to refute both von Neumann's proof and the further proof of Jauch and Piron. The approach Bell adopted was to construct, as Bohm had done previously, a simple consistent 'hidden variables' theory of quantum mechanics from which, he was able to show, all the usual statistical results of the quantum theory could be derived. Having done this, Bell asked how it was possible to do so if von Neumann's proof ruled out such a possibility. Bell was able to clarify the issue by actually showing how von Neumann's proof was related to such a theory. Bell found that one of the axioms introduced by von Neumann, to which it was assumed that a 'hidden variables' theory must adhere, was in fact an impossible axiom for any 'hidden variables' theory, which was to reproduce the results of the quantum theory, to contain. Without this axiom the contradiction between 'hidden variables' and von Neumann's conception of the quantum theory could not be shown. Thus the results of von Neumann's proof and, as Bell went on to show, Jauch's and Piron's proof were assumed in the axioms. Belinfante sums up the situation nicely when he writes that "each of these authors [of the proofs] defined hidden-variables theory by some set of postulates which then later they proved to be self-contradictory" (79).

Bell's paper stimulated Bohm to produce a new theory of 'hidden variables'. This theory was presented in a paper written by Bohm and J. Bub (80), which was published in *Reviews of Modern Physics* alongside Bell's paper. Bohm and Bub also published, in the same issue, a separate refutation of Jauch's and Piron's proof obtained by expanding on Bell's refutation of the proof (81). The fact that Bohm took the opportunity of publishing a new 'hidden variables' theory at the same time as Bell refuted von Neumann's proof indicates the influence that the proof has had on the 'hidden variables' issue.

The results of Bell's research-area mode articulation of von Neumann's proof seem to have been accepted by those physicists interested in the problem. This is evidenced partly by those previously adhering to the impossibility proofs never having published a refutation of Bell's work. The only criticism of Bell's work, published by such scientists (82), has come in the form of a sharply worded letter in *Reviews of Modern Physics* (83). In this letter Jauch and Piron claim that Bell's work is '*ad hoc*' and conclude that "It is contrary to good scientific methodology to modify a generally verified scientific theory for the sole purpose of accommodating hidden variables." Jammer (84), Ballentine (85) and Belinfante (86), in their commentaries on von Neumann's proof, all agree that Bell's paper has been the essential one in clarifying the issue. That Bell's refutation has now even become institutionalised in textbooks can be seen from the comments of L. Eisenbud in his textbook, *The Conceptual Foundations of Quantum Mechanics*. Eisenbud writes in a footnote that:

"It was shown by von Neumann, with the aid of certain rather general and apparently harmless assumptions, that hidden variables are inconsistent with the results of quantum mechanics. For many years it was believed that his 'proof' showed that hidden variables could not exist. But any theorem is no more than an expression of the hidden content of the assumptions on which it is based. With a slight change in von Neumann's assumptions, J. S. Bell showed that it is possible for hidden variables to be consistent with the statements of quantum mechanics" (87).

In other words the official-history mode articulation of von Neumann's proof is today that the proof is invalid.

Further evidence that physicists now accept that von Neumann's proof is inadequate comes from the fact that they are now questioning why the proof was considered valid for such a long period. Already the proof is being reconstructed as nothing more that just a mistake. For example, Belinfante remarks that: "The lack of validity of 31 [the axiom Bell questioned] in any decent hidden-variables theory should have been obvious to anybody by inspection" (88).

The attitude of regarding the proof as *just* a mistake and playing down its importance can be seen in the remarks of von Neumann's friend, Eugene Wigner, who was in Berlin at the same time as von Neumann and shared a professorship with him at Princeton. Wigner acknowledges that Bell has shown the irrelevance of the proof to 'hidden variables', but he goes on to claim that von Neumann himself was not convinced by the proof. Wigner writes:

"As an old friend of von Neumann, and in order to preserve historical accuracy the present writer may be permitted the observation that the proof contained in this book [von Neumann's book] was not the one which was principally responsible for von Neumann's conviction of the inadequacy of hidden variables theories " (89).

Wigner later writes: "Apparently, even mathematicians are convinced occasionally by considerations which they cannot formulate in a rigorous fashion" (90). So what was it that convinced von Neumann? Wigner writes:

"... the point which the present discussion is trying to make is that all schemes of hidden parameters which either von Neumann himself, or anyone else whom he knew, could think of ... had some feature which made it unattractive, in fact unreasonable. This was, in my opinion, the true reason for his conviction of the inadequacy of the theories of hidden variables" (91).

However, if von Neumann himself merely found such theories *unattractive*, the problem remains of what role a proof which claimed they were *impossible* played.

Since Bell's refutation of von Neumann's and Jauch's and Piron's proofs, there have appeared several further proofs. All these proofs have met with severe difficulties (92) and, in a review article of such proofs published in 1970 (93), the authors considered that all such proofs had been refuted apart from that of a mathematician, S. Gudder. Within two years Gudder's proof was refuted (94) but by this stage Gudder was himself questioning what was happening. In a paper published in 1970, he noted that Bohm's 1952 theory had never been shown to be inconsistent and this led him to remark with great clarity:

"Clearly there is something wrong here. One obviously cannot have an HV [hidden variables] theory if it is impossible" (95)!

Gudder decided, as Bell had done previously, that the root of the confusion lay in what was meant by a 'hidden variables' theory. Gudder then formulated a new 'proof', based on Bohm's definition of 'hidden variables', which showed that 'hidden variables' were *always possible*!

The transformation of a proof of the impossible into a proof of the always possible led me to formulate the title of this paper: 'What Does a Proof Do If

It Does Not Prove?' The transformation of such proofs, mainly achieved by the research-area mode articulations of Bell, Bub (**96**) and Gudder, has led to some insights into the relation between Bohm's interpretation and von Neumann's proof; these insights will be explored in the next section where I reconstruct aspects of the cognitive content of Bohm's and von Neumann's work.

The realisation that 'hidden variables impossibility proofs' do not rule out 'hidden variables' has not led to the success of Bohm's interpretation or any other such theory. Bohm's 1952 interpretation is today largely ignored and, as Bohm, who no longer subscribes to the interpretation himself, recently put it to me:

"... in general the physics community has become less and less interested in any of these questions, even points that were understood are probably sliding into obscurity for most people" (**97**).

5. Bohm's Interpretation and von Neumann's Proof — Their Cognitive Relation

In order to understand the failure to communicate over the proof it is necessary to reconstruct parts of the cognitive structure of Bohm's interpretation and von Neumann's proof. In doing this I will make use, in particular, of Bell's 1966 analysis, for the essential part of this analysis involved showing the cognitive relation between Bohm and von Neumann.

I take the central thesis of Bohm's interpretation to be that he is offering a doctrine opposed to the 'indeterminateness of state description' of the Copenhagen Interpretation. This doctrine upholds that, during the interaction of two mechanical systems, the dynamical states of the two systems cannot be well defined. This means that it becomes meaningless (as opposed to false) to ascribe a definite energy to either state. Bohm's interpretation centred on an opposing doctrine whereby it is meaningful to conceptualise the states of physical systems as being well defined. Bohm's doctrine was that, in principle, the problem of conceptualising quantum-mechanical states is similar to the problem of conceptualising states in classical mechanics; this is clearly illustrated when he writes:

"In contrast to the usual interpretation, this alternative interpretation permits us to conceive of each individual system as being in a precisely definable state, whose changes with time are determined by definite laws, analogous to (but not identical with) the classical equations of motion" (98).

Bohm was careful to stress that his interpretation was only an analogy with classical mechanics. It was analogous in the sense that the conception of classical states and of quantum states was in principle the same, as Bohm stated:

"... in our description, the problem of objective reality at the quantum level is at least in principle not fundamentally different from that at the classical level" (99).

Bohm's theory is not a classical theory because he adheres to Bohr's doctrine of the mutual exclusiveness of experimental arrangements. This doctrine emphasises the crucial role of experimental arrangements in Bohr's principle of complementarity (100). Essentially, Bohr considered that the concepts which are applicable to a given physical system depend upon the entire physical situation in which the system is located, including, in particular, the measuring apparatus involved. This means that when two incompatible quantities are being measured, for instance wave and particle properties of a system, not only are the concepts mutually exclusive but so also are the experimental arrangements to which these concepts are applicable.

This can perhaps be seen most clearly when we consider making individual measurements of the spin components of a particle. The spin components in two different directions, say σ_x along the x-axis and σ_y along the y-axis, are incompatible: that is, the operators, which are the mathematical representation of the spin components, do not commute ($\sigma_x \sigma_y - \sigma_y \sigma_x \neq 0$). This means that to make a measurement σ_x with a Stern-Gerlach magnet requires a different orientation of the apparatus from that required to make a measurement σ_y. In other words, the two different orientations form mutually exclusive experimental arrangements. To find the sum of $\sigma_x + \sigma_y$ requires a third orientation or a third mutually exclusive experimental arrangement, as $\sigma_x + \sigma_y$ is incompatible with σ_x and σ_y. The physical importance of the doctrine of mutually exclusive experimental arrangements is that individual measurements of incompatible properties cannot be added together without considering the experimental arrangements concerned.

This aspect of complementarity was not challenged by Bohm and played an integral part in the measurement theory of his interpretation. As Bohm stated:

"... in our interpretation of measurements of the type that can now be carried out, the distribution of hidden parameters varies in accordance with the different mutually exclusive experimental arrangements" (**101**).

For Bohm, as for Bohr, the role of the measuring apparatus was crucial but Bohm differed from Bohr in that for him, in principle, the state of the measuring apparatus could be precisely defined in terms of 'hidden variables'. As Bohm put it:

"We differ from Bohr, however, in that we have proposed a method by which the role of the apparatus can be analysed and described in principle in a precise way, whereas Bohr asserts that a precise conception of the details of the measurement processes is as a matter of principle unattainable" (**102**).

I have emphasised the main features of Bohm's interpretation relevant to this reconstruction. In reconstructing von Neumann's proof I will emphasise only the structure of the proof and the types of physical assumptions made. The proof is formulated in a highly abstract algebra, but the mathematics of the proof will not concern me here; the mathematics has only rarely been called into question and most authors who are technically competent to judge, today argue that von Neumann's mathematics were rigorous (**103**).

For von Neumann, a 'hidden variables' theory was a causal theory which defined the state of a system absolutely by supplying additional and numerical data — these additional data constituted the 'hidden variables'. If all these additional parameters were known then "we could give the values of all physical quantities exactly and with certainty" (**104**). A 'hidden variables' theory should be one which is "... in agreement with experiment, and which gives the statistical assertions of quantum mechanics when only ϕ [the wave function in his terminology] is given (and an averaging is performed over the other co-ordinates [the 'hidden variables'])" (**105**).

Von Neumann produced a mathematical definition of 'hidden variables' in terms of dispersion-free ensembles — dispersion-free meaning that the variables exhibit no statistical spread (**106**). Having defined 'hidden variables' he next postulated five axioms (**107**) from which the statistical results of the quantum theory could be derived via a statistical matrix. One of these axioms, 5, (**108**) was a mathematical condition on the way in which dispersion-free ensembles or dispersive ensembles were combined together. Von Neumann then showed that 'hidden variables' could not exist because he could derive no dispersion-free ensembles that could reproduce the statistical results of the quantum theory.

The proof can be regarded as involving a process of theory comparison. Properties essential for the existence of 'hidden variables', that certain statistical results should be reproduced and that dispersion-free ensembles should exist, are shown to be in contradiction with the quantum theory, the point of comparison being a statistical matrix from which the results of the quantum theory could be derived but not the existence of dispersion-free ensembles. What von Neumann should have concluded according to this reconstruction was that 'hidden variables' defined in a certain manner by him were in contradiction with his conception of the quantum theory. This does not mean that 'hidden variables' are impossible, for to assume that is to assume that current definitions of the quantum theory will always be valid and that the definition of 'hidden variables' used in the proof is appropriate.

It was the essence of Bell's work on von Neumann's proof that, by constructing a simple 'hidden variables' theory, he was able to carry out the theory comparison attempted above and was able to show which axiom of von Neumann's proof implicitly ruled out such a theory. To illustrate Bell's analysis I would like to consider how Bohm's theory related to the theory comparison attempted by von Neumann. What I intend to show is that only certain dimensions of Bohm's theory were considered by the proof, and that the impossibility of 'hidden variables' was only achieved by neglecting a crucial dimension of Bohm's theory.

The dimension of Bohm's theory that was ignored by the proof was Bohm's allegiance to Bohr's doctrine of mutually exclusive experimental arrangements. The possibility of a theory adhering to this doctrine was implicitly ruled out by the fifth axiom of the proof. This axiom expressed a certain mathematical rule that 'hidden variables' had to obey. This axiom states that for arbitrary observables, $R, S,$ ..., and arbitrary real numbers, $a, b,$ ..., we must have

$$\langle aR + bS + ... \rangle = a\langle R \rangle + b\langle S \rangle + ...$$

for all possible states or ensembles in which the averages must be calculated.

This axiom articulates the requirement that the average of the sum of two observables be equal to the sum of the averages taken separately. Now it is a property of dispersion-free states that the eigenvalues of such states are equal to the expectation values for such states (expectation values are the average values of observables, and eigenvalues refer to the individual values of possible results of measurements). To illustrate this property of dispersion-free states it is helpful to conceive of quantum-mechanical measurement as the actualisation of a potentiality. The quantum state, described by a wave function, can be regarded as a potentiality which, on measurement, is actualised into a definite state. This state is called an eigenstate and the observable can have one of several values called eigenvalues. Each individual measurement or actualisation leads to a different eigenvalue and it is not possible to predict the individual eigenvalue the actualisation will produce. However it is possible to predict from the theory the expectation value or average value of many such measurements, this being calculated from the wave function. Dispersion-free states, however, are described by a uniquely defined wave function and hence each actualisation leads to the same eigenvalue. The expectation value for many measurements (of a particular type) therefore equals the eigenvalue, as the dispersion-free states actualise into the same value for each measurement.

This property of dispersion-free states, when expressed in terms of axiom 5, means that the eigenvalues (now the right hand side of the equation in axiom 5) must obey a simple linear relationship, and, for $a = b = 1$, that the results of two successive measurements on R and S must equal the sum of the eigenvalues of R and S.

However, a 'hidden variables' theory that is to account for the sum of individual measurements made by mutually exclusive experimental arrangements, as Bohm's theory was designed to do, cannot obey axiom 5. This is because such measurements depend on the choice of experimental arrangements, which means that the sums of such measurements are not linearly related to the eigenvalues. In the example of measurements on the spin of a particle, the sum of the two components, $(\sigma_x + \sigma_y)$, could only be determined by a third measurement. The result of the measurement, an eigenvalue of $(\sigma_x + \sigma_y)$, would be the result neither of adding an eigenvalue of σ_x and an eigenvalue of σ_y nor of adding any linear combination of them. That the ensemble average or expectation value of many measurements of $(\sigma_x + \sigma_y)$, $\langle(\sigma_x + \sigma_y)\rangle$, should be equal to the sum of the averages of two other measurements involving different experimental arrangements, $\langle\sigma_x\rangle + \langle\sigma_y\rangle$, is apparently a peculiar and non-trivial property of quantum states **(109)**. Thus, axiom 5, although true for quantum states, could not be applied to dispersion-free states that were required to reproduce individual measurements.

Bohm's interpretation, as already stated, was in agreement with Bohr's doctrine of mutually exclusive experimental arrangements. The proof did not relate to Bohm's theory because the proof had tacitly assumed that a 'hidden variables' theory did not obey the doctrine and thus a crucial dimension of Bohm's theory was ignored. The fact that Bohm's theory was in line with Bohr's doctrine of mutually exclusive experimental arrangements, although clearly stated by Bohm, has, as Jammer described it, "almost universally been ignored" (110). Bub (111) has also pointed out that it has not generally been recognised that Bohm's theory was highly non-classical, as any theory adhering to Bohr's doctrine of mutually exclusive experimental arrangements inevitably must be.

Since Bell's work, some of those responsible for formulating 'hidden variables impossibility proofs' have made explicit the type of theory they have been trying to eliminate. For instance, Jauch and Piron in 1968 wrote that their definition of such a theory had been the same as von Neumann's "and all other discussions of the hidden variables problem known to us" (112). Misra, another author of such proofs, has, since Bell's work, also started to question what he calls his 'tacit assumptions' (113) concerning the nature of 'hidden variables' theories. He admits that one such assumption is to neglect Bohr's doctrine of mutually exclusive experimental arrangements. This assumption is made in the spirit of preventing 'hidden variables' from dissolving into 'a fog ot mysticism' and to make the search for them 'a meaningful scientific pursuit'.

6. An Explanation of the Failure to Communicate

The 'hidden variables' controversy and the special role played by von Neumann's 'well known' (114), 'formidable' (115), 'celebrated' (116), and 'famous' (117) proof have not passed without several suggestions emerging for their appropriate analysis. The political aspect of the dispute had been suggested as being important by Jammer (118), and the religious aspect by Belinfante (119), but neither author develops these ideas in any detail. In analysing the role of von Neumann's proof I feel it is necessary to go beyond Jammer's historical reconstruction (120); nor do I feel one should rely, as Belinfante does (121), on there being "some magic in his arguments that could fool people into believing that *his* definition of a hidden-variables theory would be the only correct one rather than the obviously inappropriate one" (Belinfante's emphasis).

The communication problem between Bohm and von Neumann has recently been analysed by Bohm himself (122). He does not deal specifically with von Neumann's proof and his analysis is mainly directed towards more general communication problems, although he does produce an analysis concerning the differences between von Neumann and other quantum physicists over the cognitive object of the 'measurement problem'. Bohm's conception of science as perception-communication and his attempt to explain the cognitive differentiation between von Neumann's and other approaches in terms of a 'habit of thinking' (123) and 'tacit' (124) and 'subliminal' (125) differences in individual judgements, indicate that he seeks mainly a psycho-linguistic explanation of communication failure. I regard this lack of sociological emphasis as the main weakness in his account (126), but nevertheless he has drawn attention to important problems in need of sociological explanation. For instance, his remarks on the stabilisation (127) of confusion are in need of sociological extension. Also he has indicated that his psycho-linguistic analysis is related to the metaphysical commitments of scientists. In particular he has accounted for the adverse reaction to his own work as being the result of most scientists being committed to the language of dynamics (128). In analysing the role of metaphysical commitments in the 'hidden variables' controversy below, I will make use of some ideas on metaphysics which are, I believe, fairly close to Bohm's, but which are not hampered by the linguistic analogy. In particular I will consider scientists' metaphysical commitments in terms of Georgescu-Roegen's concept of arithmomorphism (129).

So far, in dealing with the communication problem between Bohm and von Neumann, I have focussed on the specific object of von Neumann's proof. Of course there are other objects which illustrate this communication breakdown, such as, for example, the 'measurement problem' in quantum mechanics. By concentrating on a specific cognitive object and considering its transformation and mode of articulation, I believe more understanding of the detailed social and cognitive processes involved can be achieved. I am not denying that specific failures to communicate are linked to other developments and my outline of the social preconditions for the controversy to occur was an attempt to draw such links. The relation of the cognitive object to other developments in science is, as I have already suggested, to be found by elucidating the various components of scientific activity. In particular I would like to consider the relation of· the metaphysical component to the cognitive object of von Neumann's proof. It is, I believe, the metaphysical divisions identified in this case study which are most important in considerations of how this particular dispute is linked to wider developments.

There is a special need for caution in analysing the metaphysical component of science, which stems from the difficulties in imputing metaphysics. Scientists' metaphysical commitments are rarely articulated and, when articulated, are often expressed in a confused or contradictory manner. This leads to the problem of deciding which is the more important commitment, the explicit commitment to a particular metaphysical doctrine or the implicit commitment which can be imputed from other cognitive commitments. This problem is particularly pressing when considering commitments to general philosophical positions. For example, it might appear to be promising to analyse the 'hidden variables' controversy as a conflict between Bohm's realism and Bohr's, Heisenberg's and von Neumann's instrumentalism. Although Bohm claimed in his 1952 paper that his interpretation was based on "the simple assumption that the world as a whole is objectively real" (130), the question immediately arises as to what brand of realism it was to which Bohm was committed and how far his work was based on this principle. For example, Bohm's adherence to Bohr's doctrine of mutually exclusive experimental arrangements, a doctrine which some philosophers have considered to be a relational doctrine (131), could be considered as going beyond the realist assumption Bohm outlined in 1952. Apart from the philosophical problems of imputing Bohm's position, in order to reconstruct Bohr's Heisenberg's and von Neumann's positions one would need to carry out an extensive historical analysis which would involve one in the philosophical disputes as to what these positions were (132).

Narrowing down from general philosophical positions to specific commitments, one such important commitment in the 'hidden variables' issue might be considered to be causality. Paul Forman, in his account of the development of the quantum theory in the Weimar Republic, chooses to centre his analysis on causality, a metaphysical commitment he considers to be related to styles of thought in the Weimar Republic (133). However, it is not clear how Forman has overcome the problem of what physicists mean by causality; the fact that scientists express belief in the 'causal principle' does not mean that they may not use quite a different notion of causality in their scientific work.

Causality has been notoriously confused in the 'hidden variables' controversy. For example, von Neumann claimed that his proof meant that "there is at present no occasion and no reason to speak of causality in nature" (134) at the same time as maintaining that "it would be an exaggeration to maintain that causality has thereby been done away with" (135). Von Neumann's contradictory position has not always been realised by physicists who, as Jammer (136) and Feyerabend (137) have noted, have considered that von Neumann had done away with causality for ever.

Bohm, in his 1952 paper, refers to the laws which govern quantum states as being, in principle, causal and continuous. It is not clear what Bohm meant by causality in this context and he has told me that his notion of causality then was not well articulated (138). There is evidence that some physicists have understood the interpretation as advocating a return to the determinism of classical mechanics (139). This view of Bohm's work has been enhanced by Bohm and some of his supporters referring to the interpretation as the *causal* interpretation (140). Bohm's views on causality were not fully articulated until his book, *Causality and Chance in Modern Physics* (141), was published in 1957, by which time he was referring to his 1952 paper as the "so-called causal interpretation" (142).

Apart from the problem of imputing what was meant by causality in this context there is also the problem of relating the metaphysical principle to other social and cognitive structures. It might be tempting to relate causality to the use of von Neumann's proof by hypothesising that those formulating and using the proofs considered that a 'hidden variables' theory must be causal and hence of a classical or phase-space type and thus could not possibly adhere to Bohr's doctrine of mutually exclusive experimental arrangements. This attempt to link causality to von Neumann's proof would only be justified if it was apparent that those using the proofs to reject Bohm's interpretation were aware of the crucial importance of Bohr's doctrine in relation to the proof. The role of Bohr's doctrine was, however, not articulated until 1966, by Bell, well after the interest in Bohm's interpretation had abated, and there seems to me to be little evidence indicating that causality was important in the cognitive assessment of the validity of von Neumann's proof.

The main problem with causality appears to be that it has, in this dispute, been treated as 'window dressing'. That is, it is difficult to ascertain the underlying divisions by considering causality, because physicists seem to produce cognitive objects which they then call causal or acausal rather than basing their work on any commitment to a particular notion of causality. If causality is used in this manner, then it is difficult to see how social constraints, such as physicists' work situations, relate to causality and to communication breakdown.

Bohm himself has told me that the causality issue has been comparatively unimportant in the controversy (143). The present author considers that causality may have been important in the context of von Neumann's original formulation of the proof but that the communication breakdown over the proof cannot be explained in terms of causality.

I would like now to consider another approach to ascertaining the relevant metaphysical components in the 'hidden variables' controversy. This approach is based on the concept of arithmomorphism introduced by Georgescu-Roegen in his book, *The Entropy Law and the Economic Process* (144). Arithmomorphic concepts are concepts that are amenable to logical (in the narrow Aristotelian sense) sifting. Georgescu-Roegen argues that logic can only handle a restricted class of concepts, that is arithmomorphic concepts. This is because "every one of them is as discretely distinct as a single number in relation to the infinity of all others" (145). In introducing the notion of arithmomorphic concepts, that is concepts which are logically discrete and additive, he is particularly interested in distinguishing such concepts from dialectical concepts, that is concepts which emphasise forms and qualities. Dialectical concepts are specifically defined as concepts which violate the Principle of Contradiction 'B cannot be both A and not-A' (146). He argues that dialectical concepts are as relevant to science as arithmomorphic concepts and that the barring of dialectical concepts from science leads to a situation of 'empty axiomatisation' (147) and 'arithmomania' (148).

It is not my intention to elucidate or defend Georgescu-Roegen's analysis of science (149), but I do intend to make use of his concept of arithmomorphism, because I believe it provides an important means of characterising cognitive objects which helps to illuminate the communication breakdown over von Neumann's proof.

I believe that Bohr's emphasis on experimental arrangements via his principle of the mutual exclusiveness of experimental arrangements is an example of a dialectical concept. If the case of complementary properties of waves and particles is considered, Bohr's doctrine can be seen to violate the principle of contradiction. That is a particular quantum system, (B), can be described in terms of waves, (A), and particles, (not-A), depending on the choice of experimental arrangements. The failure of von Neumann's proof to capture Bohr's doctrine can then be understood as a failure to express a dialectical concept. That is, I am suggesting that the mathematical and logical form of von Neumann's proof was such that it could only handle arithmomorphic concepts, and that von Neumann ignored Bohr's doctrine because a dialectical concept could not be expressed in terms of his proof. The whole essence of von Neumann's proof is axiomatisation, that is, there are a few basic propositions (axioms) from which the rest of the 'theory' is deduced. In order for axiomatisation to work, the process of deductive reasoning must be used and there must be deductive chains linking the 'theory' to the axioms, but if logic depends, as Georgescu-Roegen asserts (150), on the property of discrete distinctness in concepts as well as in symbols, then no axiomatic proof can manipulate a concept such as Bohr's doctrine, which emphasises the continuation or 'wholeness' of apparatus and quantum system.

The difficulty of capturing Bohr's doctrine in a logical proof or axiomatic system is nicely illustrated by the quantum logician Misra. As stated previously, Misra formulated an impossibility proof which he realised was not in line with Bohr's doctrine. Misra makes explicit his reasons for doing this when he writes:

"... this line of thought [questioning the validity of 'hidden variables impossibility proofs'] can be pursued profitably only when an *alternative mathematical description* of states, ... has been outlined" (151) (my emphasis).

Misra essentially seems to be saying that, although he realises his assumptions are inadequate, other assumptions cannot be expressed in the mathematical form of a proof, and that it is better to have incorrect assumptions expressed axiomatically, than to have assumptions which cannot be put in the axiomatic form.

The lack of communication over the 'hidden variables impossibility proofs' can be seen as resulting from differing approaches to the mathematical characterisation of cognitive objects. That it is differing mathematical approaches that lie at the heart of failures to communicate in quantum physics seems to have been realised by Bohr. Feyerabend writes:

"Bohr would on occasions be critical of von Neumann's approach which, according to him, did not *solve* prolems, but created *imaginary difficulties* ... I also had the impression that he definitely preferred his own qualitative remarks to the machinery of the famous 'von Neumann Proof'. Nor was he too fond of the rising axiomania ..." (152) (Feyerabend's emphasis).

The axiomania of von Neumann and other quantum logicians seems to be symptomatic of the condition identified by Georgescu-Roegen as arithmomania. An analysis of the approach of the school of quantum logicians to other cognitive objects in the quantum theory would provide further evidence of arithmomania (153). Their approach to the quantum theory has met with severe criticisms recently (154) and their arithmomania is, I think, clearly revealed in a recent confession by the quantum logician, Guenin, who, in writing about axiomatic restrictions, mentioned that:

"To be honest, we have to say we do not know at all if this restriction has any physical meaning; we have made it only to be able to solve the problem mathematically" (155).

The importance of differing mathematical approaches in physics in the context of von Neumann's proof has been stressed by Ballentine who writes:

"I would contend that Misra's abstract algebraic approach, and the proposition-lattice theoretic approach of Jauch and Piron ... impose only *abstract mathematical* conditions whose physical implications are obscured by their abstractness. The danger inherent in such an approach is underlined by the 34 year interval between von Neumann's abstract attack on the hidden-variable problem and Bell's demonstration that one of his assumptions was physically unreasonable, and even impossible" (156).

If the cognitive differentiation over von Neumann's proof can be understood in terms of differing mathematical approaches, it remains to be shown how these mathematical approaches are related to the different components of scientific activity and to the dynamics of communication breakdown. In analysing the dynamics of communication breakdown I have suggested that two modes of articulation are important, the research-area mode and the official-history mode. I would like next to consider how arithmomorphism relates to these modes of articulation.

The commitment to arithmomorphic concepts can be regarded as a kind of metaphysical commitment. However, in the research-area mode of articulation this commitment will be sterile unless it can be used to define and resolve an area of uncertainty. That is, I regard the most important component of science in relation to arithmomorphism, in the research-area mode, to be the research technique. The reason why I wish to stress the research technique is that it seems to be the component which is most closely related to scientific work. It is the research-technique level which most constrains the transformation of cognitive objects which characterises the research-area mode of articulation.

The failure of Bohm and von Neumann to communicate in their research-area mode articulations can be explained in terms of their differing research techniques. Von Neumann was a mathematician committed to unifying and 'making rigorous' the various approaches to the quantum theory by using the research technique of axiomatisation. Bohm was a theoretical physicist committed to developing new theories by considering the ontological and epistemological basis of physical concepts. Bohm's research techniques mainly involved the development of qualitative considerations and dialectical concepts, which could be expressed mathematically but not within the framework of axiomatisation. These differing techniques led to the confusion over the validity of the proof. The 'stabilisation' of this confusion occurred because scientists could not suddenly change research techniques. Scientists not following the axiomatic approach could not take it up at will because it involved considerable work to learn a new research technique. I think the attitude of most physicists to von Neumann's axiomatic approach is nicely captured in this comment by Bastin. He said:

"Well, I suppose that they regard von Neumann's book as a perfectly adequate formal treatment for pedants, people who like that sort of thing. They wouldn't read it themselves but they're glad somebody has done all that hard work!" (157)

The important point here is that von Neumann's axiomatic approach to the quantum theory has, as a research area, made very little impact. Von Neumann's axiomatic approach, although often referred to by physicists as 'mathematically rigorous' (158), has not been used by most physicists, who mainly use the Dirac formalism because of its elegance **(159)**. Not surprisingly von Neumann regarded the Dirac approach to be deficient in mathematical rigor but, despite philosophers' **(160)** attempts to reinstate von Neumann, it seems that his axiomatic approach has not had a major impact on physicists actually using the quantum theory. As Hanson put it, when writing about the 'great' von Neumann:

"The plain and unvarnished fact is that physicists have made almost no direct use of von Neumann's methods in practice, nor have they bothered to try to stay within the bounds which he set" **(161)**.

Thus the 34-year stabilisation of confusion over the validity of von Neumann's proof can, I think, be explained by the differing research techniques of theoretical physicists constructing new 'hidden variables' theories, and mathematicians and quantum logicians legislating by their proofs that such theories were impossible. The reason it took 34 years to find the 'error' in the proof is that not enough physicists used the research technique of axiomatisation, and so most physicists could not investigate the proof.

However, much of the communication breakdown between Bohm and his adversaries has been in the official-history mode, rather than the research-area mode. There has been little sociological work on the official-history mode of articulation of cognitive objects but it would seem that, in this particular case, the nature of articulation in the official-history mode requires further investigation. In particular I would like to consider the role of authority structures in the official-history mode of articulation. Official history seems to me to have two important aspects to it: firstly it legitimises the past invest-ments of scientists and secondly it provides the rationalisation for allocating resources to present areas of concern. It is the first aspect of official history which seems to have been important in the case of Bohm. The attacks on Bohm by the quantum elite can be regarded as part of what Bourdieu calls the conservationist strategy to be followed by the elite to ensure continual return on their investments. Bohm, by advocating a heterodox interpretation, was challenging the elite's authority by questioning the legitimacy of their previous investments in the interpretation of quantum theory. The official-history mode articulation of von Neumann's proof can be regarded then as an attempt to maintain a particular authority structure.

Authority structures in science are closely related to metaphysical commitments and the particular authority of von Neumann's proof, I think, lies in the commitment generally in physics to arithmomorphism. The authority of the proof stems from the fact that it is a logical, mathematical object as opposed to the qualitative considerations raised by 'hidden variables' theorists such as Bohm. As Jammer puts it:

"Von Neumann was hailed by his followers and credited even by his opponents as having succeeded in bringing the foremost methodological and interpretative problem of quantum mechnics down from the realm of speculation into the reach of mathematical analysis ..." (162).

Jauch and Piron (163) similarly claim that the importance of their proof is that the problem of 'hidden valiables' has been "brought from the speculative level". The phenomenon that the more abstract and arithmomorphic the object the more authority it commands has been noted by Lakatos when considering the official-history mode of articulation of mathematicians. He writes:

"Many *working* mathematicians are puzzled about what proofs are for if they do not prove. ... *Applied* mathematicians usually solve this dilemma by a shamefaced but firm belief that the proofs of the pure mathematician are 'complete' and so really prove. *Pure* mathematicians, however, know better — they have such respect only for 'complete proofs' of the *logicians*" (164) (my emphasis).

Similarly the authority of von Neumann's proof can be seen to rest in the deference shown by physicists to a logical proof. Of course, part of the reason why physicists accepted von Neumann's proof as valid may have been von Neumann's personal reputation for brilliance; as Bohm put it to me:

"... most physicists have heard of von Neumann's proof and perhaps in the past they said it must be so because they had great respect for his abilities" (165).

However this type of answer does not account for why physicists should have respect for particular mathematical abilities, especially when they are being applied in a different field.

The authority structures in modern physics and in other sciences, produced by arithmomorphism and the 'arithmetic ideal', have been analysed by Whitley (166). The relation of these authority structures to other social and cognitive structures has also been investigated. The lack of impact made by von Neumann at the research-area level, in contrast to his authority in

official history, indicates that a crucial part of the battle for authority in
modern physics occurs at the official-history level. I suggest that differing
types of official history and their relation to the 'arithmetic ideal' in different sciences is a further method of analysing authority structures in
science.

The characteristics of the official-history mode of articulation outlined in
this paper, that is, the static, undifferentiated and closed nature of the cognitive object, can themselves be seen to reflect the commitment to arithmomorphism in physics. The 'arithmetic ideal' embodied in the official-history
mode of articulation in modern physics will constrain official histories in
other sciences. Because the official-history mode of articulation is important
in the allocation of social capital of recognition, a challenge to its arithmomorphic basis is inevitably a challenge to the system of awarding capital.
As Whitley suggests (167), Bohm was not only producing a rival interpretation of quantum mechanics, but was, by his emphasis on qualitative and
physical considerations, also challenging the authority structure of physics.
The short, sharp reception that Bohm received at the hands of the elite
can be seen as the defence of an authority structure which, if overthrown,
would have led not only to loss of capital by the elite and gain of capital by
Bohm, but also to a loss of capital by those scientists following succession
strategies and to the writing of a new official history with the subsequent
possibility of resources being allocated to new research areas. The failure
by Bohm to achieve a social and cognitive redefinition is not surprising
when so much was at stake and considering that he was fighting against the
embodiment of the arithmetic ideal, the much worshipped and revered, but
little understood, von Neumann Proof.

7. Concluding Summary

In conclusion I will briefly summarise the main aspects of the communication
breakdown outlined in this paper. By identifying specific disputed cognitive
objects I have suggested that it is possible to analyse scientific controversies
in terms of the articulation of these objects. In this case I have suggested that
two modes of articulation have been important, the research-area mode and
the official-history mode. By identifying the main division in this dispute as
being over the commitment to arithmomorphic concepts I have considered

how the cognitive object in its two modes of articulation has embodied this division. I have suggested that, in the research-area mode of articulation, the 'arithmetic ideal' manifests itself in differing research techniques, which can be used to explain the failure to communicate at the research-area level. I have suggested that in the official-history mode of articulation the 'arithmetic ideal' primarily manifests itself as a metaphysical commitment. By considering the role of the official-history mode of articulation in legitimising previous investments and determining the allocation of resources to new areas, I have suggested that it plays an important part in the battle for authority. A cognitive challenge to the 'arithmetic ideal', such as Bohm's approach to the quantum theory, is therefore also a social challenge to the authority structure of science.

Just as the social preconditions for the controversy taking place can be understood in terms of social capital requirements, the form the controversy has taken (the crucial role played by the official-history mode of articulation) can be understood in terms of the cognitive challenge embodied in Bohm's heterodoxy, a challenge to the 'arithmetic ideal', an ideal which is inseparable from the social processes whereby social capital is awarded.

Notes

1. T. S. Kuhn, *The Structure of Scientific Revolutions*, Chicago: Chicago University Press, 2nd ed., 1970.
2. *ibid.*, p. 132.
3. See, for example, Margaret Masterman, 'The Nature of a Paradigm', in I. Lakatos and A. Musgrave (eds.), *Criticism and the Growth of Knowledge*, Cambridge: C.U.P., 1970.
4. See, for example, Allan Bitz, Andrew McAlpine and R. D. Whitley, 'The Production, Flow and Use of Information in Research Laboratories in Different Sciences', London: British Library Report Series, 1975.
5. See, for example, M. J. Mulkay, G. N. Gilbert and S. Woolgar, 'Problem Areas and Research Networks in Science', *Sociology* 9, 1975, pp. 187–203.
6. See, for example, J. W. Meiland, 'Kuhn, Scheffler and Objectivity in Science', *Philosophy of Science* 41, 1974, pp. 187–203.
6a. See K. R. Popper, *Objective Knowledge*, Oxford: The Clarendon Press, 1972.
7. R. D. Whitley, 'Black Boxism and the Sociology of Science', in P. Halmos (ed.), *The Sociology of Science*, Keele University, Sociological Review Monograph, 18, 1972.
8. H. M. Collins and G. Cox, 'Recovering Relativity: Did Prophecy Fail?', *Social Studies of Science* 6, 1976.
9. Roy Bhaskar, *A Realist Theory of Science*, Leeds: Leeds Books, 1975.
10. R. D. Whitley, 'Components of Scientific Activities, Their Characteristics and Institutionalisation in Specialities and Research Areas', in K. Knorr, H. Strasser,

and H. G. Zilian (eds.), *Determinants and Controls of Scientific Development*, Dordrecht: Reidel, 1975.

11. R. D. Whitley, 'The Sociology of Scientific Work and the History of Scientific Developments', in S. S. Blume (ed.), *New Perspectives in the Sociology of Science*, New York: Wiley, 1977a.
11a. H. M. Collins, 'The Seven Sexes: a Study in the Sociology of a Phenomenon, or the Replication of Experiments in Physics', *Sociology* 9, 1975, pp. 205–224.
12. For a discussion of 'official history' see Bitz *et al.*, *op. cit.*, 1975, Note 4, pp. 5–28, 194–217.
13. Collins, *op. cit.*, 1975, Note 11a.
14. David Bohm, 'A Suggested Interpretation of the Quantum Theory in Terms of Hidden Variables, I and II', *Physical Review* 85, 1952, pp. 166–193.
15. The interpretation of the quantum theory was discussed at the fifth and sixth Solvay Congresses of 1927 and 1930.
16. For a discussion of the role of paradoxes see T. J. Pinch, *Hidden Variables, Impossibility Proofs and Paradoxes: A Sociological Study of Non-Relativistic Quantum Mechanics*, unpubl. M.Sc. diss. University of Manchester, 1976. In particular the E.P.R. paradox has led to an experiment which may bring about a fundamental change in the theory, see R. A. Holt, and S. J. Freedman, 'Test of Local Hidden-Variables Theories in Atomic Physics', *Comments on Atomic and Molecular Physics* 5, 1975, pp. 55–62.
17. References to this approach can be found in Pinch, *op. cit.*, 1976, Note 16, p. 60.
18. J. M. Jauch, *Are Quanta Real?*, London: Indiana University Press, Introduction, 1973.
19. L. E. Ballentine, 'Statistical Interpretation of Quantum Mechanics', *Reviews of Modern Physics* 42, 1970, p. 374.
20. P. W. Bridgman, Review of Louis de Broglie's book, *Non-Linear Wave Mechanics: A Causal Interpretation*, in *Scientific American* 203, Oct. 1960, p. 206.
21. Pierre Bourdieu, 'The Specificity of the Scientific Field and the Social Conditions of the Progress of Reason', *Social Science Information* 14, 1975, pp. 19–47.
22. Interview with Professor Bohm, Birkbeck College, London University, 16th June 1975.
23. David Bohm, *Quantum Theory*, London: Prentice Hall International, 8th ed., 1960.
24. For details of Bohm's approach to E.P.R. see Pinch, *op. cit.*, 1976, Note 16, Ch. 6.
25. Interview with Professor Bohm.
26. *ibid.*
27. Einstein's position is set out in P. A. Schilpp (ed.), *Albert Einstein: Philosopher Scientist*, New York: Tudor, 1949.
28. Bohm, *op. cit.*, 1952, Note 14, p. 179.
29. Interview with Professor Bohm.
30. Ted Bastin, for example, commented to me that "Bohm was very much the bright boy, he had a tremendous reputation at Princeton". Interview with Dr. Bastin, Language Research Unit, Cambridge, 14th, July 1975.
30a. Bohm's subversion strategy was implicit in the unorthodox (unmathematical) approach of his book written in 1949. Bohm himself has told me that he wrote the book to try and understand the theory and by the time he finished it he realised he did not understand it! His allegiance to Copenhagen in the book was because he had not yet gained enough capital to make his dissatisfaction explicit.
31. Bohm was one of the younger generation of post-war physicists. Schrödinger, for example, who published a heterodox interpretation also in 1952, may have been ignored because he was of the pre-war generation.
32. Bohm's work was sent out for refereeing by *Physical Review*, which is unusual for

a physicist of his stature. Personal correspondence Harriet Zuckerman.

33. For details of de Broglie's interpretation see Max Jammer, *The Philosophy of Quantum Mechanics: The Interpretations of Quantum Mechanics in Historical Perspective*, New York: Wiley, 1974, pp. 44–49.
34. Interview with Professor Bohm.
35. *ibid.*
36. Jammer, *op. cit.*, 1974, Note 33, p. 279.
37. Bohm, *op. cit.*, 1952, Note 14, pp. 191–193.
38. Wolfgang Pauli, 'Remarques sur le problème des paramètres cachés dans la mécanique quantitique et sur la théorie de l'onde pilote', in A. George (ed), *Louis de Broglie: Physicien et Penseur*, Paris: Albin Michel, 1953, p. 33.
39. Werner Heisenberg, 'The Development of the Interpretation of the Quantum Theory', in Wolfgang Pauli (ed.), *Niels Bohr and the Development of Physics*, London: Pergamon, 1955, p. 19.
40. N. R. Hanson, *The Concept of the Positron*, Cambridge: C.U.P., 1963, p. 88.
41. Leon Rosenfeld, 'L'évidence de la complémentarité', in George, *op. cit.*, 1953, Note 38, pp. 43–65.
42. For an example of Rosenfeld's most potent criticisms, see Leon Rosenfeld, 'Physics and Metaphysics', *Nature* 181, 1958, p. 658.
43. Interview with Professor Bohm.
43a. Max Born (ed.), *The Born-Einstein Letters*, New York: Macmillan, 1971, p. 192.
44. *Scientific Papers Presented to Max Born*, New York: Hafner, 1953, p. 33.
45. *ibid.*, p. 13.
46. H. Freistadt, 'The Causal Formulation of Quantum Mechanics of Particles', *Nuovo Cimento Supplement* 5, 1957, pp. 1–70.
47. There was a specific objection raised by Halpern, but this was based on a misunderstanding of part of Bohm's theory. See O. Halpern, 'A Proposed Re-Interpretation of Quantum Mechanics', Letter to the Editor, *Physical Review* 87, 1952, p. 389. See also Bohm's reply, *ibid.*, p. 389.
48. Interview with Professor Bohm.
49. This approach has resulted in proposals for experimental tests to distinguish it from the quantum theory. See A. B. Datzeff, 'On Some Experiments Leading to a Revision of the Foundations of Quantum Mechanics', *Nuovo Cimento* 29B, 1975, pp. 105–123.
50. Max Born, 'Quantenmechanik der Stossvorgänge', *Zeitschrift für Physik* 38, 1926, pp. 803–827. Quote from Jammer, *op. cit.*, 1974, Note 33, p. 263.
51. This analogy is explained in more detail and extended to a derivation of the uncertainty relations in David Bohm, *Causality and Chance in Modern Physics*, London: Routledge and Kegan Paul, 1957, p. 107. This analogy, although probably acceptable to most contemporary physicists ignores the paradoxes and problems associated with the derivation of Boltzmann's H. Theorem. For details see Nicholas Georgescu-Roegen, *The Entropy Law and the Economic Process*, Cambridge, Mass.: Harvard University Press, 1971, and Phyllis Jenkin, *Structure and Contradiction in Scientific Development: The Case of Nicholas Georgescu-Roegen and the Entropy Law*, unpubl. M.Sc. diss. University of Manchester, 1975
52. John von Neumann, *Mathematical Foundations of Quantum Mechanics*, Princeton: Princeton University Press, 1955. First published in German in 1932.
53. *ibid.*, p. 209.
54. *ibid.*, p. 324.
55. *ibid.*, p. 325.
56. Jammer writes that: "Von Neumann was hailed by his followers and credited even by his opponents ...". Jammer, *op. cit.*, 1974, Note 33, p. 270.

57. Pascual Jordan, 'Die Physik und das Geheimnis des organischen Lebens', Braunschweig, 1943, p. 114. Quoted in P. K. Feyerabend, 'Problems of Microphysics', in R. G. Colodny (ed.), *Frontiers of Science and Philosophy*, Pittsburgh: University of Pittsburgh Press, 1962, p. 193.
58. *Dialectica* 2, 1948, p. 309. (Editorial of special issue on the interpretation of the quantum theory).
59. Hermann's criticism is outlined in Jammer, *op. cit.*, 1974, Note 33, pp. 272–275
60. See Note 64 below.
61. Hans Reichenbach, *Philosophical Foundations of Quantum Mechanics*, Berkeley: University of California Press, 1944, p. 14.
62. F. J. Belinfante, *A Survey of Hidden Variables Theories*, Oxford: Pergamon, 1973. Quotes from pages 34 and 24.
63. Interview with Professor Bohm.
64. Bell put forward a 'hidden variables' theory in 1966 which was consistent and capable of producing all the results of the quantum theory yet did not have 'hidden variables' in the measuring apparatus. So Bohm had shown why the proof was irrelevant to his theory but not why the proof was generally invalid. See J. S. Bell, 'On the Problem of Hidden Variables in Quantum Mechanics', *Reviews of Modern Physics* 38, 1966, pp. 447–452.
65. Rosenfeld, *op. cit.*, 1953, Note 41.
66. F. Cap, 'On the Causal Interpretation of Quantum Theory', *Nuovo Cimento Supplement* 3, 1956, p. 421.
67. Bridgman, *op. cit.*, 1960, Note 20, p. 204.
68. N. R. Hanson, *Patterns of Discovery*, Cambridge: C.U.P., 1958, p. 174.
69. Interview with Dr. Bastin.
70. Pauli, *op. cit.*, 1953, Note 38.
71. Louis de Broglie, *Une Tentative d'Interpretation Causale et Non Lineaire de la Mécanique Ondulatoire*, Paris: Gauthier-Villars, 1956, p. 66.
72. See Pinch, *op. cit.*, 1976, Note 16, Ch. 5, and Jammer, *op. cit.*, 1974, Note 33, pp. 292–294.
73. Interview with Professor Bohm.
74. Ballentine, *op. cit.*, 1970, Note 19, p. 374.
75. Jammer, *op. cit.*, 1974, Note 33, p. 272.
76. Details of Nabl's paper can be found *ibid*, p. 272.
77. J. M. Jauch and C. Piron, 'Can Hidden Variables be Excluded in Quantum Mechanics?', *Helvetica Physica Acta* 36, 1963, pp. 827–837. Quote from page 828.
78. An account of the 'loss' of such an important paper is given in Jammer, *op. cit.*, 1974, Note 33, p. 303.
79. Belinfante, *op. cit.*, 1973, Note 62, p. 4.
80. D. Bohm and J. Bub, 'A Proposed Solution of the Measurement Problem in Quantum Mechanics by a Hidden Variable Theory', *Reviews of Modern Physics* 38, 1966, pp. 453–469.
81. D. Bohm and J. Bub, 'A Refutation of the Proof by Jauch and Piron that Hidden Variables can be Excluded in Quantum Mechanics', *Reviews of Modern Physics* 38, 1966, pp. 470–475.
82. Bub has recently published a criticism of Bell's work in which he implies that Bell's argement is confused, but this criticism is only made in the context of the argument as to whether the quantum theory is a complete theory. In the context of the validity of von Neumann's proof, Bub accepts Bell's conclusion. See J. Bub, *The Interpretation of Quantum Mechanics*, Dordrecht: Reidel, 1974, p. 54.
83. J. M. Jauch and C. Piron, 'Hidden Variables Revisited', *Reviews of Modern Physics* 40, 1968, pp. 228–229.

84. Jammer, *op. cit.*, 1974, Note 33, p. 305.
85. Ballentine, *op. cit.*, 1970, Note 19, p. 374.
86. Belinfante, *op. eit.*, 1973, Note 62, p. 25.
87. L. Eisenbud, *The Conceptual Foundations of Quantum Mechanics*, New York: Van Nostrand Reinhold, 1971, p. 46.
88. Belinfante, *op. cit.*, 1973. Note 62, p. 34.
89. E. P. Wigner, 'On Hidden Variables and Quantum Mechanical Probabilities', *American Journal of Physics* 38, 1970, p. 1009.
90. E. P. Wigner, 'Rejoinder', *American Journal of Physics* 39, 1971, p. 1097.
91. *ibid.*, pp. 1097–1098.
92. For a review article concerning the difficulties encountered by these further proofs, see J. Bub, 'What is a Hidden Variable Theory of Quantum Phenomena?', *International Journal of Theoretical Physics* 2, 1969, pp. 101–123.
93. V. Capasso, D. Fortunato, and F. Selleri, 'Von Neumann's Theorem and Hidden-Variable Models', *Rivista del Nuovo Cimento* 2, 1970, pp. 149–199.
94. W. Ochs, 'On Gudder's Hidden-Variable Theorems', *Nuovo Cimento* 10B, 1972, pp. 172–184.
95. S. P. Gudder, 'On Hidden Variable Theories', *Journal of Mathematical Physics* 11, 1970, p. 431.
96. Bub, *op. cit.*, 1969, Note 92.
97. Interview with Professor Bohm.
98. Bohm, *op. cit.*, 1952, Note 14, p. 166.
99. *ibid.*, p. 188.
100. For an exellent review of complementarity see C. A. Hooker, 'The Nature of Quantum-Mechanical Reality', R. G. Colodny (ed.), *Paradigms and Paradoxes,* Pittsburgh: University of Pittsburgh Press, 1972, pp. 67–302.
101. Bohm, *op. cit.*, 1952, Note 14, pp. 187–188.
102. *ibid.*, p. 188.
103. See for example the comments of Ballentine (Ballentine, *op. cit.*, 1970, Note 19, p. 376.), and of Jammer (Jammer, *op. cit.*, 1974, Note 33, p. 303).
104. Von Neumann, *op. cit.*, 1955, Note 52, p. 209.
105. *ibid.*, p. 209.
106. Von Neumann also defined homogeneous ensembles, which were pure and could not be resolved into sub-ensembles. As a dispersive ensemble can be resolved into two or more dispersion-free ensembles, von Neumann also had to show the quantum theory contained homogenous ensembles.
107. These axioms are axiom I, p. 313, axiom II, p. 314, unspecified axiom, p. 313 (The correspondence between Hermitian operators and observables is one to one), axiom A′, p. 311, and axiom B′, p. 311.
108. Axiom B′.
109. This example is discussed in more detail by Ballentine, see Ballentine, *op. cit.*, 1970, Note 19, p. 376.
110. Jammer, *op. cit.*, 1974, Note 33, p. 286.
111. Bub, *op. cit.*, 1969, Note 92.
112. Jauch and Piron, *op. cit.*, 1968, Note 83, p. 228.
113. B. Misra, 'When Can Hidden Variables Be Excluded in Quantum Mechanics?', *Nuovo Cimento* 47A, 1967, pp. 841–859.
114. Bohm and Bub, *op. cit.*, 1966, Note 80, p. 453, Pauli, *op. cit.*, 1948, Note 58.
115. Hanson, *op. cit.*, 1958, Note 68, p. 174.
116. Rosenfeld, *op. cit.*, 1953, Note 41, p. 56; N. R. Hanson, 'Five Cautions for the Copenhagen Interpretation's Critics', *Philosophy of Science* 26, 1959, p. 332.

117. Freistadt, *op. cit.*, 1953, Note 46, p. 47, Feyerabend, *op. cit.*, 1962, Note 57, p. 207.
118. Jammer, *op. cit.*, 1974, Note 33, p. 251.
119. Belinfante, *op. cit.*, 1973, Note 62, pp. 17-19.
120. Jammer, *op. cit.*, 1974, Note 33, pp. 265-278.
121. Belinfante, *op. cit.*, 1973, Note 62, p. 34.
122. David Bohm, 'Science as Perception-Communication', in F. Suppe (ed.), *The Structure of Scientific Theories*, Urbana, Illinois: University of Illinois Press, 1974, pp. 374-391.
123. *ibid.*, p. 388.
124. *ibid.*, p. 385.
125. *ibid.*, p. 385.
126. This is the main criticism by Kuhn of Bohm's account. See 'Discussion', in Suppe, *op. cit.*, 1974, Note 122, pp. 409-412.
127. Bohm, *op. cit.*, 1974, Note 122, p. 385.
128. Interview with Professor Bohm.
129. For a discussion of arithmomorphism see Georgescu-Roegen, *op. cit.*, 1971, Note 51, Jenkin, *op. cit.*, 1975. Note 51, Phyllis Colvin, 'Ontological and Epistemological Commitments and Social Relations in the Sciences: the Case of the Arithmomorphic System of Scientific Production', this volume, Whitley, *op. cit.*, 1977a. Note 11, and R. D. Whitley, 'Changes in the Social and Intellectual Organisation of the Sciences: Professionalisation and the Arithmetic Ideal', in this volume.
130. Bohm, *op. cit.*, 1952, Note 14, p. 189.
131. See Feyerabend, *op. cit.*, 1962, Note 57, and Jammer, *op. cit.*, 1974, Note 33, pp. 197-211.
132. For an indication of the complexities of this dispute see Hooker, *op. cit.*, 1972, Note 100.
133. Paul Forman, 'Weimar Culture, Causality, and Quantum Theory, 1918-1927', in R. McCormmach (ed.), *Historical Studies in the Physical Sciences* 3, Philadelphia: Univesity of Pennsylvania Press, 1971, pp. 1-115.
134. Von Neumann, *op. cit.*, 1955, Note 52, p. 328.
135. *ibid.*, p. 327.
136. Jammer, *op. cit.*, 1974, Note 33, p. 270.
137. Feyerabend, *op. cit.*, 1962, Note 57, p. 238.
138. Interview with Professor Bohm.
139. For details see Pinch, *op. cit.*, 1976, Note 16, Ch. 4.
140. See for example, Bohm's letter to *Physical Review* in 1952 entitled 'Reply to a Criticism of a *Causal* Re-Interpretation of the Quantum Theory' (my emphasis), *Physical Review* 87, 1952, p. 389, or the title of Freistadt's paper in Note 46.
141. Bohm, *op. cit.*, 1957, Note 51.
142. D. Bohm and Y. Aharanov, 'Discussion of the Experimental Proof for the Paradox of Einstein, Rosen and Podolsky', *Physical Review* 108, 1957, p. 1072.
143. Interview with Professor Bohm.
144. Georgescu-Roegen, *op. cit.*, 1971, Note 51.
145. *ibid.*, p. 14.
146. *ibid.*, p. 46.
147. *ibid.*, p. 53.
148. *ibid.*, p. 52.
149. For an analysis of Georgescu-Roegen's work, see Jenkin, *op. cit.*, 1975, Note 51.
150. Georgescu-Roegen, *op. cit.*, 1971, Note 51, p. 44.
151. Misra, *op. cit.*, 1967, Note 113, p. 859.

152. P. K. Feyerabend, 'On a Recent Critique of Complementarity; Part II', *Philosophy of Science* **36**, 1969, p. 87.
153. See, for example, Hooker's analysis of their approach to E.P.R. (Hooker, *op. cit.*, 1972, Note 100).
154. See Hooker's criticisms in the same essay.
155. M. Guenin, 'Axiomatic Foundations of Quantum Theories', *Journal of Mathematical Physics* **7**, 1966, p. 282.
156. Ballentine, *op. cit.*, 1970, Note 19, p. 377.
157. Interview with Dr. Bastin.
158. See, for example, the remarks in the preface of C. Kemble, *The Fundamental Principles of Quantum Mechanics*, New York: Dover, 1958.
159. Jammer writes: "Yet due to its immediate intuitability and notational convenience Dirac's formalism not only survived but became the favourite framework for many expositions of the theory". Jammer, *op. cit.*, 1974, Note 33, p. 8.
160. Jammer, for instance, in the introductory chapter of his book implies that not enough consideration has been given to von Neumann's approach.
161. Hanson, *op. cit.*, 1963, Note 40, p. 124.
162. Jammer, *op. cit.*, 1974, Note 33, p. 270.
163. Jauch and Piron, *op. cit.*, 1963, Note 77, p. 827.
164. Imre Lakatos, 'Proofs and Refutations', *The British Journal for the Philosophy of Science* **14**, 1963, p. 125, footnote 1.
165. Interview with Professor Bohm.
166. Whitley, *op. cit.*, 1977, Note 129.
167. *ibid*.

PART III

SOCIAL GOALS, POLITICAL PROGRAMMES AND
SCIENTIFIC NORMS

THE POLITICAL DIRECTION OF
SCIENTIFIC DEVELOPMENT*

WOLFGANG VAN DEN DAELE and WOLFGANG KROHN

Max-Planck-Institut, Starnberg

and

PETER WEINGART

University of Bielefeld

1. The Concept of Regulation — Resistance and Receptivity of Science

The question of whether processes of scientific development can be socially directed has been discussed for several decades with no convincing conclusions emerging. The controversies have produced, however, several conceptual distinctions which form a vocabulary for the analysts of science. Distinctions are often, for instance, made between: pure research and applied research; the

---

* The aim of the present essay is to present a theoretical discussion of a study of science policy in seven fields of research. The study deals with the general and comparative aspects of the controllability of the disciplines. Analyses of the special structures and processes of the orientation of research are presented in the following case studies:

'Biotechnology' (K. Buchholz)
'Cancer Research' (R. Hohlfeld)
'Computer Science' (K. Mainzer)
'Educational Research' (E. Schmitz)
'Environmental Research' (G. Küppers, P. Lundgreen and P. Weingart)
'Heavy Ions' (K. Prüss)
'Plasma Physics' (G. Küppers)

These analyses form the basis of the theoretical treatment presented in this paper. They also indicate the scope of the literature that has been examined in preparing the present essay, and should be consulted for the evidence referred to in this paper. The individual case studies are in the process of being published, together with the comparative evaluation, and are available from the present authors.

The authors of this essay wish to express their thanks to their colleagues who undertook the case studies. This discussion is the result of the work of all those associated with the project.

The project was carried out at the 'Zentrum für interdisziplinäre Forschung' in Bielefeld. We thank the Centre for its financial and organizational support.

---

autonomy of academic research and the heteronomy of industrial or governmental science; the internalist orientation of scientists concerned with the
study of nature and the externalist orientation related to its regulation and
domination, i.e. oriented to technology. These distinctions, although conceptually not sharp, are based on contrasting cases in the history of science
such as, e.g., quantum mechanics, cancer research and agricultural chemistry.

There are a number of research fields, however, that are not easily classified
within the context of the dichotomy of basic research and applied research.
Cancer research, for example, is only superficially the application of the
knowledge of biochemistry and molecular-genetics to a social problem. In
fact, the cancer problem has necessitated investments in basic research across
the biological sciences. Similarly plasma physics is a fundamental discipline
within general physics; nonetheless its development is currently determined
by technological and economic parameters as a result of its orientation towards
the goal of controlled fusion. These examples suggest that the separation of
nomologically-oriented fundamental disciplines from artefact-oriented technologies (1) has become obsolete. In present-day science, research fields subject to the control of science policy are complex aggregates of concerns
dealing with the structure of matter, technological constructions (e.g. acceleration to extreme velocities, realisation of extreme pressures) and social
normative expectations (e.g. profitability, security, health). Thus the political
direction of science implies the initiation of special developments both in
basic research and in technology. Or, to put it another way, the strategic direction of science may assume such complexity that problem-solving can no
longer depend on the application of advances made in basic research but instead implies the production of new forms of fundamental knowledge.

In the present study, we analysed the relations between research policies and
scientific development in seven research fields in Germany. Of these, five are
in the area of the natural sciences and technology (heavy ions research, fusion
research, biotechnology, cancer research, environmental research), one may
be called a formal discipline (2) (computer science) and one is in the area of
the social sciences (educational research). We confined the analysis of external influences on scientific development to the relatively accessible and limited sphere of systematic policy requirements (i.e. explicit attempts to direct
research) omitting the entire complex of socio-economic and socio-cultural
determinants of the direction of science.

Analytically, 'policy' and 'science' are here treated as distinct with regard to ends, methods, cognitions and institutional norms. This means that the formulation and realisation of normative decisions in politics are contrasted with the primacy of knowledge as the objective of science. Both the political and scientific processes involved must be analysed at the cognitive and the institutional (social) levels. Thus science may be reconstructed as a cognitive process determined by the definitions given to subjects by the problem structure, the methodological and theoretical rules of research, and so forth. Likewise, policy-making as a process of goal-formation may be explained on the basis of the given problems, of information processing, of the weighting of interests, and of normative programs. On the institutional level of analysis, the development of scientific knowledge and political goals are social processes, as evidenced by the organisation of work, the formation of groups, the institutionalisation of social positions etc. Thus, for instance, biotechnological research is cognitively defined by the problems entailed in the artificial mutation of micro-organisms for the manufacture of industrial products and their technical cultivation in large reactors; institutionally, this may involve the setting up of new careers outside the established research systems. At each of these levels the factors which affect the form and scope of the political direction of scientific development must be defined.

The identification and analysis of the effects of science policies is not straightforward. Due to the 'universal validity' of scientific and technological knowledge one can keep track of only one line of development for which, as a rule, there is no alternative. Only the crystallisation of the objectives of a 'movement', as, for instance, of the protest against ecological damage, into a political program which articulates explicit demands for research can operationally be considered as an instance of political direction. Effects of political direction, then, are defined here as the institutionalisation of research governed by goal-definitions which stem from science policy programs. In contrast with applied research, in which the 'internal' dynamics of scientific development retains primacy and is not directly affected, science policy direction replaces the traditional regulative mechanisms by politically defined objectives (the cure of cancer, protection of the environment, and the like), or such political goals are introduced in research fields which lack an 'internal' dynamic (e.g. by giving scientific support to projects for comprehensive schools). The objective of the political direction of research is not, as in the

case of the general promotion of science, the optimal advance of science itself, but the solution of specified social, economic, military and other problems by means of scientific development.

Such goal-orientation is subject to the limits set by the internal structure of
the sciences. These limits can be defined as cognitive deficiencies and as social
resistance. They define the relationship between problem-oriented and autonomous science. Cognitive deficiencies arise when the demands made on a
particular field of research are too great for its current theoretical and methodological state. Social resistance on the part of scientists can arise when the
direction of science impinges upon social processes and mechanisms in science
which, on the one hand provide stability and continuity to cognitive processes as guaranteed by the disciplinary structures, but on the other hand induce
inflexibility and traditionalism. The degree to which the orientation and behavioural patterns institutionalised within the system of scientific knowledge
production are characterised by inflexibility indicates the resistance of
science to externally induced innovations.

2. Science Policy Program Formulation

2.1 *The Transformation of Problems*

The process of orienting science to social ends at the cognitive level entails
a sequence of transformations. Social ends have to be translated into political goals, the political goals in turn into technological norms and these into
scientific problems. We can define the stages of this transformation as follows:

— We designate as 'social' the problems which appear in the form of identifiable preferences in a subsystem or sector of society. These are economic, military, welfare, health problems, and the like.
— We designate as political goals that sub-class of social problems which become the goals of political parties, parliaments and governments. Social
   problems are translated into political programs.
— A sub-class of these political goals may become problems of science policy
   in that research and development are defined as the decisive means for
   problem solution. This transformation, as a rule, entails the operationalisation of political goals in the form of technical problems, which may be

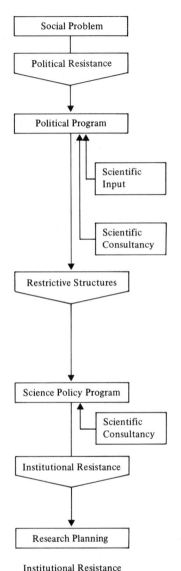

The cure of a disease, that causes more than 300 000 deaths annually (in the U.S.)

The 'battle against cancer' gained high priority in public health policies – probably at the expense of alternative programs concerning diseases of equal epidemiological relevance.

National Cancer Act 1971 providing for a National Cancer Plan, the establishment of additional cancer centres, the promotion of cancer control etc.

A precondition for the political effort was the feeling that breakthroughs in science were imminent, presaged by developments in virology, immunology, molecular biology.

Scientists participated in the initiating 'Report of the National Panel of Consultants on the Conquest of Cancer', 1970.

It was clear from the outset that political action would mainly consist in measures of science policy. Controversies within the scientific community indicated that the program formulation might have been unduly influenced by the predominance of virologists and by centralising allocation decisions with the National Cancer Institute (this applies more to the Special Virus Cancer Program of 1963, than to the Strategic Plan).

National Cancer Program Plan: Strategic Plan, defining the goals, objectives and major courses of action.

250 laboratory and clinical scientists participated in preparing the plan.

Academic orientation of the biological sciences is suspected to cause an overestimation of fundamental research; 'transfer research' is difficult to organise, environmental carcinogenesis is said to be insufficiently funded.

Operational Plan of the National Cancer Institute, individual program plans specifying research tasks.

Problems of communication between clinical and laboratory scientists (bedside orientation vs test tube orientation).

Fig. 1. **(3)** The Transformation of Problems: Cancer Research (Illustrations from the case of cancer research in the United States)

solved by the application of existing knowledge, or may become targets of scientific development.

- The sub-class of these technical problems which are targets of research must be linked to existing fields of research by research planning. They are translated into concrete research projects.
- The last transformation phase consists in the transposition of the planned project targets into effective research oriented problem solving; that is, into research capable of producing those results that were spelled out in the original problem formulation. Figure 1 illustrates the analytically distinct transformation phases in the case of cancer research.

Social problems, as understood here, may arise from the sphere of the organised public realm (citizens' action committees, trade unions, economic associations), from the sphere of politics (parliament, government, administration) and also from within the domain of science. Problem-perception is here a function of interests and values on the one hand, and of knowledge on the other. The former is evident since interests and values (ideologies in the widest sense) form a selective grid which gives priority to particular problems. More important is the fact that problem-perception is contingent on knowledge. Thus, the problem of environmental protection could only be formulated systematically in governmental programs when scientific results were available regarding the accumulation of DDT in the chain of nutrients or the long term development of pollutants in water, air, and soils. In general, given situations become problematic only when something is known about the causal factors and, consequently, about how the given state can be modified. This dependence of problem formulation on systematic knowledge with 'ideologies' operating selectively as the intervening variable remains effective in the subsequent transformation phases.

The first transformation phase is characterised by the transposition of social problems into political programs. In most cases this process of crystallisation of political issues is a highly complex process which is not clearly attributable to determinate causes. If we take the ecology debate as a case in point, it is possible to set up a chronology which shows that the concrete incidents, their scientific explanation, their treatment by the media and even the attempt to politicise them (under the catchword 'a blue sky over the Ruhr') had become a part of the public scene in Germany in similar form about five years prior to the politicisation which occurred with the adoption of the governmental environmental program. This instance is a good example of the modus operandi of what is termed the 'selectivity of politics', without, however, it being possible to specify what reasons initially prevented its politicisation. We can say, though, that the initiative of the Federal Government was partly motivated by the desire to put its politics of reform on the record.

As can be indicated by this example, the politicisation of social problems is determined by two conflicting factors:

— Dominant interests and value-orientations act as structural restrictions which selectively determine the transformation of social problems into political problems. These restrictions influence in particular the extent to which prevailing knowledge is drawn upon in political problem-perception and problem-solving.

— On the other hand, the knowledge available to the public has a delegitimising effect on the political retention of mass loyalties and thereby on existing social relations. Thus even scientific knowledge has a political complexion. New knowledge calls traditional legitimations into question.

Essentially, it is the same structural conditions which, in a more pronounced way, are operative in the next transformation phase, i.e. the transformation of a political program into a science policy program. On the cognitive level this requires the operationalisation of politics in the form of techniques which can be provided by science and technology. This is, in some ways at least, a programmatic scientification of political goals. In science policy programs therefore the economic and social problems are operationalised into technological objectives — as for instance, the construction of bacterial strains with special properties and the maintenance of their growth in large reactors (biotechnology), or controlled and continous fusion with a positive energy balance (plasma physics), or the reduction of pollutants (environmental research). Such operationalisation of social ends is exemplified by the American 'National Cancer Program'. Every objective is introduced with the phrase 'develop the means to ...' Operationalisation of political goals in terms of technical objectives is the condition for connecting problem-oriented with discipline-based types of research.

One point must be emphasised here. Besides the manifest function of the scientification of politics, namely the actual solution of political problems, the operationalisation of social ends also has latent functions. The transformation of political into scientific problems can serve to reduce conflicts in political decision making. Thus, for instance, public health policy need not adopt a program of cancer prevention, which could meet with psychological resistance on the part of the public, if 'science' promises to find a curative approach.

This second transformation phase is also subject to the operation of two structural mechanisms which influence problem-solving. The first of these are administrative structures. Administrative organisations have the task of finding solutions to particular problems. Consequently, the internal structure of ministries as well as the interdepartmental division of competences are a function of problem-perception and of political intentions. This relation, in turn, is mediated by the fact that organisational structures assume a life of their own relative to their original tasks, they become the objects of power struggles and generate 'vested interests'. The inflexibility and dynamics of these structures are hence explicable on the basis of political and organisational processes. However, at the same time, they also have a cognitive substrate and can be interpreted as cognitive processes. Consequently, the structure of the political administration, which affects the transformation of political goals into science policy programs, operates selectively with respect to problem-perception and information-processing. Aspects of a problem or whole problem-areas which do not fall under the jurisdiction of the administrative units dealing with it are ignored (**4**).

For science analogous considerations apply. The second transformation phase is characterised by an institutionalised dialogue between the administration and scientists. To formulate science policy programs the administration makes use of scientific expertise. Representatives of the scientific community are appointed to advisory boards and there formulate the conditions for the development of the science policy program: the state of research, the scientific problem-solving potential, disciplinary competences, and the delimitation of particular problems. The temporary co-opting of scientific experts into the administration must inevitably rely on institutionalised science.

A connection also exists between organisational structures (university departments, research institutes etc.) and subject areas. Organisational structures are, to an extent, the result of the institutionalisation of disciplinary fields. These administrative structures achieve a relative independence due to the emergence of vested interests in the form of career patterns, processes of evaluation and reputational structures. Adaptation to the problem-shifts arising from cognitive processes is discontinuous and problem-perception and problem-solving are selective. Thus, from the perspective of the formulation of political programs aspects of a particular problem may be ignored because no discipline is found to be 'competent' to take the problem up, or problems are reformulated in terms of the categories of the prevailing structure of science and are subdivided into separate aspects so that their interconnections are not considered.

Examples of these two fundamental selection mechanisms are found in environmental research and cancer research. With respect to environmental research, the specific jurisdictional structure of the ministries resulted in a compartmentalisation of the environmental problem into the categories of 'land', 'air', and 'water' and 'environmental technologies'. Such a division hinders the analysis of the connections between the 'media' implied by an ecological-system approach. The selection of the scientific consultants who formulated the desiderata of research followed this division. One of its consequences was that the problem of thermal pollution was selectively perceived and only heat emission into water was considered. In cancer research, the predominance of established medicine has resulted in an almost complete neglect of epidemiological research and thereby of the preventive approach to combat cancer, although this is a declared goal of the public health authorities. In addition, the institutionalised disciplinary demarcation between medicine and biology has prevented the establishment of any continous cooperation on the cancer problem.

2.2. *Indicators of direction – Norms and Institutional Measures*

The science policy program emerging from this transformation phase becomes the basis for concrete research planning (Transformation Phase 3) and marks the transition to implementation. At this point we have to discuss some properties of the concept of the political direction of science. In the first instance, it is obviously problematic to speak of the direction of science since the process described as the transformation of social into scientific problems does not take place between two systems that are isolated from one another. Institutionally, the political direction of research entails the establishment of a novel sphere of action which, in terms of systems theory, is the result of the increased 'communication loads' between the differential systems of politics and science and of the institutionalisation of new modes of communication (5). The transfer is achieved by groups which we call 'hybrid communities', since they typically are composed of scientists, politicians, civil servants and experts from industry as well as from other interest groups. In some instances, there are advisory boards, responsible to the appropriate ministry, which, because the problem-definitions and the problem-solving strategies are in the main produced by science, are almost exclusively occupied by scientists. This is the case in plasma physics. In other instances, in the phase of program formulation there are a number of thematically differential committees whose job it is to collect available knowledge about specific issues and to identify research gaps. This is the case in environmental research.

The composition of these groups, whose output was co-ordinated by the respective officials of the ministries and were then integrated into the program formulation process, differed considerably. Some of them consisted solely of administrative experts, others of scientists, administrators and industrial experts in roughly similar proportions. Others had only industrial scientist-managers as members. While the task of these committees and commissions was completed once the program was formulated, scientific consultancy was firmly institutionalized in the form of the Council of Environmental Experts (Umweltsachverständigenrat). The council has the function of providing a continous feed-back and of reformulating the program.

The case of educational research reveals another pattern. The establishment of the 'Deutsche Bildungsrat' (German Council for Education), its Committees and its executive organ, the 'Bildungskommission' (Commission on Education), represents a highly institutionalized and differentiated transformation procedure between politics and science. The Commission was composed of social scientists and representatives of the departments for education: two Ministers of Culture, the Secretary of State of the Federal Ministry for Culture and Education and representatives of the German Städtetag (convention of municipal authorities). But even the social scientists appointed as members of the Commission on Education were not only academics but also acted as politicians and as representatives of trade unions or business. The members of the Commission spelled out in greater detail the requirements formulated by the Council for Education and appointed scientists to various subcommittees, each of which dealt with particular tasks. The results of the discussion in the subcommittees were presented to the Commission which then decided whether it should formulate a recommendation. Such recommendations had the character of political program formulations.

From the institutional point of view the emergence of transfer organisations and the concomitant 'hybrid communities' as well as research planning measures, such as funding programs, setting up research centres, research co-ordination, the establishment of new departments or chairs, and so forth, are indicators of the political direction of research. For empirical analysis, however, the problem is how to draw a clear distinction between research directing measures and traditional forms of support. This is especially so because a political direction can also take the form of a support program that ties in with existing disciplines or specialties. Accordingly, if institutional measures are not an adequate indicator of direction, then we must try to identify the content and characteristics of direction at the cognitive level. In many cases the political direction of science is recognizable in the implicit definition of non-disciplinary research programs or subject areas (i.e. those that do not fit into any existing discipline or specialty).

Every field of research has a delineated universe of discourse defined by specific properties. The structures of the universe of discourse can be investigated by means of theoretical models and experimental procedures. These in turn can serve to define the research field within the disciplinary context (disciplinary matrix). Of course, no sharp boundaries can definitely be drawn around the universe of discourse or around the related action system of the scientists concerned. Yet the examples of the research fields studied show that goal-definitions established through policy planning deviate from the objectives and procedures of existing disciplines. From the perspective of the research field, however, all such goal definitions are 'external', irrespective of whether they originated in social or technical problems or from the cross fertilisation of different fields of science. The difference between 'external' influences from other disciplines (cross fertilisation) and the cases discussed here lies in the type of normative orientation adopted. Through the imposition of what were originally social goals, the 'mother-disciplines' of the research fields discussed here are obliged to reduce the level of abstraction typical of the fundamental sciences. They have to incorporate the concrete complexity of social problems to find solutions. This means that research is directed by norms oriented to the construction of concrete problem solutions, rather than to the discovery of general structures. This occurs in two phases. First, the discipline is set technical targets (plasma physics has to make a fusion reactor with a positive energy balance; cancer research has to reverse errors of cellular growth and differentiation). Secondly, the discipline is directed to social ends (e.g. fusion energy should be delivered at competitive costs).

The cases investigated exemplify how the political direction of research is to be understood. The goal of producing energy by controlled nuclear fusion requires the investigation of plasma properties under complex conditions, e.g. of plasma in toroidal geometries (which promise a positive energy balance of fusion). Without this external goal these phenomena would probably not have become the subject of the academic discipline of 'plasma physics'. Biotechnology entails the microbiological production of suitable micro-organisms and the application of engineering procedures to their metabolism in large reactors. The disciplinary goal of microbiology is the study of micro-biological metabolism in very simple model systems. This program does not entail the analysis and mutation of organisms according to industrial criteria. The environmental program modifies the subject matter of established ecology by making the interaction of man and nature within the ecosystem the central concern. In contrast, there are cases where the externally induced problem and the disciplinary concern coincide. Thus, for instance, the etio-logy of cancer is partly identical with the problem of cell differentiation and its possible control. These processess are the objects of cellular biology or embryology. This coincidence of 'disciplinary' cellular biology and cancer etiology does not, however, apply to cancer research as a whole.

In these examples — with the exception of the counter-example of cancer etiology — the subject matters of problem oriented research are non-disci-plinary. They either belong to several disciplines or they are of a compara-tively higher complexity than the respective discipline's model systems, or they entail technical norms which are not constitutive of the respective disciplinary programs.

The disciplines from which such deviations occur have different epistemo-logical status. Molecular biology, for example, can be taken as part of an 'internal' explanatory program within the natural sciences in which objects of increasing complexity (movement, heat, chemical processes, genetic infor-mation, cell-interaction, and so forth) are theoretically explained on the micro level. Currently, molecular biology constitutes a theoretical frontier within this super-paradigmatic research program. Plasma physics, by contrast, is a 'horizontal' research front. It proceeds from advanced theories in physics and does not aim to discover fundamental laws of nature but rather to make already known principles (mechanics, electro-dynamics, etc) applicable to more complex objects (technically speaking: to establish the equations of motion in the plasma). The situation is similar with regard to disciplinary chemical engineering which can be taken to be the physical chemistry of technical reactors. Its program consists of the molecular explication of the transport of matter and energy within the reactor by means of the known principles of molecular physics. In addition disciplinary chemical engineering – in contrast to the program of plasma physics – is characterised by its reference to an external technical goal.

3. The Implementation of the Program – the Institutionalization of Problem-Oriented Research

The transformation of science-policy program objectives into research planning is predominantly the task of scientists. Research planning must take into account the cognitive and institutional realities of the sciences and bring these into line with the external norms of the program objectives. It is confronted on the one hand with institutional resistance and on the other hand with cognitive deficiences. We shall first discuss the effects of the political direction of research on the cognitive structures of science.

3.1. *Research Planning and Cognitive Deficiencies*

Science policy program formulations, and more concretely, research plans, incorporate evaluations made by scientists about research fields for which an 'external' goal orientation is possible. Such planning can miscarry as a result of cognitive deficiences. A case in point is the U.S.A. 'crash program' to build a fusion reactor (Project Sherwood 1952). It was thought at the time that, on the basis of astrophysical plasmaphysics, it would prove possible to determine theoretically the essential conditions of controlled fusion, and research within the program was therefore focussed on reactor-related problems: the stabilization of the Pinch effects and methods for heating plasmas.

Compatibility between 'external' demands and cognitive capacity depends upon what phase of disciplinary development the particular field has reached. Here we distinguish three such phases:

The exploratory phase characterized by classification procedures and by trial-and-error strategies. Theoretical approaches are pluralistic and the theoretical problems do not constitute a unified research program.

The phase of paradigm articulation. Here, explanatory problems dominate research. The constellation of problems raised within the discipline is derived from attempts to simplify make consistent and universalize the theoretical models.

The post-paradigm phase − in which, after relatively uncontroversial theoretical explanations of simple models have been developed, theoretical conceptions for more complex phenomena are worked out. In each of these three phases different internal rules of disciplinary development are effective and these create different conditions for external orientation.

3.1.1. *Planning Exploratory Research*

The empirical exploratory strategies which characterize the early phase of disciplinary development can be oriented to external problems. An orientation which cannot draw on causal theories, and which provides no explanation of the problem, may be designated as 'functional' research. The development of therapy programs in clinicial cancer research is a case in point. The subject here is the regulation of cell growth in the human organism. The respective disciplines, however, have not as yet produced explanatory models for phenomena of such complexity. Human biology and Physiology do not provide an understanding of the mechanisms of cell differentiation, which are not even known for simple systems, nor do they have micro-theories of regulatory processes in the human organism. In this phase of disciplinary development 'external' problems can only be dealt with by 'functional research'. In spite of inputs from a number of disciplines (e.g. cellular biology, which can in part explain the way drugs act within the cell, or cell kinetics and immunology) therapy programs still proceed largely on the basis of trial-and-error methods. Thus, various therapy strategies are tested in animal experiments and subsequently with patients, human organisms being taken as a black box. The focus of research is the study of the reaction of the organism to various dosages, duration and combined factors of medication.

Another example of functional research is provided by environmental protection programs. Traditional ecology is largely a descriptive science which has only recently begun developing experimental exploratory techniques and the explanation of systematic causal relations. The available techniques can not be applied to 'external' problems, though ecological exploration can incorporate various aspects of environmental protection and planning by the isolation of relevant variables, determination of thresholds etc. The scope of functional research in the social sciences, however, is limited by the fact that one can conduct experiments with social structures only within narrow limits. Thus, several attempts have been made to orient educational and sociological research to the solution of planning problems of comprehensive schools without such approaches having reached the 'testability' stage of trial-and-error procedure.

Stimulating the progress of functional research is the typical form research planning takes in the first phase of disciplinary development. In this phase the orientation of research occurs in a strong form where 'external' goals are formulated for empirical strategies (e.g. screening). An indirect form of orientation exists when the subjects of exploratory research are politically defined. This type of research planning is possible because here problem-oriented explorations and explanation-orientated explorations are methodologically equivalent. In the examples discussed, functional research is at the same time an input into the disciplines. Problem-orientation and disciplinary development are compatible. Divergencies arise as soon as the exploratory strategies of the discipline are no longer oriented to phenomena because simple, idealized model-systems are available which promise speedy results.

3.1.2. *Coincidence of Theory Development and Problem-Orientation*

The paradigm articulation phase of disciplinary development is characterised by an 'internal' research program which determines the range of choice of problems and objectives, and which, as a rule, is incompatible with 'external' problem-orientation. A link between research and external problems in this phase can only be realized if internal research fronts coincide with external problem-orientations. This happens, for instance, when leukemia cells relevant for medical reasons represent at the same time, for reasons internal to science, a suitable model system for the study of cell differentiation. Research planning in this phase has to rely on identifying and making use of such coincidences. The political direction of research, by contrast, occurs when for 'external' reasons a model system is selected to explain the mechanisms of cellular biology (e.g. an epidemiologically relevant type of tumor) which is scientifically suboptimal because it is too complex and too difficult to handle. Such a selection leads to relevant tumor research, but the latter does not determine the disciplinary research front within cellular biology. What often occurs then is shift to 'transfer research', that is, to research which further develops the results attained by basic research with simplified models by applying these to the relevant and more complex problem-areas. The theoretical development of the discipline is not subject to 'external' direction here since it is subject to 'internal' rules which give little leeway, if any, to 'external' goal-orientation.

3.1.3. *Planning of Theory Development*

In the post-paradigmatic phase of disciplinary development, on the other hand, problem-orientation and the 'internal' dynamics of disciplinary development can be co-ordinated. External goals can become the determining factors of development. Our first example here is fusion-orientated plasma physics.

Plasma physics is a 'horizontal' development of physics ('extensive research'). Its goal is the extension of fundamental principles of nature to complex areas of study, in this case to the fourth state of matter. This program can be pursued by following the internal rules of the discipline, as it follows the structure of problems in extra-terrestrial physics and astrophysics (investigation of waves in plasma and of the interaction of the plasma and fields). But, in contrast to disciplinary development in the phase of paradigm articulation, the sequence of solvable problems which can be worked on in plasma physics is not determined by an 'internal' logic. So the continuation of disciplinary research can proceed according to 'external' guide-lines.

In the case of fusion research this means that the external goal of controlling fusion leads to specific disciplinary problems (e.g. equilibrium conditions, interaction with external fields) constituting the research front of plasma physics. At the same time problems are generated in fusion-oriented plasma physics, e.g. interaction with surfaces, or the properties of the plasma in configurations, which are necessary to get a positive energy balance from fusion. In the first case, direction is related to central research problems (external selection of theory fronts) while in the second case direction is related to the content of disciplinary development (the development of special theories).

Obviously, this directed research operates at two different levels of generality. The fusion-specific problems could also be taken to be problems of great complexity in plasma physics engendered by fusion-specific conditions. Nonetheless, their solution cannot be understood as a mere application of theory, at least no more so than plasma physics is simply an application of the general principles of physics. The purpose of their solution is to establish theoretical models (equations and their solutions for fusion-specific phenomena). But these fusion-specific models cannot be derived from general plasma physics theory because the basic equations of the latter are unsolvable. This is why the theoretical structure of the problems of fusion becomes part of the theory development of plasma physics. In the post-paradigmatic phase the 'internal' rules within a field are so weakly selective that theory development can proceed in accordance with 'external' guidelines.

The second example for the political direction of science in the extensive, post-paradigmatic, phase of disciplinary development is taken from cancer research: the explanation of chemical carcinogenesis. The 'external' problem here is the improvement of cancer prevention through the identification of carcinogens and through the control of their effects on the human body. The strategy consists in clarifying the carcinogenic metabolism in the cell and the interaction of reactive intermediary products with cellular macro-molecules. The program is carried out on the basis of the methods and models of molecular biology and biochemistry. Biochemistry and molecular biology (of the single cell) have reached the state of mature, paradigmatic theories. They have basic models of cellular metabolism and of regulatory processes. The development of biochemical basic research, therefore, is no longer determined by 'internal' hierarchies of problems. It develops 'horizontally', frequently in line with problem constellations which are important in medicine (e.g. the explanation of addiction and of resistance to drugs) and which have been taken up because of their 'external' relevance. Chemical carcinogenesis is such an 'horizontal' problem. The objective here is to obtain a complete biochemical model of the metabolic process in the cell which leads to cell transformation. Such a model may be considered to be a special biochemical theory.

To sum up: in the early phase of disciplinary development research planning related to 'external' problems can only initiate functional research. In the paradigmatic phase planning must rely on the coincidence of 'internal' developments and problem-orientation. In the post-paradigmatic phase research planning can influence the theoretical development of the discipline itself. It can induce basic research by determining theory fronts according to 'external' goals, and it can give rise to the development of special theoretical models.

3.2. Measures of the Implementation of Problem-Oriented Research – Institutional Resistance

The measures adopted to implement a science policy program were very diverse in the cases analysed. They ranged from mere funding (parts of environmental and educational research), through the setting up of departments and courses (in computer science) to the establishment of research centres (e.g. the Institute for Educational Research in Berlin, the Institute for Plasma Physics in Garching and the Society for Biotechnological Research in Stöckheim). The diversity of the measures arise from the necessity of institutionalizing problem-oriented research within the frame of, or parallel to, the established science system. Directed science must be connected methodologically and theoretically with existing fields of research. To this end manpower has to be recruited and stable working relationships, forms of communication and career patterns have to be set up. Planning measures must be adapted to the structure of training courses as well as to the forms of organization predominant in research (university department, clinic, industrial laboratory).

Thus failures in science policy may follow from the inadequacy of measures taken to overcome or undermine the social resistance of established science to problem-orientation. Indicators of such resistance are, for instance, difficulties in recruiting competent researchers for a particular program, a lack of response to funding programs, or the concealed substitution of program goals by deviant research interests. Some examples of these types of resistance will now be discussed.

Fusion research was institutionalized in the Federal Republic of Germany when the failure of the US crash program had become forseeable and the fundamental problems of the confinement and heating of plasma came to the fore. There were no difficulties in recruiting plasma physicists and physicists working in the field of gaseous discharge to work on these problems. Although at the time astrophysical problems were central to plasma physics, fundamental problems of fusion offered a scientifically equivalent and financially more advantageous means for disciplinary development. Conducting research on fusion did not imply abandoning the plasma physics research front at this stage. Practically the same situation prevailed in the physics of gaseous discharge which had also been concerned with technical problems for a long time. For this discipline, fusion research offered a new field of work within which its theoretical development could be continued. Both of these disciplines were extensive, post-paradigmatic research fronts of physics: scientifically and institutionally they were receptive to external orientation.

Resistance to 'external' problem-orientation, however, became perceptible as advances made by fusion-orientated fundamental research suggested a move to reactor-based large scale experiments. This move required external, administrative pressures not only because the Big Science Research Centres in Germany are structured much like university institutes and do not have a management that could effectively prevent science from becoming academically oriented, but also because problem-oriented big science presents career problems for scientists. Large scale research with complex instruments requires changes in the career-orientations of scientists. Compared, for instance, to radioastronomy where many observations can be made with one machine operated by individual scientists and results are still attributable to individuals, in fusion research the machine itself is the experiment, the success or failure of which will become evident only after a number of years.

The receptivity of mature, post-paradigmatic disciplines to social problem-orientations is also evident in cancer research. Chemical carcinogenesis is accepted by biochemists as a relevant research front. In contrast, molecular biologists resist participating in clinically relevant biological cancer research. Molecular biology is in the phase of paradigm articulation and so biologists consider the application of these techniques and concepts to experiment on higher animal systems and humans (transfer research) as a deviation from the disciplinary research front. The academic socialization of biologists puts a premium on academic science and so working on clinically relevant problems seems to be doing second-rate science.

The institutionalization of biotechnology reveals a similar pattern. The tasks defined by the science policy program for microbiology, i.e. to develop and improve industrially usable microorganisms, attracted only those scientists who had received their training at the few institutions for industrial microbiology that exist in Germany (in particular for zymotechnics). Conversely, molecular biologists rejected recruitment into biotechnology and related research projects as long as there were still jobs in fundamental research. Work on the more complex systems of industrially exploitable microorganisms does not allow application of the most advanced methods of biology and entails research with 'softer' empirical methods. It is considered intellectually less demanding and scientifically less rewarding than work at the disciplinary research front.

The institutionalization of epidemiological research in Germany reveals another form of institutional resistance. Epidemiology is an important element of scientific strategies to combat cancer which depends on access to medical data. However, this has proved difficult to ensure because clinical-medical research has resisted the integration of epidemiological approaches and methods. In Germany, the medical profession is biased towards a curative approach and is unresponsive to alternative strategies such as the statistical determination of risk factors.

This social or institutional resistance of scientists to problem oriented research depends on the 'internal' dynamics of disciplinary developments. The examples of the chemists, plasma physicists, physicists of gaseous discharge on the one hand, and of the molecular biologists on the other, indicate that resistance appears as soon as problem-orientation implies deviation from the disciplinary research program. Such resistance does not tend to arise when problem orientation is imposed upon mature disciplines. Of course, resistance to problem orientated research can be overcome by setting up new research institutions, by starting new curricula, or through financial incentives but there is still the tendency to undermine the problem-orientation of such research by conducting theoretically oriented research while claiming to be engaged on the specified problem. This could only be controlled by a management that is in close contact with the research process and is competent to judge it.

4. Disciplinary and Problem Oriented Science – Transformation of the Science System

The concept of 'disciplinary' science is normally used to refer to academically organised and relatively autonomous science, whose development is governed by an 'internal' logic and which is contrasted to problem oriented research. However, the above analysis of the structures of disciplinary development has shown that problem orientation is by no means a clear-cut alternative to disciplinary organization. Disciplines attain phases of development in which their research can be directed to 'external' problems, or, to put it another way, problem oriented research can be assimilated by disciplinary research.

The objects of problem-oriented research are frequently 'non-disciplinary'. They belong to several disciplines or lie outside the 'internal' program of the disciplines concerned. If we generalize the results of our inquiry, we can say that the forms of problem-solving examined above are more frequently determined by disciplines into which the respective problems have been incorporated than disciplines are modified by 'externally' formulated problems. Of course, the time-span considered plays a role in this. If the problem is properly defined and remains identical over time it will have an impact on the disciplines concerned or give rise to new disciplines (e.g. computer science, fusion research). Some developing relations between disciplines and problem oriented research can be briefly summarised in the following way.

Due to their complexity, social problems usually span several disciplines. As a rule, particular aspects of problems are worked on separately in different disciplines and are subsequently integrated 'additively', as is the case with the chemical, biochemical, and micro-biological aspects of biotechnology or the biological, chemical and physical aspects of environmental studies. This method indicates that disciplines can in fact assimilate aspects of the complex problem. On the other hand it also points to some resistance of scientists to working in inter-disciplinary teams, either because they fear that communication will be inadequate or that overcoming communication barriers demands too great an effort.

In some cases problem-oriented research has been integrated within the development of single disciplines. In plasma physics, the theoretical frontiers selected on the basis of the fusion problem are viewed as problems which

might have been selected for investigation at a later time even if no direction
had occurred. The same applied to several of the problem oriented specialties
in biochemistry (e.g. chemical carcinogenesis): they develop within the frame
of the disciplinary matrix, although without 'external' direction they presumably would not have been institutionalised until much later.

A special example of the integration of a problem-oriented field into disciplinary development is the theoretization of chemical engineering through
physical chemistry. Chemical engineering used to be an empirical field developing outside the framework of the scientific disciplines, oriented to the
problems of chemical production. Disciplinary advances in physical chemistry
enabled the partial reduction of technical problems to those of physical
chemistry. Currently, this technical field, at least to some extent, is developing according to standards and goals which give chemical engineering the
status of a discipline.

These varying examples of the combination of disciplinary developments
with problem oriented research indicate that the differences between these
two types of research have not disappeared. On the contrary, we have found
many examples of the opposite. For the research workers involved, the orientation of biology to tumor research means having to abandon disciplinary
scientific development. A similar argument has been advanced by some of the
sociologists and psychologists in normatively oriented educational research:
in their work they apply the results of sociology and psychology but with
little chance of developing them any further.

Problem oriented research does not replace disciplinary research but modifies it by various forms of problem incorporation. These modifications, in
turn, correspond to new forms of institutionalization and new communication structures. The 'external' problems set by science policy programs
become foci for the formation of new communities. These communities are
sometimes only organizational segmentations within an existing discipline
(e.g. nitrosamine research, chemical carcinogenesis in biochemistry, fusion-
oriented plasma physicists in the phase of problem-oriented basic research),
in part they emerge outside the disciplinary social structures (reactor research,
biotechnology, educational research, biological tumor research). In a few
cases 'hybrid communities' formally resemble the classical scientific com-
munites: they develop evaluation standards, reputation structures and career
patterns. They differ from them, however, in that the production of knowl-

edge takes place according to externally set norms. Chemical engineering is a pertinent example here.

This kind of social coherence, however, is not typical for problem-oriented research. In most cases, the fundamental problems of directed research are taken up by 'hybrid communities' consisting of several disciplines as well as of non-scientists. Often a diffuse problem will suffice to give such communities some solidarity (cancer research, environmental research, educational research). Cohesion here is not secured through scientific complexity but by the political priority given to concrete social ends. The functions of critical evaluation and reputation allocation are generally retained by the disciplinary scientific community from which the respective scientist came and which, therefore, have not become irrelevant to the scientist's orientations. Nonetheless, the 'hybrid communities' do have important functions for the organization of work in the problem-oriented fields and for stabilizing work patterns in the light of political changes. These may be summarised as:

— They organize the transfer of the results of the disciplines into problem-oriented research by journals and congresses.
— They evaluate research relating to problem-solving and create a reputational system which functions independently from the disciplinary science system and to some extent awards non-scientific reputations to scientists.
— They mediate the dependency of the scientist upon the institutions or organizations which employ him to work on the external problem.
— Social control takes the form of the appraisal of his competence by his peer group rather than of the sponsoring organization (professional versus organizational role).
— The institutionalization of a problem-community safeguards research against the tendency, prevalent in theoretically based disciplines, to abandon problem-orientation in favour of theoretical interests for their own sake.

A further possible conclusion is that the overlapping of disciplinary scientific communities by problem communities reduces the relevance of disciplinary dynamics of development and this reduction may be part of a comprehensive transformation by which disciplinary structures of the organization of scientific work are replaced by forms of organization that follow from the definition of 'external' problems.

However, if we generalize the results we have found for the cognitive structures of problem oriented research, something else is suggested. Disciplinary scientific communities and problem communities are not mutually exclusive and scientists may belong to both of them at the same time. Contrary to what we had expected, the existence of disciplinary orientations in problem oriented research is not a mere relic of tradition. Non-disciplinary norms are translated into disciplinary ones and do not erode the latter. The stability of disciplinary structures seems to be related to the significance of *theoretical* orientations in a research field. In the cases we investigated, theoretical development in science was necessary for dealing with 'external' problems. Theoretical models were needed to reconstruct politically defined problems as scientific ones. In some cases this gave rise to new disciplines (chemical engineering, fusion oriented plasma physics, chemical carcinogenesis) providing special theories for problem oriented research. In other cases where the basis for theoretical problem research was insufficient, the 'external' problem was reconstructed in terms of the various existing disciplines that contributed to the problem. Scientists continued to regard disciplinary scientific communities as their primary frame of reference and to evaluate the progress of research within the theoretical and technical framework of their discipline although their research originated from 'external' problems.

In conclusion, the introduction of 'external' goals through political direction is likely to lead to a pattern of scientific development which is different from traditionally autonomous science. This pattern is not, however, an alternative to disciplinary structures of scientific development.

Notes and References

1. H. Klages, *Rationalität und Spontaneität*, Gütersloh: Bertelsmann, 1967, pp. 76–104.
2. The terms 'discipline' and 'disciplinary' in this paper designate scientific development according to internal rules (most visible in progammes of theory construction). Sociologically, 'disciplinary science' may also be described as 'specialty'.
3. This scheme was proposed by G. Küppers. Its application to cancer research is by R. Hohlfeld.
4. cf. F. Scharpf, *Planung als politischer Prozess*, Frankfurt: Suhrkamp, 1973, p. 80.
5. cf. N. Luhmann, *Grundrechte als Institution, Schriften zum öffentlichen Recht*, Band 24, Berlin 1965, p. 19.

SCIENTIFIC PURITY AND NUCLEAR DANGER
The Case of Risk-Assessment

HELGA NOWOTNY

European Centre for Social Welfare Training and Research, Vienna

1. Scientific Purity at Work

In recent years the large scale expansion of nuclear power in several of the industrialized countries of the Western world has become an issue of increasing concern to environmentalist groups, policy-makers and a number of scientists. Reports on possible inadequacies in safety precautions combined with discussions on the likelihood of theft or sabotage of dangerous materials have received wide coverage in the mass media and have caused public anxiety. Scientists have been engaged in a number of controversies which indicate areas of genuine theoretical uncertainty as well as the lack of reliable data for specifying possible future implications of differences in radiation levels and carcinogenetic effects. A continuing debate has focussed on the role of scientists qua expert, on how to weigh present and future risks against benefits, notably of an economic kind, and on how to grant access to some form of public participation in complex technological matters (1).

The debate on nuclear power has exposed what its opponents regard as the risky side of modern science and technology, which had previously been largely disregarded by a public opting for a supportive view of science and technology. Potential risks have been articulated with skilful imagination and the likelihood of events with catastrophic consequences has attracted wide attention. Nuclear power has, in many instances, become equated with further economic expansion and growth of technologies viewed as increasingly harmful. Controversies carried out among scientists have had repercussions which far transgressed the customary boundaries of scientific polemics. Nuclear power as an issue of controversial status within science, and heated

Mendelsohn/Weingart/Whitley (eds.), The Social Production of Scientific Knowledge.
Sociology of the Sciences, Volume I, 1977. 243–264. All Rights Reserved.
Copyright © 1977 by D. Reidel Publishing Company, Dordrecht-Holland.

public debate outside, displays several unique features which make it a highly
visible — and easy — target of criticism of scientific advances in general, but it
also serves to highlight the artificiality and vulnerability of the conceptual
distinction between what passes as a scientific and a non-scientific, or trans-
scientific, issue.

In this paper a major problem emerging from this debate will be discussed.
It concerns 'scientific purity'. That is, science's ability to avoid any social or
political involvement on the grounds that this would violate the assumptions
on which scientific methods are based and its own, highly successful brand of
rationality and objectivity. It will be argued that nuclear power poses a threat,
not only in the eyes of the opponents of this form of energy, but equally to
the orthodox view that a clear-cut boundary can be drawn between a 'scientific' problem to which science has answers to give, and a social or political
problem which is beyond science's capacity or responsibility. Scientific purity
has implied the successful isolation of science, especially its theoretical
branch of 'pure' science, from the debasing utilitarianism of technology as
well as from lay control (2). Science has achieved an astonishing degree of
autonomy and of professionalization in its institutional form, based on its
control of resources and of the institutional infrastructure necessary to organize effectively the production of scientific knowledge (3). It has willingly paid
the price for its political and social non-involvement, namely the institutionalized restriction of legitimate fields of inquiry and has successfully defended
the sharp boundaries between what constitutes a legitimate object for study
and what pertains to the murky realm of politics and values. It is the pursuit
of this successful policy of non-contamination with social and political issues
which has guaranteed the purity of science and has contributed to its unri-
valled status. Scientific purity, however, has been endangered by issues connected with nuclear power. The way science deals with this threat is likely to
affect future scientific development.

The threat to scientific purity is reflected in the area of decision making
which is based on the assessment of risk. This can no longer be founded on
technological or scientific expertise alone, as experience has shown that although the distinction between technical forms of expertise and questions of
policy may still theoretically be possible, it does not work in practice. The
field of legitimate inquiry is therefore no longer assured of its fixed boundaries. Finally, the threat results from mixing up categories of thinking, types

of answers and methods of arriving at them which have so far been success-fully kept apart. "Dirt is matter out of place", is the metaphor so appropriate-ly employed by Mary Douglas (4) to summarize a society's preoccupation with pollution. In the orthodox view of the scientific purist, social values and interests are seen as out of place too, as they threaten to encroach on his con-ceptual territory. The nuclear controversy may in part be an attempt to assign a new place to social matters in a universe which hitherto has been dominated by an order which no longer seems to hold.

Another problem is related to this and can be also seen as a threat to scien-tific purity. It has to do with the protective belt which has been built up around pure science with regard to risks emanating from science and technol-ogy. What is usually referred to as a risk is a precarious balance between potential gains attached to uncertainties surrounding the event classified as dangerous, and potential losses. The procedures — cognitive and practical — used to arrive at such a judgement have been given the generic term of 'risk-assessment', consisting of a variety of methods of defining, classifying and evaluating uncertainties in order to allow individuals and groups to reach decisions vis-à-vis the danger confronting them. Risk-assessment methods operate on the culturally and socially mediated level of every day life situ-ations as much as on a more formalized level which aims at the quantification of risk and the establishment of risk ranking scales (5). Furthermore, risk-assessment consists of a subtly balanced integration of assessment of social risks, i.e. gains and losses weighted against each other on the basis of domi-nant values and interests, and technological risks, which depend on the availa-bility of scientific and technological means of precaution.

Risk-assessment, with regard to scientific purity, can be viewed as some-thing like an interval marker between the scientific domain and the social domain, which are perceived as mutually exclusive but do in fact overlap. In this paper, shifts in risk-assessment methods will be examined in an historical perspective. It will be argued that the case of nuclear power, at least as it appears to its opponents, no longer fits into the overall structure of risk assessment, neither on the cognitive, nor on the institutional level. Risk assessment functions as an important device, however, to guarantee scien-tific purity. Current attempts to challenge the conventional risk assessment model are, therefore, likely to have repercussions on scientific purity too and at least indicate the likelihood of a shift in boundaries. In the final section, the repercussions of the present debate on dangers associated with nuclear power on overall scientific development will be discussed.

2. Shifts in Risk-Assessment Methods

Taking a broad comparative view of risk-assessment methods allows us to identify a number of dimensions on which significant shifts along an essentially pre-scientific — scientific continuum have occurred. The first dimension I wish to single out is the *moral-secular dimension*. Scientific risk-assessment is the most secular expression of risk-assessment. It does not seek to state the probability of a flood in terms of the evil thought of men or the loss of hunting resources in terms of the putrid smell of a murderer, as examples from primitive societies would suggest (6).

Likewise, in the history of Western thought, the constant readiness of the Church and the clergy to attribute natural hazards to the sinfulness of the lay folk decreased from the 17th century onwards (7), although remnants of the once powerful moral urge to establish such connections undoubtedly lingered on for much longer. Scientific risk-assessment is generally free from any attempts to put the blame for the occurrence of the undesired event on people or institutions who allegedly caused it by their behaviour. The moral attribution of risk has been separated completely from risk-assessment which is carried out in the ideology of value-free science.

On a related dimension, the *personal - impersonal continuum* of risk attribution, a similar shift can be observed. In a primitive society, the physical agency of misfortune is not so significant as the personal intervention to which it can be traced and although we may find that 'drought is drought, hunger is hunger and that epidemics, child labour and infirmity are common experiences', each culture nevertheless knows a distinctive set of laws governing the way these disasters fall (8). The main links between persons and misfortunes in primitive societies are personal links. On the cognitive level of explanatory schemes in which assessment and attribution of risk takes place, we observe a shift from what Horton has called 'thou-theories' to 'it-theories' (9); from the personal attribution of risk in primitive societies to an ancestor spirit or a fellow tribesman, to impersonal forces such as germs or a chain of events which happened to go wrong without any human being's ability to interfere. As has been noted by many anthropologists (10), theories of personal causation relate a patient's condition to a whole series of disturbances in the social field, while in modern societies there is a tendency to separate the impersonal (scientific) theory of e.g., causation of a disease, from whatever social disturbances may occur.

The third dimension along which we find differences in risk-assessment is the *deterministic-probabilistic* continuum. Horton points out that in the traditional cultures of Africa, the concept of coincidence is poorly developed, as the overall tendency is to give any untoward happening a definite cause (11). Thus, when a rotten branch falls of a tree and kills a man walking underneath, a definite explanation for the calamity will be sought. The idea that the event could have been brought about through the accidental convergence of two independent chains of events is inconceivable, because it is psychologically intolerable. To entertain it would be to admit that the episode was inexplicable and unpredictable which would amount to a glaring confession of ignorance.

Horton explains the psychological intolerance of the traditional mind by contrasting it with the scientist's ability to tolerate ignorance. Concepts like coincidence, or probability stem from a willingness to face up to the inexplicability and unpredictability of such a type of situation. One can argue against Horton, however, that the concept of probability emanates precisely from an attempt to gain a better understanding, and therewith control, over the unpredictability of events. Historically, the theory of probability was developed by a series of mathematicians who used games of fortune as their basis of departure (12). Towards the end of the 17th century the idea gained acceptance that probability theory was not only useful to gamblers, but that it was also possible to calculate the probability of a chance event taking one particular form. John Arbuthnot declared in 1692 that a chance event was not merely one whose causes were not known, but that it was possible to calculate the probability of its taking one form rather than another, even when human beings were involved. He saw politics as "a kind of analysis of the quantity of probability in causal events" (13).

This change of attitude towards chance, and notably the awareness of patterns in random behaviour has left so strong a mark on our scientific culture that it allows us to adopt a different stand with regard to risk. In the language of scientific risk-assessment we are capable of calculating in advance the likely number of fatal accidents, diseases, crimes etc. (although there are great theoretical difficulties in extending probability theory to cover events whose occurrence is very low).

Science takes us still one step further in our probabilistic world view by allowing us to differentiate the workings of random forces. We can discern significant variations in the population exposed to risk and we are forced to the conclusion that it is less within the individuals' own personal power to control danger, than a function of their social characteristics which determine much more effectively to what kind and degree of risks an individual is exposed, as well as what kind of precautions are in fact at his/her disposal. From this follows the important conclusion that individuals and groups may also differ in the ways in which they perceive and evaluate risks: their risk-assessment methods may vary. Before we return to examine the case of diverging risk-assessment on the part of opponents to nuclear power, we have to ask, however, how we can account for the general shifts in risk-assessment that we have observed. From an historical as well as a comparative perspective, the shifts are linked to changes in the ways in which individuals and groups cope with uncertainty, notably in the transition from magic to science.

3. Coping with Uncertainty: from Magic to Science

Every society has developed sets of beliefs, embedded in religion, magic or science, to help individuals with their daily problems and to teach them both how to avoid misfortune and how to account for it when it occurs (14). Risk-assessment taken in its widest sense consists in doing just that. It is the identification and evaluation of events to which uncertainty is attached and it is the process of reducing uncertainty within mangeable limits (15). Today, the superiority of scientific methods of risk-assessment — consisting in our knowledge about the laws of probability as well as means of manipulating the probabilities involved — seems so evident that one might assume that it was the insight into their superior working that led the people in some parts of 17th century Europe to abandon their magical beliefs and magical modes of risk-assessment in favour of the new methods. This, however, is far from being the case. No system of risk-assessment, as we shall demonstrate below, is internally vulnerable, as any system of belief possesses an in-built self-confirming character. Once the initial premises are accepted, no subsequent discovery is likely to shake a believer's faith, for everything can be explained in terms of the existing system. Every system has developed elaborate ways of accounting for failures and errors. They possess a conceptual resilience which makes them virtually immune to external arguments (16).

The actual defence of this cognitive immunity depends, however, on social factors which may be less secure from attacks coming from a rival system. These factors can be divided into two groups: the first group consists of social practices which are destined to safeguard the system of belief and to ensure its effective protection and isolation from lay beliefs and institutions (17), while the second consists of general socio-economic changes which affect the broad structure of risk.

3.1. *Cognitive Immunity and the Credibility Context*

Risk-assessment, as any other system of belief, is contingent on social practices which effectively guarantee its credibility context which must be maintained on the part of the risk assessors, whether they are modern scientists, medical doctors, politicians or sorcerers. The need for credibility exists independently and irrespectively of the content of the beliefs, as we must assume that no system of thought is totally self-evident and devoid of the necessity of being socially transmitted and maintained (18). The mechanisms for assuring credibility are therefore quite similar: autonomy and authority of those who have obtained the monopoly of regulation of the system of belief, often accompanied by rituals destined to inspire respect, fear and credibility. Modern medicine provides an excellent example for the many ritual practices of a non-operative kind in which doctors and surgeons engage (19). A medicine man is as skiful and sensitive in maintaining his patient's confidence as any Western doctor. Likewise, the modern layman's grounds for accepting scientific explanations, despite the pervasiveness of modern science which has penetrated deeply into the thought and everyday practices of a larger sector of the population, is often not much different from the African villager's grounds for accepting explanations propounded by one of his elders (20). In both cases, the propounders are accredited agents of tradition (21).

Failure to maintain the credibility context is one of the factors which account for the emergence of the opposition against nuclear power, as will be elaborated in the next section. Scientific knowledge always reaches the lay audience via a transmission and translation process (22). While some scientific terms are readily translated into everyday language, the favourable reception of scientific ideas by the lay public is, despite the general deference of the public to the authority of science, limited by their low intelligibility and the lack of correspondence of institutionalized procedures in warranting and validating knowledge. Notably, the principle of scientific consensus, as the most effective means of validating scientific knowledge, is seen as contrasting strongly with the norms of democratic procedures for reaching consensus (23). Yet the social practices maintaining the credibility context necessary to ensure the functioning of the cognitive immunity of the system of belief, do not only depend on what is done, but also on who does what. Thus, we must not only ask how effective existing social practices are, but also how secure and unchallenged is the authority of the risk-assessors.

3.2. *The Social Embedding of Risk*

Thus, in analyzing why risk assessment procedures may differ, we must not only look at the cognitive procedures through which risk is identified and evaluated, but also at the economic and social factors which determine the overall structure in which risks are embedded. What kind of social institutions exist in a society, which either serve to protect an individual against certain risks, or which maximise other risks? What risks are acceptable to a society as a whole is not only determined by expectations of significant gains in terms of values and interests, but also by the means of protection available which promise to minimize the danger involved.

I shall now turn to examine the historical factors which were operating in the transition from magic to science in 17th Century England and which, after an initial development of magic and science side by side, made traditional modes of magical thought and risk-assessment appear increasingly outdated (24). This will throw light on concomitant social and economic changes and allow us to locate risk assessment methods within the overall socio-economic structure in which risk is embedded. As already mentioned, it is tempting to credit the scientific method and belief system with an inherent superiority to magical belief systems which ought to have been as convincing to 17th century contemporaries as they are for us.

The functionalist argument, first advanced by Malinowski, that magic occurs as a substitute activity, whenever man lacks the necessary empirical or technical knowledge to deal with problems confronting him ("magic is dominant when control of the environment is weak") does not, however, stand the test in this case. In England, as Keith Thomas convincingly shows, magic lost its appeal before the appropriate technical solutions had been devised to take its place. It was the abandonment of magic which made possible the upsurge of technology, not the other way round (25). In the late 17th century, the more general rejection of magic was still unaccompanied by the discovery of new remedies to fill the gap. Beliefs in witch-craft declined, for instance, before medical therapy had made much advance, reliance on love potions and divination fell into disuse without any immediate prospect of a technical substitute.

How, then, can we account for the transition from magic to science if we regard both systems as containing means for coping with uncertainty and reducing individual risk? This dramatic shift was based on a series of intellectual developments which amounted to a veritable paradigm change of the overall world view. The essence of the paradigmatic revolution insofar as it relates to the decline of magic, was the collapse of the vitalistic microcosm theory and the triumph of the new mechanical philosophy. With the former, the whole intellectual basis of astrology, astral magic and other foundations for the magical belief system, simply collapsed. The notion of the universe being subject to immutable natural laws meant the end of the animist conception of the universe which had constituted the basic rationale for magical thinking. The new world view proved to be decisive in its influence upon the thinking of a new intellectual elite and gradually filtered down to other parts of the population.

Various developments, like the insistence that all truth be demonstrated, a disinclination to accept inherited dogmas without putting them to the test, robbed the hold magical systems of their capacity to satisfy the new educated elite. To profess contempt for vulgar 'superstitions' became common in Elizabethan England. With the emergence of a new stratum containing the nucleus of what was to become the new and educated middle class, the magician ceased to command respect because intellectual prestige and credibility had shifted elsewhere. A new group of risk assessors had successfully established itself.

There were, however, complementary changes in the overall structure in which risks, as they typically appeared to contemporaries, were to be found.

A general and dramatic improvement of communications and subsequent changes in the mobility of the population took place which seemed to have served to break up the physical and social isolation that was one of the conditions for the thriving of magical beliefs in the countryside.

Personal attribution of misfortunes makes eminent sense in a closely knit social network in which there are few other outlets for conflict. As social relations grew more impersonal there was also less room for the type of conflict which gave rise to witchcraft accusations (26). The rise in literacy and the advent of the newspaper saw the emergence of advertisements which carried notices about lost property such as runaway servants and missing persons, thus notifying a wider public than a village wizard or town diviner could have done (27). The gulf which developed from the 17th century onwards between the educated classes' beliefs in the enlightened teachings of the new science, and the strands of popular 'superstition' which lingered on, especially on the countryside, well into the 19th or even 20th century (28) highlights the effect of these changes on the structure of risk.

Of even greater importance in changing the overall structure of risk were new forms of protection providing greater security for men of property: the growth of insurance at the end of the 17th century. Although certain schemes designed to cushion sufferers from theft, fire, sickness or other disasters had existed before that time, fire, flood, or the sudden death of a close relative could mean total disaster to most inhabitants of the period.

The first steps to provide economic security were taken by merchants and shipowners in the 14th century in Italy (when the term 'risk' was probably coined) and in England by the mid-16th. For some time the system remained rudimentary until, by the early 18th century, the situation changed as was highlighted by the foundation of two substantial joint-stock companies devoted to marine insurance in 1720 (29). Other types of insurance followed. Fire insurance developed at much the same time, primarily as a result of the Great Fire of London. Life insurance was the slowest to evolve, as it was dependent on accurate actuarial calculations of the current expectations of the insured's life (30).

It was these developments, so intimately linked to nascent capitalism as a new economic force, which made contemporaries less vulnerable to certain kinds of disaster. With it went new kinds of knowledge to supersede mystical explanations of misfortune and to make the transition from the personal, magical attribution of hardships to impersonal causes, which became one of the main themes of the Enlightenment. Keith Thomas sees the nascent social sciences taking over the former role of witchcraft by providing a new way in which the victim could blame others for his fate. Instead of accusing witches, he could attribute his misfortunes to the ways his parents had brought him up, or to the social system into which he had been born (31).

Questions about the amazing coincidence between the rise of science, religious beliefs which stressed self-reliance and self-help, aspirations which put faith into new technological solutions which were still to be invented and the emergence of capitalism, have been asked time and again before. We have gleaned bits and pieces from the historical account in order to examine the role magic and science have played in coping with risk as a form of uncertainty. From this evidence it appears that it was not the inherent superiority of scientific ways of coping with risk that brought about the decline in magical beliefs, but rather a shift in the overall structure of risk — at least for the propertied classes — offering new means of protection against certain types of risk. This was accompanied by a change along the personal-impersonal continuum of risk-assessment. By projecting the causative agent of risk outside the narrow medieval world, remedies and precautions which had been developed against them became superfluous and out-dated. They literally lost the basis on which they were founded. At the same time, a new form of compensation for losses emerged in the form of insurance. By converting risk and the implicit threat to such socially valued goods as property (fire, loss, natural hazards) and life (insurance against death) into a new medium of compensation — money — the impersonal attribution of danger found its corresponding institutionalization by the acceptance of an impersonal compensation. Likewise, the moral implications of causation of misfortune — the ethical assumption that suffering was probably due to someone's moral fault (most likely the sufferer himself) which were important means of social control — became replaced by a more secular attribution which eventually found expression in new institutions of legal, political and social accountability.

Today, against an impressive record of the achievements of science and technology in reducing traditional forms of risk, we are faced with the emergence of new types of risk. The most important question which arises from the opposition to nuclear power, both within the scientific community and outside, is whether the traditional scientific method of risk-assessment does

justice to this new form of risk. It is this question which I shall deal with in
the next section.

4. The Structure of Nuclear Risk

I have observed that the societal approach to risk has shifted along the
following cognitive dimensions, and in accompanying protective social institutions, which together characterize modern society's conventionalized model
of risk assessment:
- from moral to secular risk-assessment;
- from personal to impersonal risk-assessment;
- from deterministic to probabilistic risk-assessment.
In addition, there have been changes in social institutions designed to serve as
protection against risks, characterized by a change:
- from non-monetarized (and sporadic) to monetarized and systematized
  forms of prevention and compensation, notably in the form of insurance;
- from diffuse agents of responsibility to differentiated legal, political and
  administrative agencies of responsibility. It is my major contention that
  the risks associated with nuclear power – as seen by its opponents – do
  not fit into the overall structure of risk assessment as it has been developed
  by modern society's conventionalized model outlined above. This model,
  therefore, cannot serve its function of reducing uncertainty to a level
  which would allow the acceptance of the risks involved.

Opponents of nuclear power do not regard risk from a secularized, but
from a highly ethical perspective. The ecological movement which has provided an essential input, both on the ideological and recruitment bases, conceives itself as basically an ethical movement which appeals to man's responsibility both for his natural environment and health and well-being of future
generations. The rejection of economic growth as the major social goal also
marks a break in the unconditional faith in material progress which has been
such a powerful factor in public support of science and technology. The
engagement of churches in the public debate is yet another indicator of the
moral questions which have been raised by the opponents (32). The long-
term time perspective adopted by the opponents not only allows the projection of estimates of likely catastrophic consequences in a more dramatic way,
but can also be taken as another indicator for the kind of future-orientation

so characteristic of the need to express a moral imperative by millenarian movements (33).

On the second dimension, opponents of nuclear power see the risks as intimately related to the working of personal forces. They charge the nuclear industry, and — in varying degrees of collusion with it — the state bureaucracies, individual companies or politicians — with being responsible for negligence or disregard of safety precautions. They claim that the further spread of nuclear power installations will benefit the corporate interests of these groups exclusively and, therefore, adopt highly personalized theories of risk attribution (34).

On the deterministic-probabilistic continuum, the risks connected to nuclear power pose a challenge to the scientific community and the public alike. Rare events with practically no experiental nor experimental basis are difficult to assess in probabilistic terms. A single event — a major nuclear disaster — would probably change risk calculations drastically. It is in such conditions that risk-assessment becomes dominated by its credibility context (35). Probabilistic assessment, otherwise so entrenched in modern life, then gives way to a deterministic stand, whereby the determinant resides in the source of authority which is more credible. The open dissensus displayed by scientists qua experts in public reinforces the necessity of choosing among conflicting statements. In such situations, the public is not only more likely to choose the safer estimate (36), but also to shrink from a probabilistic assessment if additional uncertainties are added by conflicting estimates.

Nor do the two major protective institutions which have developed since the 17th century provide a compensatory mechanism in risk-assessment. Insurance as a device to safeguard against potential risks by promising monetary recompense is no longer feasible, given the high degree of uncertainty and enormous proportions of potential damage. It is also questionable whether monetary recompense alone would still be acceptable, once damage to future generations as well as the global effects of potential catastrophic consequences are considered. The only other comparable risk in contemporary life — war — has not been covered by insurance either.

Finally, there has been a significant decline in trust in those public authorities into whose legal, political and administrative competence it would fall to assume a certain degree of responsibility for risks connected with the planning, operation and supervision of safety of nuclear power plants (37). Regulatory procedures and access to the legal and political decision-making machine inside and outside government, have been severely criticized by opponents for their manifest lack of responsiveness to public demands for participation.

This latter demand, which is quite new (38), points to the emergence of a new element in risk-assessment, namely the necessity of allowing for some degree of consent of those who might eventually be affected by the negative consequences of technologies. While voluntariness, i.e. consent to risk, was previously of importance only on an individual basis, with many individuals never coming into the position of exercising such a right, it is now being demanded on the basis of citizen's rights. Voluntariness (consent) to risk has been assumed for workers through their entering into a contractual relation-ship. For the general public, the social acceptability of risk has found expres-sion in some kind of legal provisions (e.g. safety standards for chemical plants and other technological risks (39) or has been assumed to be sanctioned by general social practice, e.g. driving a car. An extension of these assumptions for the case of nuclear power has, however, met with fierce resistance. Oppo-nents have argued that consent can no longer be taken for granted and that legal and other provisions of safety precautions have been insufficient and grossly wanting. They argue further that the benefits connected with nuclear power are not worth the risk and that the risks by far outweigh what can be covered by conventional methods of accountability.

5. Risk Resistance and Standardisation of Risk

This brings us to the question of risk resistance as one possible form of socie-tal response and its causes. The fact that the case of nuclear power — as seen by the opponents — does not fit into society's conventional model of risk-assessment does not automatically mean that the risks in question have to be rejected. Adjustment to risk in the form of either taking a fatalistic view of the dangers involved or of neglecting the dangers would be an equally likely outcome. By improving risk-protective institutions, notably by improving the possibilities for genuine participation and by adopting higher safety standards (which has partly been the case as a consequence of public protest) the overall risk structure could be altered so as to accommodate the inherent character-istics of this particular kind of risk. The moral argument could partly be compensated for by making public institutions more accountable and by other means which would help to restore trust into political and administrative institutions. By developing new kinds of probabilistic calculations, part of the theoretical uncertainty could perhaps be reduced as well and the traditional credibility context be restored. Yet, despite some moderate efforts in this direction, public acceptance of nuclear risk seems still largely undecided in several major Western industrialised countries. Why?

Risk-assessment and risk-resistance are both outcomes of societal risk-assessment. As has been pointed out earlier, risk-resistance may be based on differences in value assessment, in technological assessment, or both. A difference in value assessment indicates a shift in social values and interests, altering the balance of benefits and costs in terms of dominant values. A difference in technological assessment indicates a shift in the credibility context of the (technological) risk assessors: they may no longer command full authority for the claims to manipulation of probabilities they make. Risk resistance in the case of nuclear power has various origins and most likely contains both elements.

The dangers connected with nuclear power are to be found in a domain of hypotheticality **(40)** which is admittedly inherently difficult to conceptualize and to translate into a proper societal image of risk. What is at fault is the failure of society so far to come up with a convincing, standardized image of nuclear risk which would allow us to place its alongside other conventionalized and standardized types of risk. Apart from its relative newness, a major factor in this default can be attributed to the fact that the images of nuclear risk which have been proposed at the societal level so far, are themselves highly ambiguous: they resemble pictures of optical illusion that psychologists have been fond of drawing. The societal images of nuclear risk which have been proposed display the same quality: depending on how one looks at them, the risks involved are entirely technical, in origin as well as in terms of solution to the problem they contain, or they are entirely social, depending on the functioning or lack of it of social institutions from the initial planning to the control of safeguards. This ambiguity is reinforced and enhanced by the adherence to the institutionalized division of labour between political institutions and science. Scientists claim that they can only answer scientific questions and that anything beyond them is for society to answer. Yet, society relies on science for deciding what image of risk to construct and to

maintain the boundary has become a most dangerous venture. Nuclear danger
— on its ultimate societal level — has not yet been standardized and classified
as a type of risk. In order to classify it, it has to become categorized. Yet, there
is utter confusion between categories which hitherto have been regarded as
scientific and categories regarded as pertaining to the social realm. Resistance
against nuclear risks is one manifestation for this societal confusion. Another
likely consequence seems to lie in its demystifying repercussions for science.

6. Nuclear Danger and the De-mystification of Science

In the years since World War II the external boundaries between science and
politics have been more and more difficult to maintain (41) as the growing
dependence of science on publicly approved funds and the hesitant first
steps of national scientific policies illustrate. Internally boundaries are open
to challenge as well: some scientists — albeit in a minority — have taken up
problems which they have helped to create and have critically assessed their
own research. In the case of nuclear power, dissensus, which is normally kept
within the boundaries of a discipline and dealt with following traditional
scientific norms, has been carried out publicly. An essentially scientific
controversy has thereby been transformed into a para-scientific one (42).
Some scientists maintain that we shall have to learn to live with semi-perma-
nent forms of disagreement, as the problem is too non-technical to be left to
the limited expertise of experts (43).

There are probably few other issues which can serve to highlight the
softening of boundaries to the same extent as the nuclear power issue. The
more scientific and political, economic and social issues become entangled,
the more vigorous will be the attempt on the part of the more orthodox
scientists to save the case of 'scientific truth'. But it seems likely that they
are fighting a losing battle. Risk-assessment is but one theatre in which it is
being carried out.

Even orthodox scientists concede that many of the questions and uncertainties raised in connection with the large-scale operation of nuclear power
plants cannot be answered with anything like the scientific validity scientists
are used to. The biological effect on humans of very low radiation level will
probably never be fully ascertained, simply because of the huge number of
animals required to demonstrate unequivocal effects. Estimates of infrequent

events, such as a serious reactor accident, cannot be made with the same scientific validity that one can apply to estimates of events for which there are numerous occurrences.

Problems of non-practicability, of non-feasibility for reasons of practical impossibility, problems of hypotheticality (44) which fall outside the range of what is experimentally probable, are not limited to peculiarities of nuclear power risks. Nor are they merely a problem of developing a new form of probabilistic theory, of using fuzzy set theory or other new mathematical techniques to cope with the problem. It is in a much more general sense that science has reached the limits of the experimental method and with it, many of the in-built and taken for granted assumptions gradually seem to dissolve (45).

If, however, traditional scientific validity standards (with regard to effects which are uncertain, but risky) cannot be maintained, what will be the consequences? The dramatic divergence in risk estimates, which can never be considered as only a scientific problem because legislative standards will be based on such estimates, has been exposed before the public and has contributed much to the confusion surrounding nuclear power safety standards. The public accustomed to the display of scientific unanimity and consensus, as befits any kind of real authority, has reacted with surprise and confusion.

Scientific authority is suffering a loss in its credibility. Knowledge sources are most effective when they present an image of unanimity and certainty, as actors lacking other guides use these as indicators of reliability (46). Pressure groups have taken advantage of the lack of unanimity and have employed it as a most effective weapon in undermining their opponents' evidence as well as to arouse fears and doubts which may put an end to public indifference. In such a situation, is it sufficient for scientists to appeal to the difference between science and trans-science?

If it is difficult, and perhaps impossible, to give answers in situations of genuine uncertainty, and yet society and decision-makers expect the experts to pronounce authoritatively, a retreat to a scientific vs. trans-scientific position will not suffice in the long run. Either scientists have to cut loose and shed the role of expert entirely, admitting that there is no expertise involved as the issue is too non-technical (which is unlikely as it would mean to give up too many privileges) or they will have to come to terms with the practical as well as ethical task of being responsive to politically defined problems. Perhaps they will do this by consciously incorporating some of the social premises and assumptions into their own work, i.e. by deliberately permitting an infiltration of pure science with social (political) values.

But the loss of credibility of science, changes in the public image of science and a shifting of the boundaries between science and trans-science are not the only conclusions that can be drawn from examining the impact of the new form of risk structure which is posed by nuclear power. There are accompanying social changes which place risk on a new social basis and which may mark the end of a paradigm of traditional scientific risk assessment methods:
 — the universalization of risk,
 — the loss of voluntariness and the concomitant bureaucratization of risk,
 — the irreversibility of risk
as they have become manifest through the opposition movement. Although risk emanating from new technological and scientific developments can bring to the fore sometimes violent forms of protest and can mobilize citizens and spread from country to country — thus expressing general grievances and societal concerns — we must nevertheless keep in mind that risk-producing technologies are far from being historically new. Ever since capitalism began with the large scale industrialization of Europe and the U.S. the destruction of nature has accelerated. Its visibility was however contained spatially in the new industrial centres as well as socially concentrated in the experience of those who had to live there (47).

On the technological side, risk has become universalized because its effects threaten to be of truly global dimensions. The consequences of a potential serious nuclear power accident are likely to be felt not only in the immediate vicinity but may spread both spatially and temporally through possible reproduction of genetic defects. In the 19th and 20th century risk technologies were localized largely in the sense that it was the workers in the plant, or the mining community who bore the highest risk. If one looks at accident statistics, both of voluntary risks (car accidents) and involuntary ones, certain population groups can be singled out as being more risk exposed for various reasons. With nuclear power this relationship has changed, at least theoretically. Although estimates have been made as to radius of risk exposure of a plant, for all practical considerations risks connected with this source are regarded as universalized.

Closely connected with the spread of nuclear risk, is the concomitant concentration of economic and political power which is responsible for large scale industrial exploitation of nuclear energy. While in other economic domains (multi-national corporations) this concentration has also been noticed, an additional element has entered in the case of nuclear power: concentration of control over its production results inevitably in rather drastically shrinking the extent to which the population at large can enter associated risks voluntarily. Decisions related to the siting, size and output of the plant, industrialization of the region and details of safety standards and regulations as well as their supervision pose a form of risk which is largely outside the political influence of those who care or could be affected by these decisions. Public participation in decision-making has become a demand which has been at the core of grievances articulated by the opposition movement. As the American example shows, the responsiveness of public authorities has been slow. The underlying issue of how individuals can organize themselves against well institutionalized, large scale bureaucracies with their well-established routine and their bureaucratic rationality, which predisposes them to work well in collaboration with other agencies or industry (48), is unsolved. Risk associated with nuclear power is a risk which remains under bureaucratic control, the possibility for the individual to accept the risk or reject it remains extremely limited and depends on his access to the legal-political system.

Finally, there is the irreversibility of decisions affecting risks in the sense that long-term consequences are to be faced which apparently prevent future developments. While it is true that ever since industrialization there has been relatively little concern about problems that might arise for future generations by decisions and actions undertaken at present, the additional uncertainties, in the genetic, as well as in the physical, sense of waste disposal problems, pose the new problem of their irreversibility quite clearly.

We have seen how the 17th century brought a decline of magic beliefs not in response to, but before the rise of, science. Scientific methods and beliefs were accompanied by significant changes in the economic and social sphere. In this paper I have focussed on risk-assessment as a societal approach to risk, whereby both scientific methods and beliefs as well as social evaluation have to be combined to determine a societal response. We have seen that the overall structure of risks associated with nuclear power does not fit well into the conventional model of risk-assessment.

While there is no doubt that new methods will be developed, these methods will only then be successful if the boundary between scientific and trans-scientific, socio-political questions and decisions becomes more permeable and transparent. Otherwise, science will share the fate of magic in the 17th century, if magic is defined in the words of Keith Thomas as "the employment of ineffective techniques to allay anxiety when effective ones are not available".

Notes and References

1. cf. e.g. I. Clark, 'Expert Advice in the Controversy about Supersonic Transport in the United States', *Minerva* **XII**, 1974, No. 4, pp. 416–432; D. Nelkin, 'Scientists in an Environmental Controversy', *Science Studies* 1, 1971, pp. 245–261; D. Nelkin, 'The Role of Experts in a Nuclear Siting Controversy', *Bulletin of the Atomic Scientists* 30, 1974, pp. 29–36; D. Nelkin, 'Political Impact of Technological Expertise', *Social Studies of Science* 5, 1975, pp. 35–54; H. Nowotny, 'Social Aspects of the Nuclear Power Controversy', IIASA RM-76-33 (Institute for Applied Systems Analysis, Laxenburg, Austria) 1976; H. Hirsch and H. Nowotny, 'Controversial Issues in the Exploitation of Nuclear Power', to appear as IIASA publication, Fall, 1976.
2. C. J. Lammers, 'Mono- and Poly-Paradigmatic Developments in Natural and Social Sciences', in *Social Processes of Scientific Development*, R. Whitley (ed.), London: Routledge & Kegan Paul, 1974; P. Bourdieu, 'Le champ scientifique', *Actes de la Recherche* 2, 1976, pp. 88–104, similarly speaks about 'strategies of closure' destined to mark a separation between scientific problems and the profane problems of everyday life.
3. R. Whitley, 'Changes in the Social and Intellectual Organisation of the Sciences: Professionalisation and the Arithmetic Ideal', this volume, p. 143.
4. M. Douglas, *Purity and Danger*, London: Routledge & Kegan Paul, 1966.
5. cf. H. J. Otway *et al.*, 'Social Values in Risk Acceptance', IIASA-75-54 (International Institute for Applied Systems Analysis Research Memorandum, Laxenburg, Austria) 1975; H. J. Otway and P. D. Pahner, 'Risk Assessment', *Futures* 8, 1976, pp. 122–134. The close link between the concept of risk and decision making is documented by the vast literature on risk in both the managerial field and in the psychological literature. Despite these attempts at quantification, the concept of risk remains ill-defined: it implies a rational decision-maker who is capable of arriving at an optimal decision, yet this decision-maker is usually seen as isolated from the social context. For a paper attempting to expand the narrow view of decision-making, see M. Toda, 'The Decision Process: A Perspective', to appear in *International Journal of General Systems*, 1976.
6. A. Whyte, 'The Cultural Encoding of Risk Assessment', paper prepared for the SCOPE/EPRI Conference on Risk Assessment, Woods, Hole, Mass., mimeo.
7. K. Thomas, *Religion and the Decline of Magic*, London: Weidenfeld and Nicolson, 1971.
8. M. Douglas, *op. cit.*, 1966, Note 4, p. 119.
9. R. Horton, 'African Traditional Thought and Western Science', in *Knowledge and Control*, M. Young (ed.), London: Collier-Macmillan, 1971.
10. See for instance V. Turner, *Ndembu Divination*, Manchester, Manchester University

Press, 1961; V. Turner, 'A Ndembu Doctor in Practice', in *Magic, Faith and Healing*, A. Kiev (ed.), London: Collier-Macmillan, 1964.
11. R. Horton, *op. cit.*, Note 9, p. 250.
12. F. N. David, *Games, Gods and Gambling*, London: Ch. Griffin & Co., 1962.
13. K. Thomas, *op. cit.*, Note 7, p. 785.
14. *ibid.*, p. 761.
15. A. Whyte, *op. cit.*, Note 6.
16. R. Horton, *op. cit.*, Note 9, p. 242, and literature cited there, speak about 'secondary elaborations' as the utilization of current beliefs in such a way as to 'excuse' failures in order to protect major theoretical assumptions on which predictions are based.
17. C. J. Lammers, *op. cit.*, Note 2; H Nowotny, 'Zur gesellschaftlichen Irrelevanz der Sozialwissenschaften', *Wissenschaftssoziologie*, Kölner Zeitschrift für Soziologie, N. Stehr (ed.), Köln: Westdeutscher Verlag, 1975.
18. H. Nowotny and M. Schmutzer, *Gesellschaftliches Lernen*, Frankfurt am M.: Campus, 1974.
19. J. Roth, 'Ritual and Magic in the Control of Contagion', *American Sociological Review* XXII, 1957, pp. 310–314.
20. R. Horton, *op. cit.*, Note 9, p. 262.
21. A. Whyte, *op. cit.*, Note 6.
22. S. B. Barnes, 'On the Reception of Scientific Beliefs', *Sociology of Science*, B. Barnes (ed.), Harmondsworth: Penguin, 1970.
23. A. Weinberg, 'Science and Trans-Science', *Science* 177, editorial, 1972, p. 211.
24. The following section depends heavily on the work of Keith Thomas. Given the exemplary role of England for the development of Western science we feel less uneasy in concentrating exclusively on England.
25. K. Thomas, *op. cit.*, 1971, Note 7, p. 786.
26. *ibid.*, p. 797.
27. *ibid.*, p. 779.
28. *ibid.*, p. 789.
29. *ibid.*, p. 780, the London Assurance and the Royal Exchange.
30. As first developed by John Graunt in his 'Natural and Political Observations⌋... upon the Bills of Mortality', which appeared in 1662.
31. K. Thomas, *op. cit.*, 1971, Note 7, p. 784.
32. P. M. Boffey, 'Plutonium: Its Morality Questioned by National Council of Churches', *Science* 192, 1976, pp. 356–359.
33. H. Nowotny, 'Time-Structuring and Time Measurement: On the Interrelation between Time-Keepers and Social Time', *The Study of Time II*, J. T. Fraser and N. Lawrence (eds.), Heidelberg-Berlin: Springer, 1975.
34. Such statements appear in the opposition literature. See for instance *Bürgerinitiativen im Bereich von Kernkraftwerken*, Batelle Institut, Bonn: Bundesministerium für Forschung und Technologie; Wüstenhagen, H.-H., 1975, *Bürger gegen Kernkraftwerke*. Rororo: Reinbeck/Hamburg, 1975.
35. A. Whyte, *op. cit.*, Note. 6.
36. H. M. Sapolsky, 'Science, Voters and the Fluroidation Controversy', *Science* 162, 1968, pp. 427–433.
37. Harris Survey, 'Majority Favours Nuclear', *Nuclear News* 18, 1975, pp. 31–34.
38. R. L. Crain, E. Katz and D. B. Rosenthal *The Politics of Community Conflict*, Indianapolis: Bobbs-Merrill; 1969, B. Mausner and J. Mausner, 'A Study of the Anti-Scientific Attitude', *Scientific American* 192, 2, 1955, pp. 35–39.
39. R. Williams, 'British Civil Nuclear Power: The 1974 Decision and the Growth of Opposition', mimeo., unpublished paper, Manchester University, 1976.

40. W. Haefele, 'Hypotheticality and the New Challenges: The Pathfinder Role of Nuclear Energy', IIASA RR-73-14 (International Institute for Applied Systems Analysis, Laxenburg, Austria), 1973.
41. See, among many, H. Rose and S. Rose, *Science and Society*, Harmondsworth: Penguin, 1971; J. Haberer, *Politics and the Community of Science*, New York: Van Nostrand-Reinhold, 1969.
42. H. Nowotny, *op. cit.*, Note 1, p. 1976.
43. J. P. Holdren, 'The Nuclear Controversy and the Limitations of Decision-Making by Experts', *Bulletin of the Atomic Scientists* 32, 1976, pp. 20–22.
44. W. Haefele, *op. cit.*, 1973, Note 40.
45. The claim to generalizability built into the experimental method is increasingly being limited as the opportunity for experience to be repeated under the same conditions declines as a result of the fact that the performance of experiments – such as the use of DDT in vast quantities, has altered the initial conditions. See on these points especially W. van den Daele and W. Krohn, 'Theorie und Strategie – zur Steuerbarkeit wissenschaftlicher Entwicklung', Starnberg, mimeo, 1975.
46. S. B. Barnes, *op. cit.*, 1970, Note 22.
47. R. Burger, 'Lebensqualität und Warenproduktion – zur Klassenbasis des Ökologismus', *Wirtschaft & Gesellschaft* 1, 4, 1975, pp. 9–32.
48. R. R. Alford and R. Friedland, 'Political Participation and Public Policy', *Annual Sociological Review* 1, 1975.

CREATION VS. EVOLUTION:
The Politics of Science Education

DOROTHY NELKIN

Cornell University

1. Introduction

Order, control, the maintenance of established values and organizational relationships; these are central priorities for any social system. Any deviation from a given social order tends to be viewed as threatening or 'polluting' — subject to what Mary Douglas has called "pollution behavior ... a reaction which condemns any object or idea likely to confuse or contradict cherished classifications" (1). Science has been increasingly faced with many such external threats. Despite the emphasis on the tentative nature of all classifications and the importance of continued testing of scientific theories against new empirical criteria, scientists also find themselves engaged in pollution behavior to protect themselves against dangerous intrusions.

Threats to science include the external pressures on the direction of research that inevitably follow from dependence on outside funding, and the controls that arise from concern with its ethical and social implications (2). Other threats arise from the resistance to science as a dominant world view that impinges on traditional values and suppresses essential elements of human experience (3). The proliferation of cults and sects, the interest in supernatural explanations of nature, the preoccupation with astrology and various pop cosmologies suggest the persistent tendency to question the image of science as an infallible source of truth (4).

Of the many challenges to science in recent years, perhaps the strangest is the effort of 'scientific creationists' to present creation theory as a scientific alternative to evolution theory. *Genesis*, argue the creationists, presents a viable theory of origins and should be given 'equal time' in biology textbooks. Creationists claim to be scientists. They work out of educational and

Mendelsohn/Weingart/Whitley (eds.), The Social Production of Scientific Knowledge.
Sociology of the Sciences, Volume I, 1977. 265–287. All Rights Reserved.
Copyright © 1977 by D. Reidel Publishing Company, Dordrecht-Holland.

research centers, belong to scientific societies and publish professional journals within the sociological framework of the contemporary scientific establishment. They also use sophisticated organizational and political tools to influence the teaching of science in the public school system. In response, biologists, appalled at what they perceive as a travesty of modern science and a threat to its credibility, have mustered considerable political power to maintain their control over the definition of science as it should be taught in the schools. In the course of the dispute over biology textbooks, it becomes difficult to distinguish science from politics and ideology.

This paper will describe the beliefs and activities of creationists, and the biologist's response suggesting how political and social values are imposed on science by scientists as well as by their critics. It then analyzes several fallacies that are evident as scientists try to transfer their professional expectations about science to the diffusion of scientific knowledge and to their quest for credibility in the public domain.

2. The Scientific Creationists and the 'Social Pollution' of Science

[Science] wrote an end to the ancient animist covenant between man and nature, leaving nothing in place of that precious bond but an anxious quest in a frozen universe of solitude. With nothing to recommend it but a certain puritan arrogance, how could such an idea win acceptance? It did not; it still has not. It has however commanded recognition; but that is because; solely because, of its prodigious power of performance.

(Jacques Monod, *Chance and Necessity*)

During the 1960's a group of scientifically trained fundamentalists began to reevaluate fossil evidence from the perspective of special creation as described in the Biblical record. These creationists believe that "All basic types of living things, including man, were made by direct creative act of God during the creation week described in *Genesis*" (5). They thus chose to reinterpret organic evolution according to Biblical authority.

Some creationists accept aspects of evolution theory but set limits to scientific explanations, rejecting, for example, natural selection as a causal explanation of evolutionary change. More extreme creationists deny all evolutionary processes, arguing that evolution and creation are mutually exclusive theories. Still others accept the common compromise — that there are two levels of reality, but they are concerned that the teaching of evolution denies and obscures all religious explanation and that failure to teach alternative hypotheses implies that science provides a complete and sufficient understanding of ultimate causes (6).

Among those who identify themselves as creationists are some fanatics (a botanist who claims that evolution theory is "a special argument of the devil"), disciples of traditional fundamentalist sects, several astronauts, and many solid, middle-class, technically-trained people working in high technology professions in centres of science-based industry. These modern day creationists share many of the moral and religious concerns expressed in the Scopes trial some 50 years ago, but their style is strikingly different from that of their flamboyant ancestors. Arthur Hays described the circus atmosphere in Dayton, Tennessee in 1925:

Thither swarmed ballyhoo artists, hotdog vendors, lemonade merchants, preachers, professional atheists, college students, Greenwich Village radicals, out-of-work coal miners, IWW's, single taxers, libertarians, revivalists of all shapes and sects, hinterlands soothsayers, holyrollers, an army of newspaper men, scientists, editors, and lawyers (7).

In comparison, creationist confrontations appear more like professional society debates. Indeed, they try to present their views at the annual meetings of professional organizations and in technical papers. They work within organizations with such names as the Institute for Creation Research, the Creation Research Society, and the Creation Science Research Center. For Creationists argue that *Genesis* is not religious dogma but an alternative scientific hypothesis capable of evaluation by scientific procedures. They present themselves not as 'believers', but as scientists, engaged in a scholarly debate about the methodological validity of two scientific theories. And typically the active creationists have scientific credentials and sometimes academic appointments in accredited colleges and universities. Of the 22 members of the advisory board and staff of the Institute for Creation Research, for example, 17 have Ph.D.'s (9 in physics or engineering, 7 in biology, chemistry or geology, and one in science education). Two have masters degrees in science, two are theologians and one is an M.D. Several of the advanced degrees are from major universities such as Harvard, Columbia, University of Minnesota, Berkeley, and UCLA. Nine are presently teaching in state universities, 4 at bible colleges, 1 is working at Sandia research laboratory and 8 are staff members of the Institute for Creation Research.

3. Ideology: The Bible as Science

The creationist world view rejects the theory that animals and plants have descended from a single line of ancestors, evolving over billions of years through random mutation. Creationists cannot accept the implication that natural selection is opportunistic and undirected, that selection pressures act to cause genetic change only because of immediate reproductive advantage. According to creation theory, biological life began only 5 to 6 thousand years ago when all things were created by God's design into 'permanent basic forms'. Similar to the pre-Darwinian views of Charles Lyell, the creationists 'case for design' is that all subsequent variation has occurred within the genetic limits built into each species by the Creator. Evolution is a directed and purposeful process (8). Change would not modify the original design, for nature is static, secure and predictable, each species containing its full poten-tiality.

The creationists thus differ from evolutionists in their explanations of the origin of life, the transmission of characteristics, the nature of variation and complexity, and the character of the fossil record (See Table I).

Creationists clearly are faced with a formidable amount of evidence that supports the theory of evolution. This poses a cruel dilemma; they must either admit exceptions to their beliefs which would raise doubts among their constituents, or they must maintain consistency at the risk of public ridicule. They have chosen the latter alternative and spend their energies trying to demonstrate that evidence supporting evolution is biased and in-complete, or that it can be reinterpreted to fit whatever conceptual system is convenient. For example, creationist theoreticians argue that the fossil record is far from conclusive, failing to provide the transitional forms or linkages between diverse living groups that would suggest evolution from a common ancestor.

Creationists also deny the evidence from techniques of radioisotope dating, for these techniques are based on unproven assumptions that no uranium or lead has been lost throughout the years and that the rate at which uranium changes has remained constant over time (9).

For creationists, the law of conservation of energy (that energy cannot be created or destroyed), and the second law of thermodynamics (that energy approaches increasingly random distribution) are additional proof of an

TABLE I

Alternative models

	Creation Model	Evolution Model
Theory of Origins	All living things brought about by the acts of a Creator.	All living things brought about by naturalistic processes due to properties inherent in inanimate matter.
Transmission of characteristics of living things	Creation of basic plant and animal kinds with ordinal characteristics was complete in the first representatives.	Origin of all living things was from a single living source which itself arose from inanimate matter. Origin of each kind from an ancestral form by slow, gradual change.
Variation	Variation and speciation are limited within each kind.	There is unlimited variation. All forms are genetically related.
Complexity	Sudden appearance in great variety of highly complex forms. Net present decrease in complexity.	Gradual change of simplest forms into more and more complex forms.
The fossil record	Sudden appearance of each created kind with ordinal characteristics complete. Sharp boundaries separate major taxonomic groups. No transitional forms between higher categories.	Transitional series linking all categories. No systematic gaps.

Adapted from Henry Morris, 'Creation vs. Evolution', *American Biology Teacher*, March, 1973.

initial ordering of natural processes. Similarly, the laws of quantum mechanics – that individual events (e.g., the decay of K-mesons) are not predictable – are interpreted to imply that theories of origin and change are 'fundamentally unprovable' but more likely to have occurred by design than by random mutation (10).

When pressed by contradictory evidence creationists will argue that design in nature simply exists because of the will of the Creator. They are aware of the problems in this argument, but then they claim that evolution theory is but today's creation myth, based also on faith, although it excludes consideration of a supernatural force. If one accepts a different set of assumptions, then creation theory becomes fully as workable and fruitful an hypothesis as evolution. Committed to their assumptions, creationists are able to suppress dissonant evidence (11). For those who believe in creationism, it is a distinct and coherent logical system that fully explains the world around them. "Studying the facts of physics and chemistry I find that the only way I could truly understand the present world is by the word of God and the inspiration of the Holy Spirit" (12). It is evolution theory that is the 'scientific fairy tale'.

4. Political Influence

The political influence of fundamentalism peaked during the '20s. Between 1921 and 1929, anti-evolution bills were introduced into 37 state legislatures (13) and there were increasingly successful efforts to qualify statements about evolution in those few textbooks that included discussion of the theory, or to exclude such textbooks from adoption in the schools.

One contemporary writer described the prevailing emotional hostility to science as a 'cancer of ignorance' – a repudiation of the authority and the integrity of scientists (14). But hostility was largely related to the association of evolutionary theory to disturbing social problems of the day. Evolutionary ideology, claimed William Jennings Bryan at the Scopes Trial, goes beyond simple scientific questions and bears on moral values (15). The force of this argument was great in the 1920's, a comparatively lawless period, when popular discussion suggested that the country was 'going to ruin'. Social problems were variously attributed to the weakening of loyalty to the church, and to prosperity, but also, to materialism fed by science.

The Scopes Trial also reflected the demands of parents to control the education and the values of their own children. "What right", Bryan asked, "have the evolutionists – a relatively small percentage of the population – to teach at public expense a so-called scientific interpretation of the Bible, when orthodox Christians are not permitted to teach an orthodox interpretation of the Bible?" (16) Scientists, however, had quite a different view about populist control of science curriculum. "What is to be taught as science would be determined not by a consensus of the best scientific opinion, but by the votes of shopgirls and farmhands, ignorant alike of science and the foundation principles of our civil society" (17). They focused on the rational and logical basis of the theory of evolution as the basis for its inclusion in biology classes.

The Scopes Trial ended for a while the fundamentalists' efforts to ban the teaching of evolution. Their quiescence in part reflected the neglect of the subject in biology textbooks. A survey of the content of biology texts described the persistent, if undramatic, influence of anti-evolutionist sentiment and showed that the teaching of evolution actually declined after 1925 (18). Publishers, through the late 1930's, discouraged about market prospects and anxious to avoid controversy, ignored evolutionary biology. As late as 1959, public school biology teaching was still dominated by 'antiquated religious traditions' (19). One hundred years after the theory of evolution by natural selection was established and accepted by the scientific community, it was just beginning to form an integral part of the public school biology curriculum. It was not until 1968 that the last law forbidding the teaching of evolution was ruled unconstitutional (20). But even as the courts challenged the old legislation forbidding the teaching of evolution, the 'scientific creationists' were gathering momentum for a renewed attack on the new biology courses based on evolutionary assumptions that were introduced in their public schools.

These creationists have been able to exercise a remarkable influence on local school boards, state curriculum committees, and state legislatures throughout the country (21). Textbooks used in most parts of Texas still make no mention of evolution and in Tennessee, legislation requiring equal time for creation theory in biology courses was passed in 1973 (to be struck down 2 years later as unconstitutional) (22).

Events in California suggest how creationists influence educational policies. The California Board of Education publishes a Science Framework to guide the selection of textbooks in public schools. This Board has included among its members a number of people sympathetic to creationism, and in 1969, after years of political pressure, it unanimously voted to revise the Science Framework to recommend that both evolution and creation be taught as alternate scientific explanations for the origin of life.

All scientific evidence to date concerning the origin of life implies at least a dualism or the necessity to use several theories to fully explain relationships ... While the Bible and other philosophical treatises also mention creation, science has independently postulated the various theories of creation. Therefore, creation in scientific terms is not a religious or philosophical belief. Also note that creation and evolutionary theories are not necessarily mutual exclusives. Some of the scientific data (e.g. the regular absence of transitional forms) may be best explained by a creation theory, while other data (e.g. transmutation of species) substantiate a process of evolution ... (23).

Thus 45 years after the Scopes Trial, the guidelines for a state educational system that serves one million children included a formal recommendation to teach creation theory.

The California Science Advisory Committee that had written the original draft was horrified by the revision. "The changes, though small in extent, have the effect of entirely undercutting the thrust of the 205-page document ... offend[ing] the very essence of science, if not religion" (24). The implications began to be evident in 1971 when the curriculum commission selected specific biology textbooks to be used in the schools. California buys nearly ten percent of the nation's textbooks and many publishers were quite willing to adapt to the recommendations. One proposed replacing a section about Leakey's archaeological discoveries of primitive man with a reproduction of Michelangelo's Sistine Chapel painting of the Creation and a drawing of Moses.

There followed a deluge of letters, petitions, resolutions, and position papers from people representing all sides of the issue until in December 1972, the State Curriculum Committee announced that it had found a way to ensure the neutrality of science textbooks. The committee proposed to eliminate all scientific dogmatism, to avoid any discussion of ultimate causes, and to indicate the conditional nature of all discussion of evolution theory. A special committee screened and edited 30 biology textbooks. As it turned out, their changes were not only unobjectionable, but indeed called attention to much unnecessary dogmatism. Their changes were accepted by the board. Later, a revised science framework was published that avoided the question of 'equal time'. Creationists complained of the arrogance and the authoritarian power of the scientific establishment and continued their appeals.

In all the history of science, never has dogmatism had such a firm grip on science as it does today with reference to evolution theory. Evolutionists control our schools, the universities and the means of publication (25).

5. Pollution Behavior: The Scientists Respond

I don't know very much. I just know the difference between right and wrong.

(George Bernard Shaw, in *Major Barbara*)

Evolutionists were incredulous that creationists could exert influence on the
definitions and boundaries of science as taught in the schools. "It just does
not make sense in this day and age." Incredulity led to amused disdain. The
British journal, *Nature*, confidently offered free subscriptions to the first ten
biologists who could claim that their present observations were inconsistent
with the commonly accepted views of evolution (26). A Stanford biochemist
placed the creationists' argument "in the same arena as those advanced by the
Flat Earth Society" (27). Facetious remarks were abundant. It was proposed
that Bible publishers insert a sentence in *Genesis* to indicate that "scientific
method rejects the supernatural approach to explaining the universe" (28). A
biologist and member of the State Advisory Committee inquired if a scientific
course on reproduction should mention the stork theory (29).

One biologist satirized creation theory by examining it critically as a
serious scientific hypothesis. In a masterful exercise in Biblical exegesis that
reminds one of Darrow's famous cross examination of Bryan at the Scopes
Trial he pointed out problems of accuracy revealed by scholarly disagreement
about different versions of the Scripture. He noted internal contradictions in
the account of creation in *Genesis* and practical impossibilities involved in
literal interpretation of the Bible. How can one explain in rigorous scientific
terms the practical difficulties involved in the Noachian myth: the migration
of animals, the necessary size of the Ark, the coexistence of species? (30)

The creationists' public claims of scientific verity were especially embarras-
sing to biologists. Until recently scientists have rarely aired their disputes in
public. Careful of their external image and eager to avoid political interference,
they try to avoid public exposés of arguments among themselves. Control is
maintained through informal internal communications, and through a peer
review system that determines research funding and the acceptance of papers
by journals. Creationists, however, claimed publicly to be scientists and they
adopted the language and forms of science. Yet they ignored the constraints
imposed by the norms of the scientific community by seeking external
political judgements of the validity and justice of their arguments.

As creationists persisted in their efforts to influence textbook selection, the biologists' amusement gave way to defence. If creation theory was placed on an equal footing with Darwinism, it would further water down the understanding of what science was about. Thus, scientists countered creationist ideas and political demands with their own ideological arguments and political strategies.

6. The Ideological Defence

Biologists called the arguments for design based on the intricacy and beauty of nature 'spurious and irrelevant'. Belief in an intelligent designer is "as blasphemous as it is far fetched" (31). Admitting that much evidence for evolution theory is circumstantial and incomplete, they defended evolution theory as a useful model with solid support from the sum of evidence accumulated in such diverse disciplines as genetics and biochemistry (32). The creationists responded to these arguments by asserting that Biblical authority presents an equally useful model that is also confirmed by evidence.

A major confrontation took place in November 1972 at the public hearings on the California textbooks guidelines. It promised to be a circus but bureaucratic procedures (five minute limitations on speeches) and the creationists' efforts to present themselves as scientists, set a tone of sober debate. Engineers appointed to curriculum development commissions somehow lack the fire of fundamentalist preachers. Yet the ironies were striking. "Witnesses from each side appeared in each others clothing", observed a journalist amused by the spectacle of scientists speaking for creation theory and theologians supporting science (33). The 23 witnesses for *Genesis* included only 3 Baptist Ministers, but 12 scientists and engineers. The evolutionists, on the other hand, called forth only 4 scientists. Their other witnesses included Presbyterian, Episcopal, and Mormon Ministers, Catholic and Buddhist Priests, and a Rabbi; all testified for the need to separate science and religion.

Evolutionists and creationists each claimed the other based its beliefs on faith; each group argued with passion for its own dispassionate objectivity; and as in the Scopes Trial each group brought its social and political concerns to the discussion of science curriculum. Scientists as well as creationists bemoaned the moral, political, and legal implications of the alternative ideology. The influence of scientific assumptions on religious equality, as well as on educational practice, concerned both groups. And as each side defended its position and criticized the other, their arguments were strikingly similar. Indeed, the debate assumed aspects of a battle between two dogmatic groups as the anti-dogmatic norms of science faded with the effort to convey the validity of the theory of evolution (Table II).

TABLE II

Contrasting arguments of Creationists and evolutionists [a]

Creationist Argument	Evolutionist Argument

ON SCIENTIFIC METHODOLOGY

Creation theory is as likely a scientific hypothesis as evolution. Neither theory can be supported by observable events, neither can be tested scientifically to predict the outcome of future phenomena, nor are they capable of falsification. Evolutionists, while claiming to be scientific, confuse theory and fact. And it is unscientific to present evolution as a self-evident truth when it is based on unproven *a priori* faith in a chain of natural causes. Based on circumstantial evidence, evolution theory is not useful as a basis for predicton. It is rather, "a hallowed religious dogma that must be defended by censorship of contrary arguments". The situation is a trial of Galileo in reverse. [b]

Creationism is a "gross perversion of scientific theory". Scientific theory is derived from a vast mass of data and hypotheses, consistently analyzed; creation theory is 'Godgiven and unquestioned', based on *a priori* commitment to a six-day creation. Creationists ignore the interplay between fact and theory, eagerly searching for facts to buttress their beliefs. Creationism cannot be submitted to independent testing and has no predictive value, for it is a belief system that must be accepted on faith.

ON MORAL IMPLICATIONS

Man is a higher form of life made in the image of God. To emphasize the genetic simularity between animals and man is socially dangerous, encouraging animal-like behavior. As a 'religion of relativism', evolution theory denies that there are absolute standards of justice and truth and this has disastrous moral implications.

"Tampering with science education by insisting on the priority of feeling over reason, of spontaneity over discipline, of irrationality over objectivity, the honorable man wrecks his own ideals. By attempting to redefine science for his own purposes, the honorable man finds himself in the company of a young hippie radical representing the counter-culture, who indiscriminately is throwing out a life of reason based on objectivity and thus gives himself license to live carelessly and dogmatically." [c]

Table II (continued)

ON POLITICAL IMPLICATIONS

Evolution is a scientific justification for 'harmful' political changes. The evolutionary philosophy which substitutes concepts of progress for the 'dignity of man' has been responsible for "some of the crudest class, race and nationalistic myths of all times: the Nazi notion of master race; the Marxist hatred for the bourgeoisie; and they tyrannical subordination of the worth of the individual to the state."[a]

Creationism is a form of right-wing conservatism, as evident in the role of Reagan appointees in the California Board of Education. "Attempts to legislate belief systems through controlling printed materials in the public schools have frequently been a part of fascism."[e]

ON LEGAL IMPLICATIONS [f]

Public schools cannot legally deal with questions of origin that are the domain of religion. They infringe on constitutional rights as guaranteed under the 'establishment of religion' and 'free exercise' clauses of the first amendment, the 'equal protection' and due process clauses of the fourteenth, and constitutional guarantees of freedom of speech. Teaching evolution amounts to the establishment of 'secular religion' interfering with free exercise of fundamentalists' truths and violating parental rights. Moreover, restricting the teaching of alternate theories violates the free speech right of teachers.

Exclusion of creation theory in science classes is justified by the first and fourteenth amendments. It is unconstitutional to teach children in a way that would blur the distinction between church and state. Creationism is non-scientific and religious, and therefore to include it would amount to 'the establisjment of religion'. Imposing non-scientific demands would restrict the freedom of teachers to teach and students to learn. To require equal time for doctrines that have no relation to the discipline of biology would impose unconstitutional constraints on the teacher's freedom of speech.

ON RELIGIOUS EQUALITY

To select one set of beliefs over another is to suggest that one group of people is superior to another. Creationists are s persecuted minority. In view of the wide range of beliefs among Americans, teaching evolution is divisive and inequitable and reflects the dogmatism of an established group. "Science has been oversold in Western culture as the sole repository of objective truth ... the authoritarianism of the medieval church has been replaced by the authoritarianism of rationalistic materialism."[g]

Creationist demands that their beliefs be taught in public schools represent the tyranny of a minority; a few people are using democratic protections to subvert majority interests. To teach creation theory would violate the beliefs of other religious groups. Justice, in this case, would also require teaching hundreds of other mythologies reflecting the belief of the American Indians, Hindus, Buddhists, Moslems, and so on. Religions can co-exist with science because they operate at a different level of reality.

Table II (continued)

ON SOUND EDUCATIONAL PRACTICE

Education in biology is "indoctrination in a religion of secular humanism". It is a breach of academic freedom to prevent the teaching of arguments that have withstood challenges for 6000 years. "Science demands that our children be taught an unproven, undocumentable theory. There is neither a scientific nor moral base upon which to refuse our school children access to another, much documented theory – the theory of *Genesis* creation." Sound educational practice requires teaching creation as an alternate theory so that students can decide what to believe for themselves.

To include creation theory in scientific classes would be poor pedagogy leading to ridicule and rejection of both science and religion. If creation were presented as an alternate hypothesis, even less would be taught about science than is taught today. Furthermore, it would be a breach of academic freedom to require to teach what is essentially a belief system. In-depth studies of the relationship between science and religion are too sophisticated for public schools. It is sound educational practice to focus on an accurate presentation of scientific fact and leave the teaching of religion to the home.

---

[a] *Sources:* From statements at the *Public Hearings on California Biology Textbooks,* Sacramento, November 9, 1972, and from the *BSCS Newsletter*, November 1972, unless otherwise indicated.
[b] John N. Moore, 'Evaluation, Creation and the Scientific Method', *American Biology Teacher*, 35 (January 1973); and editorial, *Christianity Today*, 17 (January 1973.)
[c] David Ost, 'Statement', *American Biology Teacher*, 34 (October 1972), p. 414.
[d] Carl Henry, 'Theology and Evolution', in R. Mixter (ed.), *Evolution and Christian Thought Today* (Grand Rapids; Eardmans, 1959), p. 218.
[e] Ost, *op. cit.*
[f] Discussion of the legal issues appears in F. S. LeClercq, 'The Monkey Laws and the Public Schools: A Second Consumption?' *Vanderbilt Law Review,* 27 (March 1974), p. 209–42.
[g] Duane Gish, 'Creation, Evolution and the Historical Evidence', *American Biology Teacher*, 35 (March 1973), p. 140.

7. The Political Defence

The National Association of Biology Teachers (NABT) organized the political and legal opposition. NABT is a national organization devoted to the improvement of biology teaching. It has about 8000 members, mostly high school and junior college teachers, and its journal, *The American Biology Teacher* is distributed to about 13 000 subscribers. Increasingly dismayed by the California events, in March 1972 NABT organized a committee to plan legal action, and retained legal counsel in California hoping to prevent the Board of Education from implementing the *Science Framework*. During the following spring and summer, NABT tried to arouse the interest of the scientific community. It set up a Fund for Freedom in Science Teaching, receiving contributions of about $12000 to support its legal and organizational activities, and it organized a reponse from professional societies.

The prestigious National Academy of Sciences was moved for the first time to interfere in an issue involving a state decision. In October, 1972, the Academy issued a strongly worded resolution (**34**):

Whereas the essential procedural foundations of science exclude appeal to supernatural causes as a concept not susceptible to validation by objective criteria: and

Whereas religion and science are, therefore, separate and mutually exclusive realms of human thought whose presentation in the same context leads to misunderstanding of both scientific theory and religious belief; and

Whereas, further, the proposed action would almost certainly impair the proper segregation of the teaching and understanding of science and religion nationwide, therefore

We ... urge that textbooks of the science, utilized in the public schools of the nation, be limited to the exposition of scientific matter.

The American Association for the Advancement of Science also 'vigorously opposed' the inclusion of creation theory in science textbooks.

Scientists have built up the body of knowledge known as the biological theory of origin and evolution of life. There is no currently accepted alternative to scientific theory to explain the phenomena. The various accounts of creation that are part of the religion and heritage of many people are not scientific statements or theories. They have no place in the domain of science and should not be regarded as reasonable alternatives to scientific explanation for the origin and evolution of life.

The American Anthropological Association was less vigorous — for some members argued that it would be absurd to offer any response to creationists' demands. The Association eventually urged legislative and administrative bodies "to reject all efforts for the compulsory introduction ... of statements reflecting religious and philosophical beliefs subject to different orders of verification into biology textbooks."

The Academic Senate of the University of California condemned the creationists' statement in the *Science Framework* as a 'gross misunderstanding' of the nature of scientific inquiry. Finally, nineteen California Nobel Laureate scientists petitioned the state board to leave the teaching of evolution, the only theory based on scientific evidence, intact (**35**).

Despite the formal response from scientific societies and a general dismay at the revival of creationism, many individual scientists were reluctant to become involved. Some were sensitive to political accusations from school-boards, and preferred to stay insulated from the controversy in order to avoid interference in their own work. Others were simply uncomfortable with any public activity such as talking to reporters, writing letters to editors, or appearing at hearings. A few voiced their concern about opposing a minority group. One biologist, for example, called the NABT fund "the fund for suppression of incorrect theories". Although far from believing in creation theory, this scientist had no desire to outlaw a controversial point of view from the public school system. "Darwin by this time is quite immune to overthrow from fundamentalist attacks, and it isn't going to harm a single child to be made aware that there are divergent opinions available on the subject." He supported an open comparison of creationists and Darwinian arguments. "I am not in favour of the suppression of dissenting opinions" (36).

NABT soon discovered that its own membership included creationists. Letters poured into the Washington D.C. office. "I do not support your editorial position and the vicious scientific attacks on the creationists." "I feel the fund is being misused to try to force everyone into one mould. It is worse to block false approaches than to tolerate them." One writer suggested that the fund would be used to "promote atheism and agnosticism in the schools". It should be called a HUSH fund ('Help us to Silence Him'). "It is a campaign to close the mouths of those who espouse theories other than those of evolution."

NABT also found itself caught in the middle of a debate concerning its editorial policy. Should the Journal consider publishing creationist articles? Should it print letters from creationists? For several years the Journal did include occasional creationist articles qualified to indicate that they did not reflect the NABT view. The editor felt that their bias and lack of logic would be obvious and self defeating. By 1972 this editorial policy brought a deluge of criticism from scientists about the Journal's lack of discretion. "Creationists' goals are obviously to discredit science and scientists." The Journal should not present such 'trash'. By November 1972, as the California situation reached its climax, the Journal stopped publishing creationists' articles although it continued to include a few letters.

A similar discussion took place when NABT organized its 1972 convention. Should creationists be allowed to hold a formal session at this meeting? Some scientists felt that it was necessary and appropriate to include creationists.

Creationists will prosper and multiply on martyrdom, but will perish on exposure. Are we so insecure? Will we let our exasperation with the creationists irrationality provoke us to become irrational ourselves? (37).

From a different perspective, a NABT regional director felt that creationism should be discussed as an important social issue that bears on science teaching (38). Others, however, strongly opposed a creationist panel, for allowing creationists a voice at the professional society meeting would suggest their legitimacy: they are "religious missionaries, concerned primarily with converting classrooms by ... smuggling religious dogma into classrooms in a Trojan horse" (39).

After November 1972, biologists were increasingly reluctant to acknowledge the creationist movement. The 1973 NABT convention did not mention the controversy and biologists consistently refused to debate creationists in hopes of avoiding any activity that would suggest the scientific legitimacy of the movement. Many tried to discredit the movement by questioning the credentials and competence of those who claimed to be scientists. They were, claimed the biologists, only 'engineers'. "They are educated at Bible Colleges." "They are false authorities", "Dullards", "Rejects from the space age." "Is it legal to misuse professional titles?" "Creationists get their doctorates in a box of cracker jacks." "It is a publishers racket." "As phony as a $3 bill." "A way to subsidize religion." Scientists commonly described the work of creationists as 'rubbish', or 'garbage'. Terms that unintentionally, but engagingly suggest the concern with pollution.

8. Analysis

Most social systems find means to preserve their integrity, to resist pressures from marginal groups. Some primitive societies develop rituals that give visual expression to accepted forms of social relationships. Some animals deposit secretions to mark the territorial limits of their community and to ward off intruders. Scientists have means (such as the peer review system and a set of accepted norms) that help to preserve the boundaries of their enterprise by controlling the behaviour of scientists. But these mechanisms operate as if science were by definition an autonomous interprise. The scientific community is ill-equipped to deal with the external political pressures that become important as soon as they begin to cope with the diffusion of scientific research **(40)**. Thus, when unable to ignore persistent challenge, scientists often take refuge in reasserting the neutral character of their work and the irrelevance and irrationality of political, social, or religious considerations. The scientific society petitions against the teaching of creation theory, for example, emphasized the neutral character of science and its distinction from philosophical or personal beliefs. Scientists also appealed to rationality, assuming that people see science from the same perspective as scientists themselves. The persistence of controversies concerning scientific theories raises a number of questions about these assumptions which we will describe as 'misplaced neutrality' and 'misplaced rationality'.

9. The Fallacy of Misplaced Neutrality

In their defense of evolution theory, scientists emphasized the neutral and apolitical character of science. Yet a major aspect of their objection to the creationists was a frankly political concern about external professional control over the definition of science as it would be taught in the schools. Just as scientists in the 1920's had worried about 'shopgirls and farmhands' determining what is to be taught as science, so evolutionists in 1970 fought the influence of lay opinion. "The State Board's repudiation of its own committee in favor of a lay opinion from the audience should ultimately become a classic example in textbooks on school administration of how *not* to proceed with the development of standards", claimed an evolutionist **(41)**. "Why are comments related to science made by high-priced technicians such as medical doctors and by persons in related fields of technology more readily acceptable as statements of science than those made by scientists themselves?" complained another **(42)**.

The concept of neutrality loses its significance when scientists seek to diffuse their ideas to the public. While scientists may be neutral in the day-to-day developments in their laboratory, relying on impersonal procedures of verification, science education can not be evaluated simply according to neutral impersonal criteria. The very origin of the new biology curriculum was political; a part of the post Sputnik effort to modernize science education in order to foster American technological supremacy in the cold war (43).

As science is diffused through the educational system it is invariably invested with social meaning. For the public it may be efficacy more than evidence that effects the credibility of science. Acceptance may be based on evaluation of its influence and potential implications. Scientists themselves have assumed a congruence between scientific knowledge and values. Nineteenth century biologists had perceived their studies as a means to prove the existence of God through evidence of design and purpose in nature. In fact, the most active resistance to Darwinian evolution came from scientists themselves (44). Later scientists described evolution theory as a 'naturalistic religion' and as 'a secure basis for ethics' (45). More recently a tendency to relate scientific knowledge to values is evident in efforts to extend the concepts of biology and ecology to generalizations about man and society (46). In this context the concept of neutrality and the distinction between science and its ideological and social content has little significance. Indeed, science becomes a cultural process in which theories develop in close relationship to contemporary values and ideologies (47).

Nevertheless, the individualistic tradition in science leads its practitioners to minimize the importance of their underlying non-scientific values and assumptions. Indeed, scientists would be paralyzed if they constantly had to question hypotheses that lie deeply embedded in the structure of their disciplines. Forced to defend their assumptions against attacks on the values conveyed by science, most biologists were frustrated, for they had long dismissed these as irrelevant to the 'neutral' scientific endeavor.

10. Fallacy of Misplaced Rationality

As scientists argued against the demands for 'equal time', they noted the practical and historical problems in a literal interpretation of *Genesis* and the many facts that contradict the creationists beliefs. They accused creationists of simply repeating their arguments as if repetition could establish verity. When factual arguments and direct criticism failed to turn the creationists away, scientists responded defensively with their own kind of fundamentalism, emphasizing the rationality of science and the weight of evidence that supported their authority. Their arguments assumed a kind of literalism and realism when dealing with the religious claims of their critics, apparently forgetting that science itself is approximate and metaphoric. This literalism on the part of scientists when confronting opposition nearly matched the attitudes of fundamentalists and hindered both scientific and political communication (49).

Convinced of the rationality and merit of their methods, scientists are constantly dismayed by the popularity of non-scientific approaches to nature. In 1975, for example, hundreds of scientists signed a statement criticizing astrologers. They were puzzled that "so many people are prone to swallow beliefs without sufficient evidence", and concerned that "generations of students are coming out without any idea that you have to have evidence for your beliefs" (50). The persistence of creationism is a reminder that beliefs need no evidence; that indeed, people are most reluctant to surrender their personal convictions to a scientific world view.

For those whose personal beliefs are threatened by science the social and moral implications that can be drawn from a scientific theory, its threats to the idea of absolute ethical values, clearly may assume far greater importance than any details of scientific verification. Indeed, increased technical information is unlikely to change well-rooted beliefs because selective factors operate to guide the interpretation of evidence, especially when the nature of such evidence is poorly understood (51). Creationists, as we have seen, avoid, debunk, or disregard information that would repudiate their preconceptions, preferring to deny evidence rather than to discard their beliefs. A great deal of social reinforcement helps them to maintain their views in the face of repeated frustration. Opposition only augments the strength of their religious convictions, and their desire to see these convictions represented in the educational system.

Scientists responded to the creationists demands by denying the conflict between science and religious values; they brought clergymen to public hearings to argue the compatibility of religion and science and, more important, to emphasize the necessity of separating the two domains. Yet, the recurrence of textbook disputes suggests that the treaty between science and religion based on the assumption that they deal with separate domains may be but another convenient but unrealistic myth. Religion as well as science purports to be a picture of reality, a means through which people render their lives and the world around them intelligible. People seek in their beliefs about nature the values that will guide their behavior. The heart of the religious perspective, argues Clifford Geertz, is "not the theory that beyond the visible world there lies an invisible one;... not even the more diffident opinion that there are things in heaven and earth undreamt of in our philosophies. Rather it is the conviction that the values one holds are grounded in an inherent structure of reality" (52). For many people religion may be more likely than science to provide a satisfactory explanation of reality on which to base their values.

Faith in science persists only when it satisfies a social need. If science loses credibility, people will grope for more fulfilling constructs. Science threatens the plausibility of non-rational beliefs, but it has not removed the uncertainties that seem to call for such beliefs. Creationism thus fills a social void for its adherents. By using representations that are well adapted to the 20th century, by claiming scientific respectability while arguing that science is as value-laden as other explanations, creationists offer intellectual plausibility as well as salvation, and the authority of science as well as the certainty of scripture.

Such pressures on science are likely to continue. While rationality and neutrality may serve to guide the work of scientists within their disciplines, they will have to tolerate the inevitable influence of politics and ideology on the evaluation and acceptance of scientific ideas in the public domain.

Notes

1. Mary Douglas, *Purity and Danger*, Harmondsworth: Penguin Books, 1966, p. 48.
2. See discussion of these pressures in Dorothy Nelkin, 'Changing Images of Science', Harvard University Program on Public Conceptions of Science, *Newsletter* 14, January 1976
3. See John Passmore, 'The Revolt Against Science', *Search* 3, November 1972. See also Theodore Roszak, *Where the Wasteland Ends*, New York: Doubleday, 1972. There is now an extensive literature on current concerns with science. See, for example, J. Ellul, *The Technological Society*, New York: Knopf, 1956; V. Ferkiss, *Technological Man*, New York: Braziller, 1969.
4. Christopher Evans, *Cults of Unreason*, New York: Farrar, Strauss and Giroux, 1973, discusses some of these cults and their relationships to science. The pop-cosmologies of Velikofsky and Von Daniken have had enormous appeal ('The Chariots of the Gods' sold over 20 million copies) especially to people seeking scientific explanations that leave room for supernatural intervention.
5. Brochure from the Creation Research Society.
6. To some extent these beliefs can be associated with various organisations. The

members of the American Scientific Affiliation do not deny evolution but have argued that it is taught in too dogmatic a way. Dissidents from the ASA with more rigid anti-evolution positions broke away to form creationist organizations.

7. Arthur Garfield Hays, 'The Scopes Trial', in Gail Kennedy (ed.), *Evolution and Religion*, New York: D.C., Heath, 1957, p. 35.
8. See John N. Moore and Harold Slussher, *Biology: A Search for Order in Complexity*, Grand Rapids: Zondervan Publishers, 1970, p. 422. Also, see review by Wyatt Anderson, Rossiter Crozier and Ronald Simpson in *The Georgia Science Teacher* 13, 1974, pp. 15–18.
9. Duane Gish, 'Creation, Evolution, and the Historical Evidence', *The American Biology Teacher* 35, March 1973, pp. 23–27.
10. Ronald S. Remmel, 'Randomness in Quantum Mechanics and its Implications for Evolutionary Theory', Testimony to the California State Board of Education, November 19, 1972.
11. See the work on cognitive disssonance by Leon Festinger, *A Theory of Cognitive Dissonance*, Evanston: Row Peterson, 1957. The relationship between beliefs and the interpretation of scientific information is discussed by S. B. Barnes, 'On the Reception of Scientific Beliefs', in Barry Barnes (ed.), *Sociology of Science*, Harmondsworth: Penguin Books, 1972, pp. 269–291.
12. Letter in *Acts and Facts*, November/December 1973.
13. Anti-evolution laws were passed in Mississippi (1926), Arkansas (1928), and Texas (1929).
14. Chester H. Rowell, 'The Cancer of Ignorance', *The Survey*, November 1, 1925.
15. See selection from the Scopes Trial in Gail Kennedy (ed.), *Evolution and Religion*, New York: D. C. Heath 1957.
16. *Ibid.*
17. S. J. Holmes, 'Report', *Bulletin of the American Association of University Professors* 13, 8 December 1927.
18. Judith Grabiner and Peter Miller, 'Effects of the Scopes Trial', *Science* 185, 6 September 1974, pp. 832ff.; and Cornelius Troost, 'Evolution in Biological Education Prior to 1960', *Science Education* 51, 1967, pp. 300–301.
19. Hermann J. Muller, 'One Hundred Years Without Darwinism are Enough', *The Humanist* XIX, 1959, p. 139.
20. The last three states to repeal the 'monkey laws' were Tennessee, Arkansas, and Mississippi. See W. Dykemann and J. Stokely, 'Scopes and Evolution – the Jury is Still Out', *New York Times Magazine*, March 12, 1971, pp. 72–76, and the *Science Teacher* 33, September 1966, p. 17.
21. Bills for 'equal time' for creation theory have been introduced in the state legislatures of Tennessee, Georgia, Kentucky, Arizona, Michigan, and Washington. Most legislative efforts failed for legislatures hesitate to intervene in local educational policy. Textbook critics tend to concentrate on Textbook committees (which exist in 22 states) of local school boards.
22. The Tennessee Legislation reads as follows:

> Any biology textbook used for teaching in the public schools which expresses an opinion of, or relates to a theory about origins or creation of man and his world shall be prohibited from being used as a textbook in such system unless it specifically states that it is a theory as to the origin and creation of man and his world and is not represented to be scientific fact. Any textbook so used in the public education system which expresses an opinion or relates to a theory or theories shall give in the same textbook and under the same subject commensurate attention to, and an equal amount of emphasis on, the origins

and creation of man and his world as the same is recorded in other theories
including, but not limited to the Genesis account in the Bible.

Amendment to the Tennessee Code Annotated Section 49–2008, April 30, 1973.
Passed by the Tennessee House of Representatives by 69–15, and the Senate by
28–1.
23. California State Department of Education, *Science Framework for California Public Schools*, Sacramento, 1970, p. 106.
24. Paul DeHart Hurd, a spokesman for the committee, cited by Walter G. Peter III, 'Fundamental Scientists Oppose Darwinian Evolution', *Bioscience* 20, July 1970, p. 1069.
25. Duane Gish, 'A Challenge to Neo-Darwinism', *The American Biology Teacher* 32, February 1973, p. 495.
26. *Nature* 239, October 20, 1972, p. 420. Two scientists immediately responded to the challenge.
27. David S. Hogness, Statement at a meeting of the California State Board of Education, November 6, 1972 (mimeographed).
28. John E. Summers, M. D., Statement at hearing of the California State Board of Education, November 9, 1972 (mimeographed).
29. Ralph Gerard, Statement at hearing of the California State Board of Education, November 9, 1972 (mimeographed).
30. John A. Moore, 'On Giving Time to the Teaching of Evolution and Creation', *Perspectives in Biology and Medicine* 18, 3, Spring 1975, pp. 405–417, delivered at AAAS annual meeting, San Francisco, March 1974.
31. G. Ledyard Stebbins, 'The Evolution of Design', *The American Biology Teacher* 35, February 1973, p. 58.
32. *BSCS Newsletter* 49, November 1972, p. 3; For discussion of the nature of proof and explanation in biology, see Michael Ruse, *The Philosophy of Biology*, London: Hutchinson, 1973.
33. Nicholas Wade, 'Creationists and Evolutionists: Confrontation in California', *Science* 178, pp. 724–792.
34. National Academy of Scences Resolution, October 17, 1972. Note that this was approved by only 35 of 60 members attending the October meeting.
35. The above resolutions were reprinted in the *BSCS Newsletter*, November 1972.
36. The quotes in this section are from correspondence to the NABT in late 1972.
37. Memo to NABT, November 28, 1972.
38. Letter from Wendell McBurney to Jerry Lightner, December 22, 1972.
39. *American Biology Teachers Journal*, April 1974, p. 246.
40. The lack of an ethic to govern scientists' relationships outside the scientific community is discussed by Joseph Haberer, *Politics and the Community of Science*, New York: Van Nostrand Reinhold, 1969.
41. William Mayer, 'The Nineteenth Century Revisited', *BSCS Newsletter*, November 1972.
42. David Ost, 'Statement', *American Biology Teacher* 34, October 1972, pp. 413–14.
43. In 1960 the NSF funded the Biological Sciences Curriculum Study at the University of Colorado to develop a modern approach to teaching of biology. This was a part of the massive federally funded program for the reform of pre-college science curriculum.
44. The historian Charles Gillispie talks of the 19th century debate over Darwinism as "one of religion in science rather than religion versus science" in *Genesis and Geology*, Cambridge: Harvard University Press, 1951.

45. Julian Huxley, *Evolution in Action*, New York: Harper 1953; and C. H. Waddington, *The Scientific Attitude*, London: Penguin Books, 1941.
46. See, for example, the recent work by E. O. Wilson, *Sociobiology: The New Synthesis*, Cambridge: Harvard University Press, 1975. R. M. Young, in 'Evolutionary Biology and Ideology: Then and Now', *Science Studies* I, 1971, pp. 177–206, dicusses these tendencies to extend biology; and in particular the implications of the work of Ardrey and Lorenz.
47. This point is well-developed by a study examining the history of the study of genetics in relation to widely held beliefs during different periods. See W. Provine, 'Genetics and the Biology of Race Crossing', *Science* 172, November 23, 1973, pp. 790–98.
48. Yaron Ezrahi uses this term to describe a similar fallacy in the Jensen Controversy. See 'The Jensen Controversy: A Study in Ethics and the Politics of Knowledge in Democracy', in C. Frankel (ed.), *Controversies and Decisions*, New York: Russell Sage, 1976.
49. Donald T. Campbell, 'On the Conflicts Between Biological and Social Evolution and Between Psychology and Moral Tradition', *American Psychologist* 30, 12, December 1975, p. 1120. Campbell notes that "scientists hold up for religious discourse the requirement for a direct realism, a literal veridicality, even though they may recognize that this is impossible for science itself."
50. Statement by Paul Kurtz, editor of *The Humanist*, in justifying the statement by 186 scientists calling astrologers charlatans who have no rational basis for their beliefs. See *The Humanist*, October/November 1975.
51. Leon Festinger, *A Theory of Cognitive Dissonance*, Evanston: Row Peterson, 1957.
52. See discussion in Clifford Geertz, *Islam Observed*, New Haven: Yale University Press, 1968, and *Interpretation of Culture*, New York: Basic Books, 1973. Note that scientists as well as laymen often assume a congruence between scientific knowledge and values. This is most evident in ecology and population studies where it is assumed that increased knowledge will change values and behavior.

INDEX

294 *Index*